MW01625521

Religion and Charity

Free markets alone do not work effectively to solve certain kinds of human problems, such as education, elderly care, or disaster relief. Nor have markets ever been the sole solution to the psychological challenges of death, suffering, or injustice. Instead, we find a major role for the nonmarket institutions of society – the family, the state, and social institutions. The first in-depth anthropological study of charities in contemporary Chinese societies, this book focuses on the unique ways that religious groups have helped solve the problems of social well-being. Using comparative case studies in China, Taiwan, and Malaysia from the 1980s on, it identifies new forms of religious philanthropy as well as new ideas of social "good," including different forms of political merit-making, new forms of civic selfhood, and the rise of innovative social forms, including increased leadership by women. The book finally argues that the spread of these ideas is an incomplete process, with many alternative notions of goodness continuing to be influential.

ROBERT P. WELLER is Professor of Anthropology and Research Associate at the Institute on Culture, Religion and World Affairs at Boston University.

C. JULIA HUANG is Professor of Anthropology at National Tsing Hua University, Taiwan.

KEPING WU is Associate Professor of Anthropology at Sun Yat-sen University, Guangdong.

LIZHU FAN is Professor of Sociology and Director of the Globalization and Religious Studies program at Fudan University, Shanghai.

Religion and Charity

The Social Life of Goodness in Chinese Societies

Robert P. Weller

Boston University

C. Julia Huang

National Tsing Hua University, Taiwan

Keping Wu

Sun Yat-sen University, Guangdong

with Lizhu Fan

Fudan University, Shanghai

CAMBRIDGE
UNIVERSITY PRESS

University Printing House, Cambridge CB2 8BS, United Kingdom

One Liberty Plaza, 20th Floor, New York, NY 10006, USA

477 Williamstown Road, Port Melbourne, VIC 3207, Australia

314-321, 3rd Floor, Plot 3, Splendor Forum, Jasola District Centre, New Delhi – 110025, India

79 Anson Road, #06-04/06, Singapore 079906

Cambridge University Press is part of the University of Cambridge.

It furthers the University's mission by disseminating knowledge in the pursuit of education, learning, and research at the highest international levels of excellence.

www.cambridge.org
Information on this title: www.cambridge.org/9781108418676
DOI: 10.1017/9781108290821

First published 2018

Printed in Great Britan by Clays Ltd, St Ives plc

A catalogue record for this publication is available from the British Library.

Library of Congress Cataloging-in-Publication Data
Names: Weller, Robert P. (Robert Paul), 1953- author.
Title: Religion and charity: the social life of goodness in Chinese societies / Robert P. Weller, Boston University, C. Julia Huang, National Tsing Hua University, Taiwan, Keping Wu, Sun Yat-sen University, Guangdong, with Lizhu Fan, Fudan University, Shanghai.
Description: Cambridge, United Kingdom ; New York, NY, USA : Cambridge University Press, [2018] | Includes bibliographical references and index.
Identifiers: LCCN 2017043718 | ISBN 9781108418676 (hardback)
Subjects: LCSH: Religion and sociology – China. | Charity – Religious aspects. | Charities – China.
Classification: LCC BL60.W445 2018 | DDC 306.60951–dc23
LC record available at https://lccn.loc.gov/2017043718

ISBN 978-1-108-41867-6 Hardback

Contents

Figures

Acknowledgments

This project was made possible initially by a generous grant from the Chiang Ching-kuo Foundation for Scholarly Exchange in 2005. We are very grateful for their help. In addition to the field research, their support included funding a conference in 2008 at the College of Humanities and Social Sciences, National Tsing Hua University, Taiwan (NTHU), at which we were able to present some of our preliminary findings. Particular thanks are due to all the participants on that occasion, especially to our discussants: Fredrik Barth, Wei-an Chang, Tan Chee-Beng, Ying-chang Chuang, Hsin-Huang Michael Hsiao, Paul Katz, David Palmer, and James Wilkerson. We also thank Rosalyn Wan-jung Chao of the Institute of Anthropology and the Research Program in Gender and Society at NTHU for administrative support. Smaller portions of the conference were funded by Taiwan's Ministry of Education through a grant to Julia Huang. Portions of later field research were funded by Fulbright and Guggenheim grants to Robert Weller, and by grants from the National Science Council and NTHU, and a visiting scholarship from the Asia Research Institute (ARI) at the National University of Singapore (NUS) to Julia Huang, which were much appreciated. The ARI of NUS funded Keping Wu for an update fieldtrip and provided an opportunity for the coauthors to meet in person during the Religion and Development in China roundtable. We are grateful to ARI and to all the funding agencies for their support.

The actual process of writing was closely collaborative. One result of this is that we did not each write a chapter based on our own work. Instead we chose the more collaborative – and hopefully more intellectually rewarding – path of writing chapters on themes that cut across our field sites. Each of us contributed to every chapter. Given that we were on different continents most of the time, we also owe thanks to Skype, which was vital in easing our dozens of joint conversations, arguments, and eventual agreements. For support during the writing process, we are especially grateful to the Harvard-Yenching Institute, whose fellowship to Keping Wu allowed us to collaborate in person, and to the Ho Center for Buddhist Studies at Stanford University and the Center for Chinese Studies at the University of California, Berkeley, for granting Julia Huang visiting scholar affiliations during the writing period.

The Fairbank Center at Harvard University awarded us a grant to fund a book manuscript workshop in 2014, at which a great number of our colleagues very generously read an early draft and provided us with critiques that were thoughtful, challenging, and extremely helpful. We will not take the space to thank everyone individually, but especially want to express our gratitude to those who went over the entire manuscript with a fine-toothed comb: Elisabeth Clemens, Deborah Davis, Nara Dillon, Richard Madsen, and Johanna Handlin Smith.

Finally, and most importantly, we want to thank everyone in Lukang, Malacca, Suzhou, and the many other sites we visited for our research, who gave us gifts of their time and knowledge. The number of people is far too great to list individually, but we hope you know that we continue to feel grateful that you were willing to give in this way, in addition to all the other forms of your generosity, which are the subject of this book. We tried to express our thanks at the time to each of you, but we also know that some debts cannot be repaid.

1 Engaged Religions, Industrialized Philanthropy, and the Social Life of Goodness

In the early 1990s one of us flew to Taiwan as part of a delegation invited by the Ministry of Foreign Affairs. Mixed in among visits to politicians and think tanks in Taipei, the Ministry brought us to what appeared to be a small temple in Hualian on Taiwan's poor eastern coast. We were there to visit a Buddhist nun, the Ven. Cheng Yen (证严), at the Still Thoughts Abode, the headquarters of her Buddhist Compassion Relief Tzu Chi (慈济) Foundation.[1] Sitting in a small, quiet courtyard in front of a typical temple hall, the group had a long talk with her about Buddhism and charity. She was soft-spoken, and no one interrupted the serenity of the occasion. The temple appeared, at least at first, no different from many other old-fashioned Buddhist temples urging people to follow the bodhisattva path of helping others.

The surprise that followed came not so much from talking with Cheng Yen as from a serendipitous glance through a partially open door on our way out. Sitting inside were rows and rows of young women, each clicking away at a computer terminal and entering information about donations. Suddenly it became clear that this was not an ordinary temple, nor did the group represent Buddhism as usual. In retrospect, the enormous parking lot was already a clue that something quite different was happening here.

At that time, none of us knew much about Tzu Chi, nor had any of us begun to think about the topic of this book. In fact, however, the group was in the midst of an extremely rapid development, already well on its way to gaining the millions of followers in countries all around the world that it would have by the end of the decade. With its huge corps of volunteers, Tzu Chi would soon be the largest nongovernmental organization (NGO) in Taiwan, and a major actor in Taiwanese and global health care, emergency aid, and poverty relief.

[1] We use pinyin as the default for all romanization from Mandarin. We make exceptions when groups or individuals have established a different convention in English (as with Cheng Yen or Tzu Chi), which we follow. Where there are already alternate conventions in English (which is especially common in Malaysia, e.g., Cheng Hoon Teng), we follow those conventions. In general, we use Chinese characters instead of pinyin, but make exceptions for some terms that we prefer not to translate.

This brief visit raised many of the questions that inform this book. Why would a charity-based Buddhist movement expand so very rapidly at this historical moment? Why would the Ministry of Foreign Affairs think that such a place should be highlighted for foreign visitors? What kinds of ideas had to change for this form of Buddhism to be able to shape itself around the production efforts of millions of people volunteering to do good, and the backstage construction of massive computer banks?

As we will see, Tzu Chi was by no means unique. Our interest in religious charity began with a much broader ethnographic puzzle that extended across our field research with Chinese people in mainland China, Taiwan, and Malaysia: beginning in the late twentieth century and continuing today, religions undertook a far more active role in providing public goods in each of these communities (and many others) than they had earlier in the twentieth century. Why?

Much (though not all) of this new activity took a form that we might call "industrialized philanthropy."[2] We use this term to indicate three related phenomena. First, the scale was large, in some cases larger than ever before in Chinese history, involving millions of people all around the world. Second, the production and distribution of philanthropic goods were increasingly rationalized and bureaucratized in ways that included accounting methods, reporting responsibilities to boards of directors, recruitment and organization of members, uses of the media, and above all relations with governments. Finally, such philanthropy became disembedded from local social life and personal social connections, and relied instead on a new sense of self as something able to make autonomous and independent decisions, which are rooted in transnational and cosmopolitan notions of universal goodness. Such a self could materialize those values through voluntary donations of time and money. This notion of selfhood, seen as both universal and autonomous, parallels the shaping of identity documented in industrialized societies since the classic work of Max Weber and Émile Durkheim. That initial quick trip to Tzu Chi's Still Thoughts Abode showed all of these characteristics.

Of course, much of the literature about philanthropy focuses on precisely such industrialized forms, to the point that their goals, organizational structures, and notions of identity seem universal and natural. They sometimes seemed natural to our informants as well, such as when they talked about "doing good" (行善 or 做善事) as if it included only things like poverty relief, education, or medical care to needy strangers. As we hope to show, however, there is nothing natural about this notion of goodness or its organizational carriers. It is the historical product of a particular moment.

[2] We are grateful to Elisabeth Clemens for suggesting this term.

There are many other ways of conceptualizing and responding to human need. For earlier generations and in other contexts, doing good in Chinese societies could equally mean helping educate only the sons of one's lineage, providing burial services for fellow immigrants, releasing animals from captivity, collecting and ritually burning scraps of writing, or conducting rituals to appease the dead souls that ensue after war or natural disaster. Industrialized philanthropy typically includes none of these things. Ideas about goodness have their own social and historical lives, and our goal here is to understand how and why those ideas and their organizational forms began to trend toward the industrialization of philanthropy in multiple Chinese societies, especially beginning in the 1980s.

At first glance the prospects for socially engaged Chinese religions appear discouraging. No religious tradition has an important formal political role in any current Chinese society, and the twentieth century brought repression of many forms of religion. Until very recently, religions in Chinese societies also never created national-scale private institutions to provide such goods, with the partial exception of Christians during the brief missionary heyday of the late nineteenth and early twentieth centuries.[3] As we will discuss, religions had actually long been involved in various aspects of "the good" in Chinese history, but this was challenged in the twentieth century by massive secularization projects that tried to reduce religion to spiritual functions alone, and by changing notions of goodness that made many of those earlier activities seem irrelevant. By the 1980s, however, in each of the different political systems we will examine, the most radical secularizing trends began to reverse, and religions found ways to accommodate changing notions of goodness.

This has been most obvious in China, where the Cultural Revolution (1966–1976) reduced public religious activity to almost nothing. The state was to be the only significant public actor and there was no place for religious charity, or even for religion. By the 1990s, however, not only had religion surged anew almost everywhere, but temples, churches, and mosques again supplied all kinds of public goods. They built museums, arboreta, schools, and old age homes. They have been active in emergency relief as well, most remarkably after the devastating Sichuan earthquake of 2008.

Taiwan never had as severe a repression of religion as the mainland, but the change there too was almost as striking. When one of us first conducted field research in Taiwan in the late 1970s, temples provided no direct social services, although they quite obviously concentrated some basic social capital. Nevertheless, the situation today looks very different. Enormous new Buddhist organizations have built universities and hospitals. The Tzu Chi

[3] Nevertheless, a widely diverse array of engaged religious activities existed throughout the late imperial period. We review some of these in Chapter 2.

Foundation, mentioned in our opening anecdote, has been especially successful at delivering medical and emergency aid all around the world. Even local temples to gods are taking on a far wider range of social activities than they had several decades earlier. They typically provide scholarships for local students, arrange emergency aid for needy families, and donate garbage trucks and fire engines to their local governments. The dynamics of these changes have been rather different from what happened on the mainland, but they have been just as rapid.

Malaysia, which had by far the longest colonial history among our field sites, nevertheless felt the least pressure for religion to adjust to Western models. In some ways it maintained more features of late imperial religious organization, though with significant adjustments for the Chinese population in Malaysia as members of an ethnic minority. Dutch and British colonial rulers used forms of indirect rule, which actually reinforced the role of temples and their leaders in the local Chinese communities. It also encouraged temples to retain more of their traditional forms of social engagement than happened in Taiwan or China under all their twentieth-century regimes. Post-independence policies to protect Islam and to keep clear lines of separation among ethnic groups encouraged Chinese temples to continue meeting broader social needs. Only in the last few decades has the government allowed more space for organizations to move out of an ethnically Chinese bunker, and only with limited success so far, as we will discuss.

Goodness

Religious actors involved in charity work in all three of our field sites used very similar languages of industrialized philanthropy to describe their goals and organizational structures. Given their deep differences in political structures and social histories, this was unexpected. The various religious traditions (Buddhism, Daoism, Christianity, Islam, temple-based worship) themselves add further layers of significant variation in the potential forms and structures of "goodness," but most of our informants downplayed this too, at least at first. Instead they seemed to share the broad moral outlook that characterizes much of the literature on modern philanthropy everywhere in the world: philanthropy should, for instance, include medical clinics, but not the laying on of hands; burying the dead, but not caring for their lost souls; monitoring and aiding the poor, but not giving handouts to beggars. It should be both counted and accountable. We found this equally in our interviews with Christians and Buddhists, democrats and communists. This image of goodness, however, is not inherently natural, and is a relatively recent development in each of our cases, as we will discuss in the chapters that follow. Goodness, that is, has its own social life.

That social life has moved from the late nineteenth century when Buddhists inspired "benevolent halls" (善堂), Catholics specialized in orphanages, and everyone helped primarily people with whom they already had existing social connections. By the middle of the twentieth century (especially on the mainland) religion did very few of these activities. In the contemporary era engaged religions had changed again, so that all religions now deliver similar packages of medical aid, emergency relief, and education to a universal public of those in need. Volunteering has become a core idea to bring followers into these activities, implying a new kind of relationship between religion and follower, between philanthropic organization and the public, and between self and society. Organizational transparency has changed from temples posting names of large donors on their walls to modern accounting systems subject to audit by various state agencies.

The convergence toward industrialized philanthropy is certainly not hegemonic, however, and began to dominate engaged religions in our regions starting only from the 1980s. Before that, we saw far greater differences from one political system to another and from one religious tradition to another. One of our primary goals is to understand how this partial convergence became so strong in the late twentieth century, but also to keep an eye on those aspects of engaged religion that have been able to resist the trend.

We will argue that the contemporary image of goodness is by no means the universal truth that most people involved in these engaged religions (and in secular NGOs as well) seem to take as natural and obvious. It is instead a social construction, uniquely shaped by the times and spaces in which it spread. Our primary concern is thus with the evolving social life of goodness. In that sense we are contributing to what Joel Robbins has recently described as an anthropology of the good, which may offer ways of "helping us do justice to the different ways people live for the good, and finding ways to let their efforts inform our own."[4]

In taking this position, we are aligning ourselves with an anthropological approach that sees morality as something multiple, contextual, and constructed.[5] The world of religious philanthropy in China involves a commitment that, for most people, goes beyond and (for many) seeks to counteract the moral implications of their everyday lives. Such people fit easily with James Laidlaw's definition of ethical conduct as shaped by their "attempts to make of themselves a certain kind of person, because it is as such a person that, on reflection, they think they ought to live."[6]

[4] Robbins, "Beyond the Suffering Subject," 459.

[5] See, for example, Robbins, *Becoming Sinners*; Oxfeld, *Drink Water, but Remember the Source*.

[6] Laidlaw, "For an Anthropology of Ethics and Freedom," 327.

A language of moral breakdown has become very common in China as an explanation for everything from high-level corruption to undergraduates who do not study hard – although it is also important to recall that almost every important Confucian movement since the beginning has also been phrased as an antidote to moral breakdown.[7] Similarly, the anthropology of morality has recently begun to focus on moral breakdowns as privileged zones to provide a view of people's ethical agency.[8] Moral breakdowns involve a crisis that forces people to call their moral assumptions into question. A contrasting approach, however, involves looking at the ethical worlds that people simply take for granted during their everyday lives – an experiential morality rather than a discursive one. For our purposes, however, the distinction between moral breakdowns and experiential morality may be overdrawn, because most of the actions of everyday life can put ethical assumptions at risk. Any action contains the potential to call our moral assumptions into question. Much current ethical discourse thus continues without a strong sense of breakdown, especially in the worlds of engaged religion that we are examining.

One final theme we share with the recent literature on morality is its concern with the politics of modern states. Both the worlds of NGOs and of religions are often imagined as independent from politics, and they often present themselves in such terms as well. Nevertheless, this is deeply problematic both for religions and NGOs, especially when we try to understand them historically in Chinese societies.

On the side of religion, it is important to remember that the modern Chinese term for religion (宗教) is only about a century old, having been coined in Japan to translate the English word "religion" and its equivalents in other European languages. It was brought to China from there. This coincided with state secularization projects, especially under the Guomindang (GMD, also sometimes abbreviated as KMT) in China and Japanese colonial rule in Taiwan, which sought to remove religion from political and broader social life. In the process of limiting religion to the realm of the spiritual, of course, this project also required the creation of "religion" as a category.[9] Understood in roughly Protestant terms as something based around belief (rather than ritual), inscribed in sacred texts, and organized around voluntary congregations, this new slot for religion fit only uneasily in the Chinese social world. Islam and Christianity worked well enough, but Buddhism and Daoism undertook some significant institutional adjustment to make the change. Other potential

[7] Yan Yunxiang provides the most ethnographically grounded such argument; see Yan, *Private Life under Socialism*.

[8] See, for example, Zigon, "Moral Breakdown and the Ethical Demand."

[9] Many scholars have recently pointed to these processes, which have been documented especially clearly in Goossaert and Palmer, *The Religious Question in Modern China*, 2011.

candidates, such as Confucianism or the temple-based religion that characterized so much of local Chinese life, remained outside the system and were often condemned as outmoded and (especially for temple religion) superstitious. Until these changes of the twentieth century, aspects of what we now call religion pervaded all parts of life, including those organizations dedicated to meeting the welfare needs of the general population. The idea of a distinctly *religious* philanthropy is modern in China, but acts of worship and of charity have long been interlinked.

Any assumption that there is something apolitical about the NGO side of philanthropy is equally problematic, as several contributors to the anthropology of morality have pointed out. Peter Redfield, for example, writes that even "antipolitics," meaning the nongovernmental sector that self-consciously avoids state control (like his primary case of Doctors Without Borders) "faces political judgment, under which mere charity can never be enough."[10] Writing in the same volume, Didier Fassin says:

> The presence of a moral vocabulary in political discourses is definitely not new and one could even ague that politics, especially in democracies, has always included moral arguments about good government and public good, fairness and trust, as well as moral condemnation of all sorts of evil. Yet, the current moralization of politics as a global phenomenon imposing its moral obviousness should be regarded as an object of inquiry in its own right.[11]

That is, for both of these authors, even "private" moralities have inevitable political consequences, just as politics has moral consequences. Furthermore, these mutual shapings of goodness have intimate ties to what Redfield calls "historically liberal expectations of personhood, biopolitical norms of health, and secular understandings of the frame of moral action."[12]

Much of our argument is about how the moral and institutional structures of industrialized philanthropy – something similar to what Redfield is pointing to – have come to dominate religious (and other) charity, although we will turn toward the end of the book to alternative ideas of goodness that continue to provide an important counterpoint. As we will discuss in the chapters that follow, this approach leads to important implications for theories of globalization, social capital, and state–society relations.

Timing

Most people agree that free markets alone do not work very effectively to solve certain kinds of human problems, such as education, elderly care, medical care,

[10] Redfield, "Humanitarianism," 454.
[11] Fassin, "Introduction: Toward a Critical Moral Anthropology," 10.
[12] Redfield, "Humanitarianism," 464.

or disaster relief. Nor have markets ever been the sole solution to the psychological challenges of death, suffering, or injustice. Instead, we find a major role for the nonmarket institutions of society – the family and other very personal networks, the state, and intermediate social institutions such as religious groups or NGOs.

Before the 1980s Taiwan's autocratic regime tended to emphasize the core role of the family in dealing with these problems. The state there dedicated its efforts to military affairs and economic development, and generally left social issues to be worked out on their own. At the same time, many intermediate social organizations were discouraged because an independent society could foster political problems for the regime. This left the family as the chief actor, with the state providing mostly moral support in the form of reiterations and reworkings of Confucian family values.

Mainland China during this period discouraged intermediate social organizations even more powerfully. Its answer to welfare needs, however, emphasized the state far more than the family. It was the state that guaranteed employment, health, and retirement, especially for urban workers. The most radical moments, such as the communal food preparation and child care of the Great Leap Forward (1958–1961), undermined even basic functions of the family. During those periods, Confucian values became objects of attack instead of propaganda priorities.[13]

Of our field sites, only Malaysia encouraged social organizations to deal with welfare issues directly, although, as we will discuss, those efforts were bunkered into ethnic and religious enclaves. In the last few decades of the twentieth century, however, we can see a steady increase in the role that religious organizations played in addressing problems of social well-being on a large scale, and a steady industrialization of philanthropy. Our study explores the nature and timing of the change in China, Malaysia, and Taiwan. Our comparative approach allows us to ask whether the particular religious tradition makes any difference, and how varying political systems influence the ways that religions engage with society.

What caused one very particular image of goodness and its form of institutionalization to dominate in diverse Chinese societies beginning in the late twentieth century? Part of the answer lies in events that affected all three of our field sites roughly simultaneously. First, all three places experienced rapid economic growth at that time. The 1980s marked the beginning of the market reforms in China, and thus the beginning of a long period of rapid growth, above all in the lower Yangzi region on which our study focuses. It was also the decade in which people began to refer to Taiwan's economy as "developed"

[13] For a summary of relevant policy changes in China and Taiwan, see Laliberté, "Religions and Philanthropy in Chinese Societies Since 1978."

instead of just developing, and during which Malaysia also experienced rapid economic improvement. These changes do not automatically lead to an increase in religious philanthropy, or to large-scale philanthropy of any kind. They do, however, make such action possible by increasing disposable incomes enough that charities have a stable source of donations, and by freeing some people from labor sufficiently to volunteer their time.

Second, both mainland China and Taiwan experienced a significant political loosening during this period, as they ceased acting as symbols for the two sides of a Cold War that would soon disappear. Although they remain very different from each other – one an electoral democracy and the other a single-party state – the changes in both cases fostered a greatly increased space for social organizations of all sorts, including the ones we focus on here. Malaysia's political system did not change as clearly during the period, but did see a strengthening of the affirmative action policies that favored Malays over Chinese, and whose effects included encouraging the Chinese community to rely on its own resources. Thus in very different ways and for different reasons, all of our cases saw an increased role for social organizations in general and philanthropies in particular during this period.

Third, crucial technological changes beginning in the late twentieth century greatly eased communication. This had a wide range of indirect effects on religious philanthropy. It became much easier to know what organizations were doing elsewhere and what successful groups considered to be best practices. It also became possible to organize people and to raise funds in new, more flexible ways instead of relying on word of mouth or the mail.

Fourth, mobility also greatly increased during this period. This includes both international population flows and internal migration. To some extent, as we will discuss, international flows were direct carriers of religious philanthropic institutions, renewing ties among Malaysia, Taiwan, and the Chinese mainland that had been important through the early twentieth century, but that had greatly declined during half a century of Cold War and limited resources. Internal mobility, especially from the countryside to cities, probably had an even greater influence in fostering the attitudes and senses of self that accompany industrialized philanthropy. This is primarily because such mobility disembedded people from rural communities and their strong webs of social connection, encouraging them instead toward looser networks (facilitated by new forms of communication), a more autonomous sense of self, and new kinds of religious activities.

In the chapters that follow, we will explore three primary dimensions of these changes and their timing: political variation and the processes of what we call political merit-making as they have evolved across our field sites (Chapters 2 and 3); the effects of multiple waves of globalization (including both migration and new forms of communication), especially as they have encouraged people to develop a new sense of self and of the good, which we will call "civic selving" (Chapter 4); and the way the changes of the 1980s and beyond helped encourage innovation in forms of religious philanthropy and in conceptions of the good, creating new sets opportunities and limits that shaped the development of the field (Chapters 5 and 6). We will return in Chapter 7 to the problem of alternative views of goodness – ideas of the good that challenge, accommodate, and coexist with the universalizing and industrializing model that has tended to dominate. Let us expand very briefly on each approach here, but leave most of the relevant discussion to the chapters that follow.

Changing Regimes and Political Merit-making

Some work suggests that social organizations take over when the state fails to provide needed social services. This "state failure hypothesis" argues that the nongovernmental service sector (including engaged religions) moves in when states are unable to meet their people's needs. None of our cases involve weak states in a literal sense, however. These states are not without problems, but are fiscally strong and preside over relatively successful economies. An alternate route to the rise of social organizations providing welfare, more relevant to our cases, is "state retrenchment." This can occur when states choose to contract their welfare activities on the basis of principle, as in the United States under Ronald Reagan, or the more recent West European contraction of the welfare state in many countries.

In China, the state today certainly provides fewer social goods than it did before the reform era that began in 1979. The change occurred partly for fiscal reasons, but primarily because of China's move to embrace market mechanisms instead of central planning for many aspects of life. Education and medical care, for example, rely on free market processes now in China more than in many other countries. Public services thus offer an arena in which NGOs, including religious ones, can earn the support of the state by providing for social needs. Before democratization, Taiwan offered a comparable space, mostly because its developmentalist state was unwilling to divert resources into welfare functions.[14] Indeed, this is exactly the niche that initially allowed for the growth of Tzu Chi and other forms of Buddhist charity. After democratization, Taiwan has actually moved in an opposite direction to some extent, as many politicians began to support increased state welfare spending as a way of pleasing the electorate. The end result is a roughly similar mix in both places, but through quite different mechanisms. Only Malaysia showed little

[14] The usual term of retrenchment, of course, may be a misnomer for this, because this state had never been invested in providing these services. It was instead a kind of neoliberal regime, before this term was widely used.

change, because so much of the responsibility for social welfare, especially for the Chinese community, had already been delegated to social groups since colonial times.

Thus, as we will discuss, each of these relatively strong states has chosen to allow significant social space for civil associations that serve their needs, although the mechanisms differ significantly among our cases. Our comparative approach allows us to explore some of the effects of political differences on how this space develops. As we shall see in Chapters 2 and 3, the effects of democratization versus authoritarian rule are not as straightforward as is sometimes assumed in more theoretical formulations. For instance, our material complicates the idea that groups act on more universal ideas of goodness when they are competing for votes, or that state interference from authoritarian regimes reduces the effectiveness of philanthropies.[15]

We will also discuss the related idea that independent social institutions – the building blocks of civil society, including nonstate religions (i.e., all religions in these Chinese contexts) – exist in inherent tension with the state, as a kind of zero-sum game. This idea goes back at least as far as Tocqueville's view that civil associations in the early United States served as an important brake on the potentially tyrannical power of any state.[16] Yet this view completely fails to capture much of the actual dynamic of religious charity that our research shows, where the relation with the state is often cooperative rather than contentious.

In Chapter 2 we begin to spell out this analysis by discussing how a shared repertoire of varied forms of religious engagement evolved in the different political environments of China, Malaysia, and Taiwan during the twentieth century, leading to patterns that do not entirely fit expectations about the effects of democracy or electoral rule. Chapter 3 turns to the specific adaptations of the 1980s and beyond as we began to see all three places making more room for religious philanthropy, and all three adopting and adapting the rhetoric of a universal good. In every case the state has been a crucial shaper of engaged religions, as governments try to shape religious space and as religious groups themselves pursue state blessings – a process that we call *political merit-making*.

Earning political merit is crucial in each of our field sites, although the specific methods differ given the varied nature of the regimes and the local histories. As we will explain, we see a primarily defensive form of merit-making in China (where worries about state intervention shape nearly every form of religious engagement), a more mutualist form in Taiwan (where the politicians

[15] See, for example, Cammett and Issar, "Bricks and Mortar Clientalism"; Fuma, *History of Chinese Benevolent Halls and Associations.*

[16] Tocqueville, *Democracy in America.*

may gain as much as religious groups from the interaction), and an enclaved form in Malaysia (where state boundaries around ethnic groups are tightly drawn, but religious groups have wide options within those boundaries).

Globalizations, Competitions, and Selves

In Chapter 4 we begin to explore the spread of particular forms of religious philanthropy characterized by notions of a universal good, embodied through cosmopolitan volunteers driven by generalized feelings of love, and institutionalized to be large-scale, accountable, and rationalized. These are the processes we are calling the industrialization of philanthropy, and in this chapter we will be especially concerned with how they grow hand in hand with a particular idea of the self, which we will call "civic selving." While these "industrializing" developments by no means exhaust the field of religious philanthropy, they have become dominant modes in recent decades across all of our field sites and well beyond. In part this is a story of successive waves of globalization that began in the late nineteenth century. We should remember, however, that "globalization" as an analytic concept is simply shorthand for a complex process of imitation, resistance, accommodation, and adaptation. We will begin to dismantle some of these processes in Chapter 4.

The first big wave of globalization relevant to our topic was Protestant missionizing, which stressed philanthropic activity, especially from the latter part of the nineteenth century on. Global charities such as the Red Cross and YMCA – which themselves were directly or indirectly inspired by new trends in North American and European religious charity during the nineteenth century – also entered Asia at this time. It is thus tempting to see Protestantism as the primary instigator of these changes, especially because many of the techniques of selfhood now common appear so consistent with Protestantism. Nevertheless, we will argue that such an explanation is partial and misleading. This is most obvious in the temporal discontinuities that separate the initial missionary effort, which largely died out, from the changes that occurred many decades later. We will also argue that adaptation of these imported forms of engaged religion was never straightforward, but involved a great deal of interaction with already existing ideas from various Chinese traditions – interactions that took place first in Europe and then in Asia.

Another tempting explanation would be the wave of "neoliberal" reforms that became so important around the world, especially as promoted by the United States and the International Monetary Fund in the 1980s – exactly the period in which the changes we observed began. This decade brought a strong move, beginning with the Reagan and Thatcher regimes and then spreading globally, to reduce the state's role in welfare and to increase the role of social organizations, including religious groups. In the United States, this ushered in a continuing debate over the proper role of "faith-based initiatives." This term usually refers in practice to the religious provision of social services and education, with no more than partial funding coming from the government. Proponents argued that churches have a store of social capital and a moral basis that makes them more efficient and effective providers of such services, although opponents responded that it violated the legal separation of church and state in the American Constitution.[17] Such arguments are distinctly American, although issues of how church and state relate to each other have been important almost everywhere since the spread of yet another wave of globalization – the idea of secular states built into most Asian constitutions from early in the twentieth century.

An explanation based on the spread of neoliberalism does a better job of explaining the timing of the changes we see than one based on missionary influence. Nevertheless, we will argue that it is incomplete for several reasons. First, none of the states we are looking at is ideologically neoliberal; that is, none is actively trying to reduce the welfare role of the state to a minimum. The Chinese state has indeed stepped back from its older socialist project of encompassing everything, but it still remains starkly visible in every aspect of life in a way completely inconsistent with neoliberal goals.[18] In addition, both Malaysia and especially Taiwan have moved toward greater state intervention in welfare during this period – just the opposite of what a simple globalization story would suggest. This increase in state welfare activities has accompanied rather than dampened a simultaneous growth in engaged religion, as we will discuss.

Even if we take a narrower view of neoliberalism as the interpolation of the self as an autonomous and independent individual fully responsible for her own welfare, we need to recognize that such ideas combined in our Chinese cases with ideas that already existed. Chapter 4 shows how there were already important karmic and cultivational discourses about the nature of goodness, which continue to shape engaged religions in all of our cases. And as others have discussed, the rise of the idea of the autonomous individual has a longer history in Chinese societies than any form of neoliberal influence.[19]

Finally, we need to recall that the changes of the 1980s – new forms of communication, greatly eased mobility both within and across nations, increases in disposable income – occurred in our region at roughly the same time as neoliberal ideas were spreading, but that they cannot be reduced to neoliberal governance. They did, however, help to shape "cosmopolitan" identities for many people in our region, meaning that people can now easily conceptualize

[17] For a very useful discussion of the issues, see Wuthnow, *Saving America?*
[18] Nonini, "Is China Becoming Neoliberal?," 2008.
[19] See, for example, Yan, *Private Life under Socialism.*

themselves translocally and transnationally even without ever leaving home. They may listen to American hip hop, watch Korean soap operas, and practice yoga while never leaving the places where they were born.

These various waves of global influence have certainly been important, but as we will show, so have internal dynamics of competition and emulation among different religions, which take place largely within the confines of Asia and always in dialogue with existing discourses and institutions. It is this combination of environmental factors and competition that has fostered a particular kind of subjectivity that reaches across all our religious traditions: a generous and loving self, resonating with cosmopolitan ideas about a universal and unbounded good – "civic selving."

Networks, Innovation, and Divergences

In Chapter 5 we take another angle on the problem, asking how engaged religious groups mobilize the social resources they need to function, from networks of donors to teams of volunteers, and how this has changed. We explore the way that temples and churches can serve as reservoirs of social capital, especially in local communities and neighborhoods. Even new transnational forms of religious philanthropy have produced such ties both within their leaderships and through their local branches. The establishment of effective social networks has been a key to the functioning of much engaged religion in Chinese history, and continues to be important today.

Yet these reservoirs also have a strong tendency to maintain the status quo, because the powerful men of the community (and it is usually men) build religious ties along with all the other networks that they mobilize to maintain their positions. That is, such men tend to be nodes in networks of strong social ties. This can work well in encouraging religious groups to provide social services, but such strong ties also provide very little incentive to innovate – the status quo works in their favor. In addition, their visions of social service tend to remain within their own spheres of influence, limited to the interests of their own communities. Something similar develops as well in new groups, even those that developed recently out of very different kinds of networks (and occasionally run by women). By asking how industrialized philanthropy differs from other forms of the gift economy in Chinese societies, we hope to illuminate the possible roles of social capital.

Chapter 6 turns to the other side of the problem of social networks – if they are strong and stable as they become realized in religious philanthropy, how can we explain the kinds of innovation we see in social mobilization, including the development of industrialized religious philanthropy in the 1980s? Stability and innovation are never easy partners. The new kinds of engaged religious networks now mobilize people on far larger scales and in different ways than were previously possible. Our findings repeatedly focused our attention on the important roles of women in innovating these new kinds of organizations. Just as striking was the great increase in at least the avowal of universalist goals for religious charity – a willingness to help anyone in need anywhere in the world.

Alongside religious philanthropy constructed from strong social capital, our cases thus show the importance of new networks built out of the ability to cultivate social innovations that may undercut existing social capital. We will discuss several different mechanisms through which this can occur. Groups are sometimes able to catalyze dormant social ties, like those of gender or class, to mobilize people in new ways. In other cases, they are able to repurpose existing networks or connect across networks to create something new. Finally, with religious groups in particular we can see the importance of vertical ties to a charismatic leader, which can foster completely new networks. These appear to be the key techniques that have encouraged new roles for women and new concepts of the good over the past several decades. As we will discuss, they have been aided particularly by increased mobility, rapid urbanization, and a general weakening of older village- and neighborhood-based forms of social control.

Much of our discussion throughout the book focuses on theoretical and empirical questions raised by our observation of increasing similarities in engaged religions over the past few decades, across both religious and political lines. In Chapter 7, however, we open the question of what happens beyond the image of universal goodness that has become so widely shared. In fact, many other versions of the good continue to exist in our field areas. Just one has come to dominate, but the alternate moralities implied by the others continue to be important. In some ways, the more open field for religious philanthropy has actually encouraged diversity because groups are trying to differentiate themselves from what others do.

Research Orientations and Methods

To pursue these questions, the authors undertook field research at multiple locations. Our goal in choosing sites was to capture the kinds of variation involved in our broad questions – primarily variation in religious tradition and in regime type. We make no claims to be representative. Chinese society is so large and so varied, especially if we look beyond China's national borders, that our qualitative and contextual methods will never be representative.[20] The

[20] There are many other places, of course, that could have been added. Singapore and Hong Kong, for instance, share a British colonial history with Malaysia, but with very different ethnic mixes. Other Chinese communities exist all over the globe in virtually every kind of political regime. We are not, however, trying to create a typology of political systems, but to use some case studies to show the types of political influences that have been important in shaping religious philanthropy.

choice is instead intended to illustrate how religious charity develops in varying local and historical contexts.

We concentrated on just three of China's many religious traditions: Christianity (in both Catholic and Protestant forms), Buddhism, and the less institutionalized worship at local shrines ("temple religion," for lack of a better term). We chose these three because they have been the most rapidly growing traditions in mainland China and occupy important positions in Taiwan and Malaysia as well. We have been less systematic about the others – even obvious cases with important charitable traditions of their own, like Islam – simply because of limitations on our own time, resources, and knowledge. We will, however, make occasional comparative comments, especially about Daoism and Islam.

Chinese popular worship at local temples is extremely widespread. It has revived faster than anything else in China today, and has long been important in all Chinese societies. Worshipping a variety of spirits, it has intimate ties to community life and has shaped widely influential values such as filial piety, loyalty, and a sense of local identity. Large, organized Buddhist groups, especially in the newer forms that have grown so rapidly, seem to have thrived first in Taiwan, but have now spread through Chinese communities around the world. Many of these have a strong emphasis on philanthropy. They stress changing the character of adherents toward a this-worldly Bodhisattva ideal of dedication to helping others. Christianity has been active in China, with Catholics coming during the Ming Dynasty and establishing a permanent presence, and Protestant missionaries coming from the early nineteenth century on. Its rapid recent growth on the mainland – as in much of the world – makes it important to study. Not all villages have churches, but where they exist they have been important in building up social goods, often through joint efforts of the congregation. Christianity, Buddhism, and local temple worship are represented at each of our field sites, although in quite different proportions.

Although we will continue to use the term, we should note again that the category of "religion" (宗教) is deeply problematic in Chinese societies, taking on something like the modern Western meaning only in the early twentieth century. Some of the material we discuss is officially recognized as religion only in some of our field sites; temple worship is considered religion by most people in Taiwan, for example, but not on the Chinese mainland. Even the less troubled designation of Buddhism or Daoism as religions carries some problems if we imagine the category is really the same as the English term. Clergy aside, few people consider themselves Buddhists or Daoists in the same ways that Christians consider themselves Protestant or Catholic; terms like "conversion" are problematic when applied in such contexts. Others have told the story of how "religion" came to be such an important category in Chinese societies over the past century, of the problems it creates in understanding pre-twentieth-century practices and many of their modern continuations, and of the continuing political and social consequences of the category.[21] We will continue to use the term anyway, however, because of its political importance in all three places we studied, and because of the lack of useful alternatives in English.

We will often refer to the phenomena we are studying as "engaged religion" rather than "faith-based organizations," which is the most common term in the literature.[22] This is in part because the reduction of religion to faith – that is to beliefs rather than to rituals and other embodied practices – does not do justice to the full range of Chinese religiosities. In addition, the emphasis on "organizations" implies that something like secular NGOs are the most important carriers of these ideas. We prefer not to make this assumption. As we will discuss briefly in the conclusion, though, "engaged religion" as a term has its own dangers. In addition to the problem of "religion" as a category, the term can be taken to imply separate religious and social spheres that engage with each other. Although this is not inaccurate as a description of the relationship that modern state policies tend to assume in China, Malaysia, and Taiwan, it is not a useful way of thinking about earlier Chinese forms of social engagement, which never drew such a strong distinction between society and religion. We thus intend "engagement" only in a broad and loose sense.

We should also note here that one religious group receives particular attention in the text that follows: the Buddhist Compassion Relief Tzu Chi Foundation, with which we began this chapter. Tzu Chi was founded in 1966 by the Ven. Cheng Yen with an explicit mandate to foster a Buddhism that could create a Pure Land on earth by motivating everyone to help others. They began with just thirty housewives and six nuns on Taiwan's poor and isolated east coast, but expanded extremely rapidly in the 1980s, quickly establishing branches across the island and soon around the entire world.[23] In 2014 they claimed approximately ten million members in fifty countries and regions.[24]

We do not discuss Tzu Chi at such length simply because it is so large. The organization was a major presence in all our field sites in Malaysia, Taiwan, and China. Furthermore, it exerted a strong influence on the activities of other groups. Few made an explicit point of saying that they had imitated techniques and strategies from Tzu Chi, but as we will discuss, the borrowing seemed clear anyway, sometimes even in the names of some of the organizations themselves.

21 Most notably, see Goossaert and Palmer, *The Religious Question in Modern China*, 2011.

22 We do not engage with their arguments here, but note that there is also a lively debate around the term "engaged Buddhism." See, for example, Queen and King, *Engaged Buddhism*.

23 For details, see Huang, *Charisma and Compassion*, 2009.

24 "Buddhist Tzu Chi Foundation Fact Sheet."

In each state our research centered on a city or town and its surrounding area. In China, the main site was Suzhou and its nearby urban centers. We sometimes extended this through the entire Jiangnan region, from Hangzhou to Nanjing. These are all large cities in China's coastal south, with a rapidly growing economy and a rapidly urbanizing lifestyle; the entire region is now closely tied together by high-speed rail. We sometimes supplement this with material from other fieldwork in more rural parts of mainland China to capture more of the country's enormous variation, including the Handan (Hebei) region in the much poorer north of China, and some ethnically mixed areas in northern Yunnan.

In Taiwan, the focus was on the town of Lukang, which had lost its nineteenth-century place as one of Taiwan's major ports, but remained an important center of local temple worship and tourism. In Malaysia, the work was primarily in Malacca, one of the centers of the Chinese population there. The bulk of the field research dedicated to this project took place in 2006 and continued sporadically until late 2014. In several cases we also build on earlier work of the authors in those areas. Chapter 2 will describe each of the field sites in more detail.[25] In all of our cases we worked with clergy from across the religious spectrum, volunteers and others involved in the activities of engaged religions, and relevant government officials. Our primary methods were participant observation and extended interviews, although we also used some focus groups.

Much of the conceptual framework we use here – political merit-making, network innovation, industrialized philanthropy, civic selving, and the rest – developed only in the process of our fieldwork and through many joint discussions of our material. Perhaps the most fundamental issue we address is the problem of the social life of goodness, of the ways that people conceptualize and act on their varied concepts of the good. Our process of analysis pushed us increasingly toward this problem, as our field data gradually forced us to reconsider the assumption that "doing good" is something obvious and natural. This assumption runs through much of the literature on faith-based organizations and related issues, but it is wrong: there are many goods. Much of the rest of this book describes how that "natural" image of goodness has become predominant in the last few decades across all of our field sites, but

[25] Each of us took primary responsibility for one site, although there were also sometimes opportunities to work together. In China, Wu led the work in Suzhou and its region, although Weller was able to add to the material while based in Nanjing in 2013–2014, Fan added her long experience of research in and around Shanghai, and Huang added her brief research in Suzhou and Shanghai in 2005. The Handan material is from Fan, and the Yunnan work is from Wu. Huang led the research in Malaysia, and Weller took responsibility for the Taiwan site (joined for some of the time by Huang). We have collaborated very closely throughout the process, and so generally do not name individual researchers when we discuss our field data.

this is a story strongly conditioned by the particular trends and pressures of that time period, and strongly shaped by local political and social conditions. Our final chapter returns in particular to the issue of how what we will call the "image of the unlimited good" has been naturalized, but also draws attention to how incomplete that process is, with many alternative goods continuing to be influential.

2 Legacies and Discontinuities in China, Taiwan, and Malaysia

Before the modern word for "religion" (宗教) entered the Chinese vocabulary from Japan (and before that from Europe) at the turn of the twentieth century, the deity-based activity we now often call "popular religion" was integrated into general community forms and was not conceptually separated as a "teaching" (教, such as Buddhism, Daoism, or Christianity). For the sake of simplicity and convenience, we use the word religion to refer to those systematic teachings as well as the community forms of "popular religion." This chapter discusses the continuities and disjunctures of engaged religions and the public good from late imperial China to the contemporary societies of China, Taiwan, and Malaysia. "Religion" is always in the story because religious groups have been deeply intertwined in philanthropy in China throughout history.

Late imperial China is important to the current study not only because a lively array of social organizations (including lineage groups,[1] benevolent halls,[2] and redemptive societies[3]) emerged in the Ming and Qing Dynasties, but also because these locally engaged groups – often within a religious milieu – have survived, in varying forms and degrees, in our three different states. It is not our purpose to suggest an essentialized version of "Chinese culture" that has propelled "Chinese philanthropy," but it is our goal to set the discussion within a sociohistorical context. This contextualized view is paramount for our understanding of the forms and organizations of contemporary socially engaged religion in the three states.

Chinese religions of every kind in the late imperial period engaged with people's social lives in ways that extended well beyond temples and their rituals. In some ways, the current increase in such activities in all three states is not new, but connects to a tradition that had been curtailed through the secularizing strategies of states dedicated to their own visions of modernity. As we demonstrate later, this connection to the past is especially clear in the cases of Taiwan

[1] Faure, *Emperor and Ancestor*.

[2] Leung, *Charity and Jiaohua: Philanthropic Groups in Ming and Qing China*; Smith, *The Art of Doing Good*.

[3] Duara, *Sovereignty and Authenticity*, 2004.

and Malacca. One surprising finding is that Chinese society in Malacca, though it is geographically the most removed from China and has by far the longest colonial history, most strongly resembles that of late imperial China with its vibrant array of benevolent halls and organizations reminiscent of redemptive societies. The importance of local temples and religious engagement in Taiwan makes it second in line. Mainland China, despite geographic continuity, resembles late imperial China the least in the forms and organizations of religious engagement. One of our goals in this chapter is to explain these differences in national patterns.

This chapter will also demonstrate that although we see continuities in the rise of religious work for the general good, there have been important changes since the late Qing Dynasty in how that "good" is understood, especially in the case of China and Taiwan. This stems in part from a change in the understanding of the role of the state, from a Confucian conception of the state as ultimately responsible for the welfare of its people to something resembling a neoliberal image of the state as a guarantor of a smoothly functioning market with limited social responsibilities. Thus, for example, emergency relief over long distances took place in the late Qing either generally through the state, or through sojourning elites who would send help home through their particularistic ties (such as benevolent halls). It is only recently that we have seen religious organizations, strictly defined, take on this role for groups beyond their own immediate supporters and home communities.

Lastly, this chapter establishes that the 1980s and 1990s mark an important transition in the timeline of engaged religions in Chinese societies. This is clearest in the cases of China and Taiwan. Before the 1980s, either religious groups' activities were disrupted for political reasons or religious-based charities remained locally bound – providing aid only to their immediate neighborhoods or members. By the 1990s, however, not only had such engaged religions expanded their scope, but new transnational and de-territorialized organizations also emerged and began to influence the ways that local religious groups perceived their own possibilities of social engagement. Owing to the timing of these changes, the bulk of this book will be devoted to the discussion of post-1980s developments in the three states.

We will begin with a brief account of engaged religious groups in late imperial China and beyond, focusing on benevolent halls and societies (善堂 and 善会) in the Ming and Qing, redemptive societies in the 1920s to 1940s, and Christian missionary philanthropies (such as the YMCA) prior to the 1950s. This section largely summarizes existing historical studies, primarily to make three points: (1) rather than a simple legacy of uninterrupted institutions, the Chinese past offers a repertoire of possible discourses and practices of engaged religion based on a history of ongoing change; (2) this changing nature of engaged religious groups could never be separated from a constant rebalancing of state/society relations and changing economic resources; and (3) philanthropy consistently intertwined with religious life throughout the period.

From there we offer a brief description of the most recent developments in China, Taiwan, and Malaysia, focusing on the different political landscapes and the important transitions in the 1980s and 1990s. We will argue that a shared legacy of late imperial socially engaged religions and the particular sociopolitical histories of the past century together shaped the different pictures that we see today. Throughout this chapter and the next, we will also attend particularly to how the political differences among our three cases have shaped the history of religious engagement.

Engaged Religions and the Public Good in Late Imperial and Republican China

State and religion were key players in philanthropic activities and institutions that emerged throughout late imperial and republican China. Writing in 1912 at the dawn of the Chinese Republican Revolution, Yu-Yue Tsu (朱友渔) remarked that "the popular character and control of philanthropic institutions cannot be too strongly advocated" and he treated popular participation in philanthropy as a sign of the "practical democracy of the nation."[4] Though Tsu, a converted Christian, recognized that "philanthropy … received tremendous encouragement and development by a close alliance with religion," he conceded that the idea of philanthropy had to "dissociate itself from religion" and become a "social virtue."[5] Core to his understanding of Chinese philanthropy was the evolution from charity to mutual aid and ultimately civic betterment.[6] Yet we know that deities and gods were often central to Chinese benevolent societies and trade associations at least in the mid-nineteenth century, both as focal points of legitimation and as means of mobilization. Religious organizations have been part and parcel of such social engagement throughout the history of Chinese people. Tsu's hope for a purely secular spirit of charity was a distinctly twentieth-century phenomenon.

Long before the emergence of organizations such as benevolent halls and societies in late imperial China as major players facilitating social relief, the Chinese state already played important roles in social welfare provision. This could be traced to the *Book of Rites* in the Han Dynasty (202 BC to AD 220), which clearly stated that the Chinese state was responsible for two kinds of relief: disaster relief and the caretaking of widowers, widows, children without fathers, and elderly people without children (鳏寡孤独).[7] It is safe to say that

[4] Tsu, "The Spirit of Chinese Philanthropy: A Study in Mutual Aid," 28.

[5] Ibid., 15.

[6] Ibid., 29–30.

[7] Fuma, *History of Chinese Benevolent Halls and Associations*, 34–41.

such policies toward "the needy" started at least by the Han Dynasty, which was the first Chinese state to use Confucianism as the ruling ideology, and continued throughout the rest of Chinese history. However, notions of the "needy" shifted. Disaster relief was always important to the state, but poverty relief and other aspects of the modern concept of social welfare such as care for the sick, disabled, elderly, and orphans were not always covered by state policies.

According to Angela Leung, religious groups organized relief for the poor and the sick from the Liang Dynasty (late fifth century) to the beginning of the Song Dynasty (mid-tenth century) for "theological and philosophical reasons" or when inspired by imperially sponsored Buddhism.[8] Fuma Susumu holds that even in the Song Dynasty (960–1279) nominally state-run charities such as Futian Yuan (福田院), Anji Fang (安济坊), and Yangji Yuan (养济院) were all actually run by Buddhist monks. Juyang Yuan (居养院) of Huizhou, for instance, was officially managed by the state in the Song Dynasty, but was in reality a small temple run by monks.[9] Thus, at least by the tenth century, Buddhists were engaged in promoting charity through collective action and large-scale institutions, and even state-run charity had powerful religious connections.

It was not long, however, until the state came to perceive the large land ownership and wealth of Buddhist monasteries as a threat and came up with a series of measures to contain that power, often by subsidizing the temples with state funding. By the tenth century, many such temples were forced to close down, as the state took over the leadership of institutions such as hospitals while putting social elites in charge of daily management.[10] The Song court continued this practice and played an increasingly prominent role in social welfare provision. Even then, however, religion never ceased to be a player. The famous Fan Lineage Charity (范氏义庄) established by Fan Zhongyan (范仲淹, 989–1058) during the Song Dynasty, for example, modeled its charitable estate on the permanent endowment lands in Buddhist monasteries.[11]

While Song participation in social welfare provision can be seen as an effort of moral governance (德政), the Ming court (1368–1644) clearly used it in part as a tool of social control to deal with large numbers of urban poor and people displaced by wars and disasters.[12] Again, though religious groups were not initiators of this welfare provision, they were certainly "engaged" in such activities. For instance, the Ming court official Lü Kun (吕坤) ordered any disabled men between thirteen and fifty years of age to spend one year in a Buddhist monastery to learn skills they could use to making a living, such as

[8] We will return to Buddhist understandings of charity in Chapter 6.
[9] Fuma, *History of Chinese Benevolent Halls and Associations*, 39.
[10] Leung, *Charity and Jiaohua: Philanthropic Groups in Ming and Qing China*, 32.
[11] Ibid., 43.
[12] Ibid., 44–45.

folk singing, fortune telling, sewing shoes, and writing letters. The goal was for them to learn the Confucian virtues of ritual propriety (礼) and righteousness (义).[13] Even in such state-run charities, the engagement of religious groups and sites was obvious.

In addition to the kinds of charitable causes that would be recognized anywhere in the world, a number of organizations were dedicated to causes with more uniquely Chinese features, typically drawing on specifically Buddhist or Confucian thought. These included, for example, Life Releasing Societies (放生会), which freed captive fish and animals; Cherishing Writing Societies (惜字会), which collected and ritually burned scraps of paper with writing on them; Chastity Societies for Widows (清节堂), which supported widows, especially younger ones, who refused to remarry, and so forth. These societies promoted Buddhist ideas of compassion and merit-making as well as Confucian ethics of filial piety. They may not be considered philanthropies in the modern sense, but they constituted the "good" at that time. These examples show one way that the content of "goodness" has shifted over time.

Benevolent halls and societies became prevalent in the centuries of the Ming (1368–1644) and Qing Dynasties (1644–1911). William Rowe's study of nineteenth-century Hankow, for instance, depicted a lively picture of benevolent halls engaged in public welfare provision such as soup kitchens, provision of smallpox vaccinations, schools for the poor, and lifeboat brigades, generally shifting orientation from ritualized respect for the dead to the care of the living.[14] Echoing Tsu, who regarded them as the sprouts of democracy in China, Rowe saw these benevolent halls as grassroots organizations infused with Confucian values, constituting a public sphere with "de facto autonomy" from the state.[15] Fredric Wakeman Jr. attacked the argument, however, arguing that these organizations all thought of themselves as acting on behalf of the state and therefore it was not civil society at all.[16] Fuma went even further to say that the sheer size of these organizations at the grassroots level blocked the top-down modernizing processes that succeeded more thoroughly in other Asian states such as India and Japan.[17] For our purposes, it is enough to note that charity, religion, and state control were intimately intertwined, however we might judge the balance between civil society and state penetration.

Angela Leung's study of charitable organizations of the Ming and Qing Dynasties, which were initiated primarily by local elites and merchants,

[13] This is from Lü Kun's *Shi Zheng Lu* (实证录). Thanks to Joanna Handlin Smith for pointing this reference out to us.

[14] Rowe, *Hankow*, 91–186.

[15] Rowe, "The Public Sphere in Modern China."

[16] Wakeman, "The Civil Society and Public Sphere Debate."

[17] Fuma, *History of Chinese Benevolent Halls and Associations*, 646–647.

points out that a Confucian civilizing and moralizing orientation was a crucial motive behind such charities.[18] She counted 973 institutions for the care of baby orphans (育婴堂), 399 for the elderly and sick (普济堂), 216 for young widows (清节堂), 589 benevolent halls for delivering coffins, 338 general charities, and 743 unclassified ones in the Qing dynasty alone.[19] By confining her analysis to a Chinese society that had not yet been influenced by Western (Christian) notions of charity, Leung was able to trace crucial changes in this period, which she summarizes as institutionalization, bureaucratization, and the consolidation of the Confucian social elite through such practices (which she calls 儒生化).

Joanna Handlin Smith's study of late Ming benevolent societies through the writings of five important literati draws a partially different picture from Leung.[20] She sees their main motivations as their hope to establish closer ties with local society and their desire for self-cultivation. In contrast to Leung's focus on the influence of Confucian status, Smith describes how some of the organizations gathered in Buddhist temples and resembled voluntary religious groups in organization. Some of her benevolent society founders dabbled with Buddhism but later distanced themselves from it.[21] Like the other studies, however, she does not emphasize charity work initiated and practiced by religious organizations, which is our primary interest here.

Let us turn to the example of the Tongshanhui ("Society for Sharing Goodness," 同善会), one of the most important and influential benevolent societies of the Ming–Qing Dynasties.[22] Tongshanhui could be traced to 1590, when the Confucian scholar Yang Dongming (杨东明) founded this organization in Henan to realize his belief in *shengsheng* (生生), meaning that human beings are all connected to the universe that is ever reproducing. Therefore, it is important to care for other fellow human beings, especially when they are needy. The real flourishing of the Tongshanhui, however, appeared in the lower Yangzi River delta, the so-called Jiangnan region, because of its wealth and urban environment. By the late Ming, the Tongshanhui established branches in eight Jiangnan counties. Soon its organizations reached to Shanghai and throughout the provinces of Jiangsu, Zhejiang, Fujian, and beyond.

[18] Leung, *Charity and Jiaohua: Philanthropic Groups in Ming and Qing China*. She argues that her subject of study is nonreligious and non-state-run charities in order to emphasize the rise of the Confucian class through bottom-up charitable organizations, but her description reveals that those groups are not completely free of either religious influences or state interferences.

[19] Ibid., 2.

[20] Smith, *The Art of Doing Good*.

[21] Ibid., 81.

[22] Fuma, *History of Chinese Benevolent Halls and Associations*, 78–125; Smith, *The Art of Doing Good*, 43–154; Leung, *Charity and Jiaohua: Philanthropic Groups in Ming and Qing China*, 152–159.

Founded by literati who had retired from official posts or were without official titles, their source of income came from two areas: real estate donated by wealthy founding members and monthly membership fees. The society met two or four times a year, varying by individual branches. One of the main activities in those meetings was to deliver teachings on good behavior, often in heavily Confucian terms. To push this moralizing message further, the Tongshanhui did not allow giving aid to the people who worked for the *yamen* (衙门, bureaucratic offices), monks and Daoists, butchers, or unfilial sons who squandered away the family fortune. That is, they did not emphasize universal care but embarked on a Confucian moral mission.

A record in Fengjing Township (枫泾镇) of Jiangsu province shows that the Tongshanhui hosted a ten-day teaching session every month, with three days in the hall and seven days in different Buddhist monasteries.[23] However, they failed to repeat this pattern successfully in poor or rural areas. An official tried to replicate the Tongshanhui in Tongle County of Fujian province, for example, but the voluntary donations did not work because people were too poor and its rural environment also made the lectures hard to deliver. The association there thus gradually evolved into something forced onto the villagers by the local government. In 1776, the Tongshanhui of another poor county (Zhenhai, 镇海) in Zhejiang province also gave up on the moral teachings and on the delivery of food, clothing, money, and medicine. They were able to afford only the free burial of roadside corpses. Benevolent societies such as the Tongshanhui could maintain their particular operational model only in towns and cities where large numbers of people lived and a great amount of wealth existed.[24]

Such benevolent halls and societies played extremely important roles in providing social services to the needy, and it is clear that both religion and the state were key players. Angela Leung noted that Tongshanhui began as a symbol of the opposition between local society and the state from the late Ming through the Shunzhi period in the early Qing (1638–1661), but had become a symbol of the legitimacy of Qing governance by the Qianlong period (1711–1799). Beginning around that time, the Qing state grew increasingly involved in the management of benevolent halls and societies, from giving out permit badges (照验牌), to allocating physical buildings and appointing heads of such societies.[25]

Furthermore, the Tongshanhui no longer paid respect to the locally important Five Sages (五贤) as they had in the Ming, but made offerings to Wenchang (文昌), a national deity for Confucian scholars, in the Qing.[26] In the Qing,

[23] Fuma, *History of Chinese Benevolent Halls and Associations*, 92.

[24] Ibid., 91.

[25] Leung, *Charity and Jiaohua: Philanthropic Groups in Ming and Qing China*, 155–157.

[26] Ibid., 159. Wuxian refers to Mencius, Xunzi (荀子), Yangxiong (扬雄), Wang Tong (王通), and Han Yu (韩愈).

other benevolent halls also worshipped deities, whether or not they had ties to formal religious groups. The infant orphanage (育婴堂) in Nanxun County of Zhejiang Province worshipped Bixia Yuanjun (碧霞元君), a deity who protects mothers and babies (also much favored by the Qing court); in Gaoyou (高邮) of Jiangsu Province the orphanage worshipped Guanyin; in Suzhou, it was housed in the Daoist Xuanmiao Guan (玄妙观) and in Nanjing, the Buddhist monk Huixin was one of the initiators. The case of Tongshanhui demonstrates that both state and religion became increasingly prevalent in the operation of the benevolent halls.

One other prominent feature of the benevolent halls was the participation of women. Leung remarked that women participated directly or indirectly (through their sons) in the founding of a number of benevolent halls for young widows. These halls were so numerous and successful that Christian missionaries later emulated their practices and offered protection for young widows.[27] The widows' hall in Shanghai even had female managers (司事). Within lineage charities (义庄), widows of high prestige often oversaw the caretaking of young widows in the lineage.[28] Infant orphanages in the early Qing also hired a large number of wet nurses working outside their homes.[29] Even though they were not able to challenge the Confucian patriarchal system, these groups did offer some women a way to make a living outside their homes and sometimes to make a social impact.[30] As we turn to the Republican Period, we will see that women also played important roles in the redemptive societies of the time; they have again been important in the past few decades, as we discuss in Chapter 6.

Religious philanthropy in the Republican period (1912–1949) experienced "the rise, on the basis of local charities (*shantang*) of the Qing period, of larger, pan-Chinese organizations."[31] Prasenjit Duara coined the term "redemptive societies" to refer to those "larger, pan-Chinese organizations," which were "determined to save the world from strife, greed, and warfare, and which affected the lives of many millions of followers in the first half of this century."[32] Some of the famous redemptive societies included the Daodehui (道德会, Morality Society), Shijie Hongwanzihui (世界红卍字会, World Red Swastika Society), Tongshanshe[33] (同善社, Fellowship of Goodness), Zailijiao (在理教, Teaching of the Abiding Principle), Shijie Zongjiao Datonghui (世界宗教大同, Society for the Great Unity of World Religions), and Yiguandao (一貫道, Pervasive Way). All of them engaged in charitable work and were

[27] Ibid., 218.
[28] Ibid., 7, 234–235.
[29] Ibid., 7, 120–121.
[30] Ibid., 235.
[31] Goossaert and Palmer, *The Religious Question in Modern China*, 2011, 79.
[32] Duara, "The Discourse of Civilization and Pan-Asianism," 117.
[33] This is not to be confused with the benevolent society Tongshanhui (同善会).

strongly religious in character. The World Red Swastika Society, for example, was founded in 1921 by the spirit writing society called Daoyuan (道院) and claimed 7 to 10 million members in 1937. Moreover, these societies developed large networks throughout China. The Fellowship of Goodness apparently had more than a thousand branches throughout regions of China proper and Manchuria in 1923.[34] Prominent features of such societies were syncretism, sectarianism, and philanthropy.

> The modern redemptive societies inherited the mission of universalism and moral self-transformation from this syncretism. At the same time, these societies also retained the association of the older syncretic societies with sectarian traditions, popular gods, and practices such as divination, planchette, and spirit writing. … In this way they continued to remain organically connected to Chinese popular society.[35]

The redemptive societies established a wide range of philanthropic institutions and charitable enterprises in the Republican era. Komukai Sukurato called these groups "religious-style charitable societies" (宗教性的慈善会).[36] Much like benevolent halls in the late Ming and Qing, they were also very much interested in cultivating public morality through their teachings. The New Religion to Save the World (救世新教), for example, not only established hospitals, orphanages, refugee centers, schools, factories, and farms employing the poor, savings and loan associations, and engaged in road and bridge repair, but also set up libraries, newspapers, and lectures to spread its teachings. The World Red Swastika Society, modeled after the Red Cross, engaged in disaster relief as well as the establishment of professorships of Esperanto in Paris, London, and Tokyo. The Zailijiao, with twenty-eight centers in Beijing and Tianjin in 1913, and forty-eight centers in Tianjin alone by the late 1920s, devoted itself to drug rehabilitation using herbal medicines and self-cultivation techniques; they claimed to have brought more than 200 opium addicts to full recovery each year.[37] The Tongshanshe offered meals and beds to refugees in Shandong, established schools to teach the Four Books and Five Classics, and even ran English language night schools in Yantai, Shandong.[38]

Again, like the benevolent halls that were not truly politically "autonomous," the redemptive societies had an entangled relationship with the state. The Nationalist Party (Guomindang, GMD), aiming to build a modern state, took the eradication of superstition as one of its foremost tasks. This project

[34] Duara, "The Discourse of Civilization and Pan-Asianism," 117–118.
[35] Ibid., 119.
[36] Quoted in DuBois, "Before the NGO," 543.
[37] Duara, "The Discourse of Civilization and Pan-Asianism," 120.
[38] Cao, "From Famine History to Crisis Metaphor: Social Memory and Cultural Identity in Chinese Rural Society," 128.

included inventing a concept of religion modeled after Christianity.[39] Rights of freedom of religions in the Republican national constitution applied only to those who had something that resembled a church, joined voluntarily, and with a belief system based on sacred texts. Redemptive societies deviated from this model and were quickly excluded and outlawed. The 1929 Regulation on the Supervision of Charitable Organizations (监督慈善团体法) was a legal effort that prevented these charitable organizations from carrying out religious missions.[40] The Tongshanshe was eradicated in addition because of its close connections with the Beiyang government, a regime of warlords. However, other groups such as the Zailijiao were able to rid themselves of the accusation of superstition through their anti-opium work and by their ability to persuade the Republican government to accept them as social welfare organizations (公益团体).[41] Therefore, if the group was not eradicated, it was often co-opted by the government.[42] This legal framework of the GMD continued after 1949 in Taiwan. Many such redemptive societies went underground and managed to survive and sometimes thrive. For instance, the Yiguandao was outlawed by the GMD in Taiwan until 1987, but nevertheless thrived underground and became one of the largest and most active societies in today's Taiwan and among Chinese in Southeast Asia.

The Manchukuo government, while condemning the "superstitious" aspect of these groups, "saw in them the potential for their transformation into state-controlled civic organizations"[43] and turned them into "*jiaohua* (*kyoka* in Japanese) organizations – agencies engaged in welfare and enlightenment of the people" under its supervision.[44] As a result, the societies were not "secret" in the way that the GMD or Chinese Communist Party (CCP) government would condemn. In Manchukuo, at least, they were very public:

> Records reveal the registration of, or petitions to register, a very large number of these societies between 1937 and 1945 with either the Department of Police, the Department of Social Affairs, or the Department of Rites. In some places, these societies registered with the quasi-official "Revive Asia Association" (Xingyayuan) or the "New Peoples Society" (Xinminhui). The total figure for participants or followers of all societies within a single county or city often reached beyond tens of thousands.[45]

The redemptive societies could be regarded as a continuation from the benevolent societies active in the Ming and Qing, but they surpassed those groups

[39] Goossaert, "Republican Church Engineering: The National Religious Associations in 1912 China."
[40] DuBois, "Public Health and Private Charity in Northeast China, 1905–1945," 519.
[41] Nedostup, *Superstitious Regimes*, 27–66.
[42] DuBois, "Public Health and Private Charity in Northeast China, 1905–1945," 529.
[43] Takizawa, quoted in Duara, "The Discourse of Civilization and Pan-Asianism," 124.
[44] Gluck and Garon, quoted in Duara, "The Discourse of Civilization and Pan-Asianism," 124.
[45] Ibid., 125.

in numbers of followers, scale of organization, and influence. The benevolent societies had been township or county based, but the newer redemptive societies had a much larger national and even transnational network. Both kinds of groups had similarly intertwined relationships with the state. Many heads of the benevolent societies were retired court officials or at least tried to cultivate a good relationship with local government. Some redemptive societies were more political than others by actively aligning with the Japanese Manchukuo government against the GMD or aligning with the GMD against the CCP. In both cases it was hard to draw a line between "state" and "society." Both benevolent halls and redemptive societies had religious messages and forms of organization, as well as a passion for charitable enterprises. Both of them were also interested in civilizing and moralizing the general public by offering Confucian and popular Buddhist teachings. They were interested in both doing good and imparting knowledge of "goodness."

The redemptive societies were relentlessly syncretic across what they called the five religions: Daoism, Confucianism, Buddhism, Christianity, and Islam. They provided a wider array of public goods in the turmoil of early twentieth-century China (Japanese invasion, the presence of other colonial powers, and a civil war) than benevolent societies in the Ming and Qing. They were also more innovative, for instance by establishing English language schools or girls' schools, building farms and factories for the poor, or treating drug addiction. The "goods" these redemptive societies sought were not only limited to moral teachings but also extended to the betterment of the nation through the improvement of fellow countrymen's individual bodies. Despite their extensive national and even transnational networks, however, the organization of the redemptive societies resembled popular religious groups more than the contemporary industrial philanthropies on which this book focuses most, as we will discuss later.

Women played even more important roles in redemptive societies of the Republican era than they had in benevolent societies; by this time they were "enmeshed in projects of sovereignty and governmentality."[46] The 312 branches of the Manchukuo Morality Society, for example, established 235 Virtuous Girls' Schools (贞女义学) by 1934.[47] Many women favored separate organizations, probably to limit the interference from men in the daily management of the branches.[48] Women took over the management of schools; concubines, stepmothers, neglected first wives, and other women, many of whom were Buddhists, became lecturers.[49] Like women who supported the benevolent

[46] Duara, *Sovereignty and Authenticity*, 2004, 131.
[47] Ibid., 114.
[48] Ibid., 139.
[49] Ibid., 154.

societies, they did not challenge filial values, but they valorized public or social services as "a moral obligation to society."[50] Some women even refused to get married thanks to the financial independence they could maintain through their public lectures. Using this rhetoric of moral betterment, which was promoted by the Republican state, they were able to negotiate for improved conditions for women in general. Women's active participation in charities could be seen throughout late imperial, republican, and contemporary Chinese societies and throughout all religious denominations, including among Christians.

The first Protestant Christian missionary, Robert Morrison, entered China in 1807. As a result of suppression by the Qing court, the thirty-five-year effort of the first sixty-three missionaries led to the conversion of only about twenty Chinese. But with the signing of the Nanjing Treaty (1842), Tianjin Treaty (1858), and Beijing Treaty (1860), missionaries received privileged access to China's most important cities.[51] From 1906 to 1949, the number of Protestants grew from 180,000 to nearly a million and that of Catholics (who had a much longer history in China) grew from 500,000 to 3 million.[52] They soon dominated in education and charity: by 1914, there were 8,034 Catholic and 3,511 Protestant elementary schools, plus 542 Protestant high schools and universities.[53] These Protestant universities educated and converted many of China's elite scholars and government officials.

The Christian missionary Timothy Richard played an eminent role in leading disaster relief, such as after the Great North China Famine of 1876–1879. He also initiated the building of more than 300 hospitals. By 1949, 70 percent of the hospitals in China were built by Christian missionaries.[54] In Southern Jiangsu, local residents still remember the Christian origin of many hospitals and schools. For instance, the current No. 1 People's Hospital in Suzhou was built in the late nineteenth century by the American Methodist Episcopal Mission. The current Suzhou University was originally Dongwu University set up by the same mission. These efforts became targets of emulation by some of the redemptive societies that were active at the same period, especially two "institutional innovations:" "endowed funding and a dedicated administrative structure."[55] For instance, Goossaert and Palmer see the Red Swastika Society and Daoyuan as imitations of such Christian charities.

The YMCA and YWCA are good illustrations of the social engagement of Christian groups in this period. These organizations were established in China in the late nineteenth century and soon spread throughout the country. By 1920,

[50] Ibid., 155.
[51] Li, *The History of Early Christian Missionaries to China*, 269.
[52] Goossaert and Palmer, *The Religious Question in Modern China*, 2011, 72.
[53] Ibid., 77–78.
[54] Gao, "The Positive Role of Religion in Society."
[55] DuBois, "Before the NGO," 542.

thirty provinces in China established YMCA branches including one among the Chinese students in Tokyo.[56] The YMCA in Beijing built two universities and three night schools, teaching English, Chinese, mathematics, commerce, and so forth.[57] Besides building schools, the earlier charitable programs ranged from community services (such as infant care, career training, family counseling, leadership training, sports and entertainment), public lectures in prisons and rehabilitation centers, and so forth. John Stewart Burgess, a member of the Beijing YMCA and coauthor of *Peking, A Social Survey* (1921), also helped to found the Sociology and Social Work Department of Yenching University.

Interestingly, full-fledged relief projects coincided with the localization processes of the YMCA in the 1930s. During that period, the number of Chinese people in leadership positions went up, partly owing to anti-missionary sentiment. The pre-1930s YMCA had been more interested in proselytizing. The frequent natural disasters in the early 1930s and the Japanese invasion toward the end of that decade propelled the YMCA to be more engaged in disaster relief, especially feeding the homeless, poor, women, and children; hiring able-bodied men affected by disasters to help in reconstruction; giving out loans to help the reconstruction; and so on. During the war, the YMCA took anti-Japanese positions and set up a Soldier Service Department that provided medical support for the wounded (feeding, cleaning, and even writing letters for the wounded soldiers to their families). They also helped resettling dispersed students. The YMCA was active in the anti-Japanese resistance and came under the influence of the CCP during the civil war.[58] Some of the local leaders, such as Wu Yaozong (吴耀宗 1893–1979), played prominent roles in the Christian associations in the PRC.[59]

The legacy of Christian missionaries' social engagement left a clear mark on today's Christian charities (as in the contemporary YMCA charity seen in Figure 2.1). Christians in contemporary China still uphold the narrative that Christians have always been engaged in charity, especially building schools and hospitals; similar claims are echoed by Christians across Taiwan and Malacca. However, Christian missionaries did not enter a Chinese society that was completely void of charity and philanthropy. On the contrary, as we have discussed, there was a very active scene of engaged religions side by side with all kinds of state-run relief agencies such as police offices and various government disaster relief bureaus (助赈局).[60] The point, which we will discuss

[56] Zuo, *Social Gospel, Social Service and Social Reform: A Historical Study of Beijing YMCA 1909–1949*, 72.

[57] Ibid., 98–115.

[58] Goossaert and Palmer, *The Religious Question in Modern China*, 2011, 145.

[59] Ibid., 146.

[60] Zuo, *Social Gospel, Social Service and Social Reform: A Historical Study of Beijing YMCA 1909–1949*, 253.

Figure 2.1 A YMCA daycare for disabled children in Nanjing, 2014.

further in Chapter 4, is that Christian missionary-based charities were able to make an impact only when they went through a localization process.

All three types of engaged religions that emerged in late imperial to republican China – benevolent halls, redemptive societies, and Christian charities – still exist in contemporary Chinese societies in China, Taiwan, and Malacca, in various forms, with or without interruptions. Benevolent halls were severely repressed during the anti-superstition campaigns by both the GMD and CCP. However, they managed to survive in Southeast Asian Chinese communities, such as Malaysia, Thailand, and Singapore. In mainland China they came to life again only after the 1990s, largely due to the support of Southeast Asian businessmen. To ward off charges of "superstition," many of them had to change their names to "welfare society" (福利社).[61] Tan Chee-Beng's study of such organizations in Chaozhou (Fujian, China), Malaysia, and Singapore argues that the religious element contributed to the resilience of benevolent halls: "The charity and management of the public good can be taken over by the modern state, but as religious organizations, shantangs [benevolent halls] cannot be replaced by the state."[62] The redemptive societies were equally active in Southeast Asian Chinese communities. The success of Yiguandao in both Taiwan and Southeast Asia is a case in point. Christian charities, though not the dominant forms of social engagement, are still widely found in all three Chinese societies discussed in this book. The rest of the chapter will discuss each Chinese society and its distinct connection and claim to this shared historical legacy.

China: From Mao to Post-Mao

Both the GMD and CCP maintained a Christian-based model for "religion" – they understood it to be institutionalized through an educated clergy, realized in sacred texts, and based on individual choices of personal belief rather than ritual conventions. Therefore, it was not surprising that both regimes launched campaigns against "superstitious" elements in traditional religious organizations that might block the modernization project.[63] The CCP, which was sensitive toward religious and ethnic groups in China's borderland especially during the Long March (1934–1936), and which had made alliances with various religious organization during the anti-Japanese war (1937–1945) in the form of the United Front, very much turned against religious groups after the civil war and its aftermath (1945–1957).[64] Many Muslim, Protestant, and Catholic groups seem to have sided with the GMD. Moreover, the redemptive societies were condemned as antirevolutionary societies and sects (反动会道门) and often accused of collaboration with the Japanese. They were eradicated as completely as possible. During the Cultural Revolution (1966–1976), virtually all religious practices were forced to stop or went underground, conducted mostly by women or the elderly. It was impossible for any religions to be engaged in the provision of the public good since the Communist Chinese government was supposed to be the sole provider of social well-being.

Religious policy during the Mao era left deep marks on contemporary policies on religion and religious philanthropy in China. First of all, only Christianity (Protestantism), Catholicism, Islam, Buddhism, and Daoism are

61 Tan, "Shantang."
62 Ibid., 98.
63 Nedostup, *Superstitious Regimes*.
64 Goossaert and Palmer, *The Religious Question in Modern China*, 2011, 139–165.

officially recognized as religions. Even today, only these official religions have any possibility to form legal religious philanthropic programs or organizations. Popular religious groups, which still play significant roles in local Taiwanese charity, are not officially recognized and therefore are left out of the legally defined "engaged religions" scene.[65] Redemptive societies have been basically wiped out as public actors. Benevolent societies have to become thoroughly secularized charities and have been revived only in recent years.[66] Second, since social welfare was regarded as the full duty of the state during the Mao era, religious philanthropic activities and nongovernmental organizations (NGOs) were treated with suspicion in the 1980s and even 1990s. This has also caused the deeply rooted conviction that people in need should turn to the state first and foremost as the only legitimate source of support beyond the family. Furthermore, the state would like to impose strict restrictions on other social organizations that try to step in to the state's role as the "provider" or dare to take the credit for welfare provision. This point is further elaborated in Chapter 3.

Nevertheless, none of these problems stopped religious groups from engaging in social service provision as soon as they were allowed to practice again in post-Mao China. Indeed, one could say that the moment when official religions were allowed to reinstate themselves almost coincides with the appearance of the first grassroots religious philanthropic activities. This occurred before the economic takeoff of China and before the rise of wealthy religious groups.[67]

China's economic reforms started around 1978. Though the Chinese government continues to see religions as partial competitors with Socialist ideology, the politics of religion has nevertheless gone through significant changes. The first crucial policy change that marked the transition was the famous Document 19, which was published in 1982. Often regarded as the first statement of religious freedom in post-Mao China, it allowed many religious sites to be restored and religious properties (partially) returned. Some religious sites that were considered economically valuable (for tourism) actually started their restoration a few years before the policy was published and with complete government funding and support. However, this policy specifically states that the freedom of religion not only means the freedom to believe in religion (though

65 There are a few exceptions, like the Black Dragon Temple discussed by Chau, *Miraculous Response*, 2005. Yet these temples cannot directly participate in social services but have to transform themselves into a cultural heritage or conduct their activities in the name of an individual leader.

66 Tan, "Shantang."

67 Parts of this section have appeared in Keping Wu, "The Philanthropic Turn of Religions in Post-Mao China: Bureaucratization, Professionalization and the Making of a Moral Subject" in *Modern China* (forthcoming).

only the five officially recognized ones), but also the freedom not to believe in any religions, thus containing the expansion of religious groups within specific territories by limiting evangelization. Before the second important regulation on religion appeared in 1994 ("Regulation Governing Venues for Religious Activities," which further limited religious activities strictly to certain physical sites), religious groups in China were already actively contributing to the public good.

It started with small efforts by local Buddhist temples or from grassroots-level organizations by Christian leaders. For instance, the Jade Buddha Temple (玉佛寺) in Shanghai had been a major donor to the Shanghai Children's Welfare Association since 1984, but it could be done only in the name of the former abbot Master Zhenchan (真禅), who became the honorable head of the association and founded the "Master Zhenchan Disabled Children's Welfare Foundation" in 1988.[68] This became the forerunner of a much larger endeavor. In June 2008, the charitable foundation Juequn Ci'ai Gongdehui (觉群慈爱功德会) was established in the Jade Buddha Temple. Now its services have expanded to poverty and disaster relief, community service, emergency care, and environmental activism as well as a continued commitment to children's welfare. It also accepts donations in all major foreign currencies. Amity Foundation, the Christian-based NGO, was established by a group of Protestant leaders, especially Bishop K. H. Ting (丁光训), in 1985 to engage in relief work. Ever since then, its thirty-year involvement in all kinds of developmental projects throughout China has made it the model for extensive service and professional management of NGOs with religious backgrounds.

A decade later, Shaolin Temple's abbot Shi Yongxin (释永信) founded the first legally registered Buddhist nonprofit social organization (非营利社会团体), the Shaolin Charity and Welfare Foundation (少林慈善福利基金会) in 1994. Another decade passed before religious groups' contribution to the public good was mentioned for the first time in the "Regulations on Religious Affairs (宗教事务条例)" in 2004. There has been at least a twenty-year lag between the religious groups' participation in social service provision and the state's grudging acceptance of it in the regulatory framework.

This history also shows that the engagement in philanthropy was not a top-down process. Religious individuals and groups have been pushing the boundaries all along. All these efforts accumulated into the "Advice on Encouraging and Regulating Religious Sector's Participation in Philanthropic and Charitable Activities" issued by the State Administration for Religious Affairs (SARA)

[68] It is said that Master Zhenchan's grandson (the result of his forced marriage during the Cultural Revolution) has disabilities, which was what propelled him to take up this cause. However, what the Buddhist master has done has pioneered Buddhism's engagement in social causes in post-Mao China.

in February 2012.[69] This was immediately followed by the top-down, state-directed, nation-wide "Religious Charity Week" in March 2012. This campaign, supposed to be done annually, was mandatory for the five official religions, through their respective religious associations. Supervised by provincial and municipal Religious Affairs Bureau (RAB) officers, the five official religions are expected to join hands in public fund-raising events and offer social services collectively. This is addressed further in Chapter 3.

Besides the grassroots efforts pushed by religious groups, other events have also facilitated this graduate shift of positions of the Chinese state on religious philanthropy. First of all, economic development in the 1980s poured resources into many religious groups. Granted, this process was uneven among different religious groups and there were huge regional variations. Southern Jiangsu, where we conducted our research, was among the fastest growing economic zones in the entire country. Furthermore, as the most pervasive religious influence in this region since the Ming Dynasty (and with an important history going back much further), Buddhist temples benefited first and most in this process. Second, the southeast China flood in 1991 marked the first natural disaster when the Chinese government called for not only international help but also help from other social sectors (社会各界). As a result, religious groups seized this opportunity to contribute and engage with reconstruction. The national Buddhist Association alone donated 5 million RMB (about USD $930,000) to the relief of the flood.

The famous Taiwan-based Buddhist charitable NGO Tzu Chi first started its relief work on the mainland for the southeast China flood and formally entered China in a legitimate way despite internal criticism in Taiwan for aiding the power that most threatened the island. Tzu Chi became a huge inspiration for mainland religious groups that had started their own philanthropic activities but lacked a model to follow. It also marked the start of a different era, in which the state allowed international religious NGOs to operate legally in China.

A third important development occurred in 1991, when the Chinese government called for religious groups "to facilitate socialist development." That same year the government also brought up the idea of "opening up social welfare to society" (社会福利社会化) owing to the mushrooming of individually operated social welfare institutes. Twenty-two years later, this evolved into the "Guidelines on Government Purchase of Services from Social Organizations" (关于政府向社会力量购买服务的指导意见), issued in October 2013. Most of the social organizations that the government is purchasing services from are

[69] Six state and party units participated in the making of the policy: the State Administration for Religious Affairs of the PRC, the United Front Work Department of the CPC Central Committee, the National Development and Reform Commission, the Ministry of Civil Affairs of the PRC, the Ministry of Finance of the PRC, and the State Administration of Taxation.

secular, but the change has certainly also opened up more space for religious groups to utilize government resources. For instance, religious organizations can now apply for government funding to build old age homes. However, this could be a double-edged sword. As we will elaborate in Chapter 3, some religious groups would rather give up such resources in order to maintain their autonomy in the management of such old age homes.

In comparison with the Mao era, religious groups in post-Mao China thus have much more freedom in carrying out philanthropic projects. The evolving regulatory framework, however, demonstrates that the state is still deeply involved in the regulation of such activities. The state's role has shifted from that of the direct provider of social welfare to a regulator of social service provision, often remaining backstage. This does not mean that its role has decreased. On the contrary, the watchful eye of the state is more present than ever. Social services unsanctioned by the state are hardly visible from religious groups. For instance, religious groups can organize garbage recycling but cannot support demonstrations against the building of a nuclear power plant.[70]

One prominent feature of religious philanthropy with "Chinese characteristics" is that the government tries to make sure that the credit goes to the state, instead of the religious leaders, organizations, or the deities people espouse. One of the lower level public security officers in charge of religion thus cautioned in a 2010 interview with one of us:

> Although our government now encourages religious groups to contribute – they have so much wealth anyway, otherwise they get corrupted – it's not good if the religions are doing too much. [If that happened,] they would be winning the hearts of the people who may look up to the gods made of mud or religious leaders – who are only human – as the providers! Because people are simple-minded, they do not realize that our government is making it possible for them to live the lives they have now. And we work so hard in order to make sure they are safe and provided for!

This attitude reveals that the government still views religious groups as at least partially incompatible with the state project.

The other feature of the watchful eye of the state can be seen in its increasing demand of transparency from all social organizations, including religious groups. In 2005, the Ministry of Finance issued "Regulations on the Accounting System of Non-governmental Non-profit Organizations." The regulations apply to any registered social organizations, foundations, nongovernmental and non-business associations, as well as Buddhist and Daoist temples, mosques, and churches (Article 2). But at least as of 2006, very few religious venues were using an accounting system that followed these regulations. The

[70] This is in contrast to the cases in Taiwan as shown in Robert Weller's case where a spirit medium gets possessed by Guanyin to object openly to the construction of an oil refinery in the neighborhood. See Weller, *Discovering Nature*, 105.

abbot of Lingyan Shan Temple of Suzhou, for instance, did the accounts by hand on an exercise book for a long time. Retired schoolteachers (as learned and trustworthy people) often volunteered as bookkeepers in small churches and temples. It was common for churches to post their income and expenses on the blackboard for all the members to see and for temples to write donors' names and the amounts of donations on a large piece of red paper for display to the community. But with the implementation of the regulation on accounting systems, this level of "transparency" for its own members is not enough. The state demands transparency in the form of modern accounting systems that can be audited. This model of governance demands religious groups to be "upwardly responsible."

In 2008, a policy briefing issued by the vice chair of the RAB of Jiangsu Province urged religious venues to implement the "Regulations on the Accounting System of Non-governmental Non-profit Organizations":

> By May 2008, 39 religious venues in Nanjing, such as temples and churches, have implemented the new accounting system, except the Shigu Catholic Church, Doushuai Buddhist Temple in Pukou, Hongjue Buddhist Temple in Jiangning ... In the Regulation on Religious Affairs, an entire chapter (8 articles) is devoted to regulating the property of religious organizations and venues. It both increases the protection of such property and strengthens the regulations. It clearly states that religious organizations and venues need to regulate their financial situations ... Non-profit organizations throughout the world are required to use at least 50% of their income on philanthropic enterprises. Religious groups in developed countries, including those in Hong Kong and Taiwan, also spend more than half of their income on philanthropy ... To better regulate the accounting system is to better manage the funds, caution against extravagance, promote frugality, and accumulate more funds on social charitable and philanthropic enterprises.[71]

This briefing demonstrates a top-down demand for religious philanthropy to be financially "accountable." This accountability requirement is part and parcel of the "industrialized philanthropy" model. In contrast to the state attitudes toward benevolent halls and redemptive societies, this is a new way of regulating religious philanthropy. Instead of eliminating or secularizing those practices, the current Chinese state regulates religious philanthropy through modern financial means. It facilitates and demands the bureaucratization process of such organizations.

In a nutshell, the CCP government completed the anti-superstition campaign that the GMD started in mainland China in a much more radical fashion. Most benevolent societies and redemptive societies were eradicated, and all other forms of Chinese religions were severely undermined by the end of 1970s (the

[71] www.jsmzzj.gov.cn/art/2008/12/6/art_300_4019.html, accessed on 12 September 2013.

end of Cultural Revolution), with their properties confiscated, clergy persecuted, and activities forced to stop. However, religion-initiated social engagement quickly picked up in the mid-1980s when the state began to allow greater social space. Just as in late imperial and republican China, religious groups have been pushing the boundaries of social engagement all along. And the state had to respond to their newly acquired space in public good provision. As soon as religious groups were allowed to recover some of their properties and activities in the 1980s, some of them began to be engaged in philanthropic practices. What constitutes the "good," however, has shifted since late imperial times. If the earlier benevolent societies and redemptive societies aimed at moralizing both the donor and receiver, "the good" in contemporary religious philanthropies contains a more universalizing message centered on love, as we shall elaborate in later chapters. Furthermore, state attempts to regulate the religious philanthropies through modern financial means have furthered the industrialization of philanthropies.

Taiwan: From Colonialism to Authoritarian State to Democracy

Religion and society were inseparable from the seventeenth-century beginnings of Chinese settlement in Lukang to the arrival of Japanese colonialism in 1895. It is not a coincidence that the formal separation of religion from society that began under the Japanese occupation was roughly simultaneous with the introduction of the modern Chinese word for "religion" (宗教), which itself came from Japan. Similar changes happened on the mainland as well, as we have mentioned, although the Japanese influence was of course more direct in Taiwan.

We can see evidence of these developments going back to stories about some of Lukang's earliest history. The exact origins of the town as a Chinese place are unclear, but one of its major early events was its use as a point of initial attack and later base of operations for the invading Qing Dynasty forces who captured the island from the Ming loyalist Zheng Chenggong (Koxinga). According to local legend, Admiral Shi Lang, the leader of the Qing invasion forces, had stopped to pick up a statue of the goddess Mazu at her main temple in Meizhou, Fujian. On reaching Taiwan, he established a base at Lukang because of the port facilities. In thanks for the support of local leaders, he left the Meizhou Mazu statue in the care of a local temple that allegedly dated back to the late Ming. Partly on the fame of that statue, the temple has now evolved into Lukang's most famous and powerful institution – the Tianhou Temple (天后宫), a reference to Mazu's imperial title.[72]

[72] Xu, *Lukang Gazetteer: Religion*, 115.

This story shows the intertwining of religion, society, and politics that was typical of late imperial Chinese history. We see this first in the need a military expedition felt for religious protection, and then in Shi Lang's attempt to superscribe an older and more local Taiwanese Mazu temple with his own image – a Mazu in the service of the Qing Dynasty, and clearly more efficacious than the local images, as the military victory showed.[73] We see it again in the way the temple has been able to use the story of this image to achieve a great deal of secular power over the centuries that followed. We can see the close ties between religion and government again later in the Qing, with the construction of paired official military and civil temples, led by a local holder of the *jinshi* degree in 1811. A Confucian school opened in the civil temple in 1824, and began training students hoping eventually to work as officials.[74] State, religion, and society were intermingled.

Lukang's kinship networks also linked intimately to deities. Chinese almost everywhere burn incense for their ancestors, and in some areas (including parts of Taiwan) they construct shared ancestral halls to house memorial tablets for an entire lineage, which may live together in a village. Such halls often also owned land to provide income for annual rituals. Just four surnames completely dominated settlement in Lukang town, and a total of ten made up the great majority in the township as a whole. Rarely, however, did these groups organize as traditional lineages.[75] Instead, the most common form of organization was as a "god association" (神明会).

God associations were an extremely common form of social organization in which groups organize around the worship of one or more deities, but can also carry out any other kind of activity. God associations in late imperial times were the most common vehicle for rotating credit associations, charitable groups, professional associations, and many other functions.[76] In Lukang, shared surname groups organized by worshipping gods together, often either gods their ancestors had worshipped or community deities in the neighborhoods they had emigrated from. Typically this happened in someone's home, rather than a temple or an ancestral hall.[77] In Lukang's case this may well represent an adaption to urbanized migrant life, but it shows in any case just how closely religious themes organized all aspects of social life.

Merchant associations (行郊) usually also adopted a similar structure. In Lukang these groups were organized around major commodities (oil, sugar, cloth, etc.) in some cases, and around major trading ports in others (Quanzhou,

[73] The superscription idea comes from Duara, "Superscribing Symbols."
[74] Dan, *Lukang Gazetteer: Education*, 6.
[75] The only active such hall in Lukang town currently is a Shi surname association with a global base. It was founded only in 1991.
[76] Sangren, "Traditional Chinese Corporations."
[77] Zhuang, *Lukang Gazetteer: Kinship*, 75–76.

Xiamen, etc.). In addition to dealing with issues of trade and competition, they were important charitable actors; they built bridges and roads, contributed to temple reconstruction, and donated food to the poor.[78] These groups peaked in the nineteenth century, before Lukang's harbor silted up and trade died out. All of them were founded around altars to deities, which always included Mazu among others (which varied from one group to the next), and their leaders had the titles of Incense Pot Master (炉主) and Head (头家), the same as the leaders of temple rituals.[79] The centrality of the gods became clear when one of us visited the one remaining active association, the Quanzhou Association (泉郊). While no longer a merchant guild, this group has maintained corporate wealth and a continuous membership, and they still have an active hall. Immediately on entering, one sees the altar with its ancient images, and photographs of these gods grace the opening page of the brochure the group puts out.[80] As a group, the eight most powerful associations rotated worship of the Emperor of Heaven. Like lineages in Lukang, merchant associations cannot be extricated from their links to religion.

Whatever their primary purpose, all of these groups (and many more) shared a religious institutional structure, and all provided some forms of charity. The Japanese colonial rulers of 1895–1945 gave us the first systematic surveys of local institutions. They registered sixty-six god associations in Lukang in 1923, including kinship groups, neighborhood groups, and business groups (coffin makers, Western-style tailors, and so on). After this registration, however, the Japanese discouraged this religion-based organizational form.[81] We could mark this moment, in fact, as the beginning of the broad state project of secularization, which continued after the colonial period through the first decades of GMD rule.

God associations continue today mostly on a small and informal scale, either for historical reasons (such as the Quanzhou Merchants Association) or for small and relatively informal groups such as rotating credit associations. Close links among social organization, religion, and charity, however, continue in new forms. In some cases, this involves a continuation of some of the community building functions that temples always had. A beautiful and renowned temple indexes a successful community, for example, but temples also create ties that bridge community boundaries. This is especially clear at the Tianhou temple, which is a major attraction for pilgrims from all over the island. There is a constant stream of visiting deities and their followers, with each group

[78] Huang, *Lukang Gazetteer: History*, 163.
[79] DeGlopper, *Lukang*, 163.
[80] *Introduction to the Quanzhou Guild.*
[81] Xu, *Lukang Gazetteer: Religion*, 211–242.

paying its respects (often through performances by the visiting gods themselves through possessed followers) in the front courtyard before entering the temple. On a more local scale, we can see it also in the cooperative arrangements between some temples, and in the visits deities pay to each other when the temples hold processions.

We see links between religion and charity in the revival of direct philanthropic action by religious groups. These typically include scholarships for the children of followers, emergency aid for people with a sudden financial need (often coordinated through the township government), running medical clinics, or providing public goods beyond the temple building and its religious activities. In the case of the Tianhou Temple, for instance, they have donated fire-fighting equipment and garbage trucks to the township government. They also built what people laughingly called the "five-star" toilet – a massive, clean, marble-lined, and air-conditioned public bathroom just across from the temple. In a place where public toilets are almost unheard of, and where tourist traffic is enormous, this was greatly appreciated. Even much smaller temples, however, also have scholarship funds or give small cash gifts to the old or poor at the Chinese New Year. The "good" here is restricted mostly to the community well-being. The "community" can range from temple followers and their families to the entire township.

Even though the god association has not been the primary form of formal incorporation since the 1920s, we can still see evidence of a strong link between religion and other forms of social organization, including philanthropy. The primary form for such groups since democratization has been the NGO. The Changhua County government listed sixty-eight "popular organizations" (人民团体, the legal term that covers NGOs but not larger foundations) with Lukang addresses in 2005. These include surname associations and charitable groups as well as the usual business and hobby groups (e.g., the Glass Association, two Chinese chess clubs, four Kiwanis Clubs). This seems like a large number for a township whose urban center has only 20,000 people, but in fact there are many more, smaller associations that have not registered at the county level.

These numbers do not include temples (which have a separate registration procedure), but do include several groups with close ties to temples. The Zhongyi Charitable Society (忠义慈善会), for example, began as a social group affiliated with Lukang's Zhongyi temple, which houses the god Guan Gong. They originally helped coordinate temple feasts for the followers and occasionally gave emergency aid. In 1987 they organized to provide more systematic aid, and registered with the county in 1989. Most of the original board of directors were also members of the temple committee, although there is no legal tie between the two groups. They provided roughly TWD 300,000 (about 10,000 USD) in emergency aid in 2004, held a blood drive, and gave the township government TWD 50,000 to be used as gifts for the elderly during an annual festival. This is a typical list for a group like this.[82] Though the scale of these groups is mostly limited to local communities, they are not bureaucratized and are still embedded in local social life and personal connections. However, they provide systematic aid and, after their registration with the local government (therefore submitting to further bureaucratization), they began to exhibit the characteristics of what we call "industrialized philanthropy."

These historical ties to a temple are also not unusual. The Zijidian Educational Foundation (紫极殿文教基金会) is another small NGO, in this case dedicated to providing scholarships for neighborhood high school and college students. Its name refers to the Zijidian, the central temple in that neighborhood of Lukang. The group began when a donor to the temple was convinced to dedicate his donation to educational help. The temple eventually asked the current director to help raise more funds, and they ultimately set up the new fund as an independent NGO.[83] In other cases, temples themselves still run these activities directly. The powerful Tianhou temple, for example, discussed the possibility of setting up a separate educational foundation, but decided not to, probably to avoid having to deal with the supervision that comes with official registration.

It may be that the relatively reduced political space for popular religion during the last part of the Japanese regime and the Chiang Kai-shek period was a temporary aberration, and that the current situation is a return to a historical norm. Chinese popular religion did not fare well under the most radically modernizing regimes, including both the Japanese and the GMD (both on the mainland and later in Taiwan). In Taiwan, perhaps the first sign of trouble was the end of the god worshipping association as a legal organizational form in 1923. Things got much worse with the Japanese *kominka* ("creation of imperial subjects") policy of the late 1930s, when there was a general attempt to discourage popular religion in favor of official Shinto.

Those most repressive policies ended when the GMD took the island back in 1945, but the government still campaigned against popular religion as superstitious, wasteful, and embarrassing. This eased up only after the death of Chiang Kai-shek, and especially with the gradual opening to democracy in the 1980s. Once politicians had to appeal directly to voters, temples once again thrived as centers of social capital. With the government relaxing its pressure on temples, and on the very idea of popular religion, local deities have reclaimed a central place in social networks and in providing public goods through philanthropy.

The 1980s created a very different atmosphere for engaged religions. Some of the most important groups had been founded earlier, like Tzu Chi, which began in 1966.[84] Even for them, however, the 1980s saw their first period of

[82] This is based primarily on an interview with Xu Shengxiong, who was the director when interviewed in 2005.

[83] Interview with the current director in 2005, Huang Zhinong.

[84] See Huang, *Charisma and Compassion*, 2009.

very rapid island-wide and then national expansion. In part this happened because the government became eager to have social groups take over aspects of welfare, as happened in much of the world beginning in the 1980s after the so-called Reagan and Thatcher Revolutions. We see this in the greatly increased legal space for NGOs, as well as increased religious charity. Taiwan's democratization was the other driving force, where politicians for the first time needed to mobilize religious social networks to generate local support. One important result has been the greatly increased role of religious groups such as churches and temples, or of NGOs with religious ties, in providing for the welfare of needy citizens.

What kind of "good" is being served here? The authoritarian regimes that had preceded this period allowed the maintenance of many strictly local social ties, but the public itself could exist only in service of the state. Democracy brought a reconception of this relationship, however, with a social world conceived independently from the state. This revised understanding may have encouraged charitable activity aimed at this new "public," that is, servicing a "good" that was not limited only to immediate community members.

Changes in state policy also encouraged the new vision of charity. Tzu Chi's hospital construction, which was critical to their initial expansion, received Chiang Ching-kuo's blessing in part because there was an increasing feeling that society should take more responsibility for its own welfare needs, leaving government to concentrate on defense and the economy. The change also indicates some willingness to allow surveillance functions – keeping track of needy families over the long term – to move into the social sector.

Gender may again be an important factor here. Tzu Chi's appeal has been to women above all, and they frequently talk about how they have taken the love and care that mothers offer their families and brought it to the world as a whole.[85] Nurturance for them becomes a general and abstract good, independent from the specific nurturance offered to one's children or help to one's neighbors. Men dominated all the earlier models of philanthropy that we have mentioned. Tzu Chi offers the first time we see women taking on this enormous public role, even though it is couched in the conservative terms of nurturance and family values. In this new model, women's caring and loving hearts become the dominant metaphor for a "good" that is universal, instead of men's gatekeeping for the interest of the community. We will return to the issue of gender especially in Chapter 6.

In some ways this picture of Taiwanese engaged religion that began to take shape in the 1980s was a return to the intertwined religion and social service of the late imperial period, but in other ways it also showed new understandings

[85] Huang and Weller, "Merit and Mothering."

of the "good" and institutional structures, which exhibited features of industrialized philanthropy in its scale, organizational structure, and disembedding from previous social networks.

Malaysia: From Ethnic Enclave to Ghetto Escape

Malaysia is a multiethnic society. Chinese comprise the largest minority in Malaysia, although the percentage of Chinese has been declining (from 36 percent in 1970 to 22 percent in 2012).[86] According to government statistics, 25 percent of the population of the State of Malacca was Chinese in 2012.[87] The City of Malacca is the oldest metropolis of Malaysia, with a history of multiple colonizations. Particularly as one of the three former British Strait Settlements, it preserves much of its Chinese heritage.

The earliest Chinese settlements can be traced back to the Malacca Sultanate in the fifteenth century. The majority of immigrants, however, came between the nineteenth and early twentieth centuries, mostly as laborers brought in by the British from the southeastern coast of China.[88] When Malaysia achieved independence in 1957, the Chinese became citizens of the new nation-state, yet soon found themselves excluded by the majority "sons of the soil" (*bumiputeras*). Throughout the colonial and postcolonial periods, the governments generally left the Chinese to look after their own needs. As a result, Malacca and other Chinese settlements even today accommodate an elaborate list of Chinese guilds, organizations, and associations, as well as a long history of a Chinese-language school system.[89]

The Malaysian government launched its New Economic Policy (NEP) in 1970 and has since successfully fostered a new Malay middle class to counterbalance the economic power of the Chinese in the postcolonial period. In the wake of the NEP, the government sought to promote a Malaysian national identity based on the language, culture, and religion of the *bumiputeras*. As a result, many Chinese turned inward to their community to seek social respect during the 1970s and 1980s, leading to the revitalization of Chinese religious culture. In the early years of the twenty-first century, Chinese Malaysians continue

[86] Hirschman, "Demographic Trends in Peninsular Malaysia, 1947–1975," 111. Department of Statistics Malaysia, Official Portal, Population Quick Info, "Population by States and Ethnic Group, Malaysia, 2012," pqi.stats.gov.my/result.php?token=424a2220a608bf5d524f5c546d69c1e3 (Accessed December 8, 2016).

[87] Department of Statistics Malaysia, Official Portal, Population Quick Info, "Population by States and Ethnic Group, Melaka, 2012," http://pqi.stats.gov.my/result.php?token=54f201408e25bdb18ec0d5824ac15204 (Accessed December 8, 2016).

[88] Hefner, "Introduction"; Li, *An Immigrant Town: Life in an Overseas Community in Southern Malaya*; Yen, "Historical Background."

[89] Lim, *Constructing Chinese Culture: An Ethnic-Based State and the Chinese Language Education Movement*.

to campaign for power and cultural identity through political and associative means while the government's strategies for promoting a multicultural national image persist.

The colonial "divide-and-rule" pluralist policy prepared the public arena for Chinese religion in Malaysia. The history of engaged Chinese religions in Malacca began with a temple that functioned as the colonially sanctioned court for Chinese affairs. Cheng Hoon Teng (青云亭), commonly known as Guanyin Ting, is the oldest Chinese temple in Malaysia and Singapore (built ca. AD 1600). It is obviously one of the most popular and well-endowed Chinese temples in Malacca, with nearly 50,000 square feet of land downtown and in the cemetery grounds of a Malacca suburb. Its key significance in the public sphere lies first in its history as the Chinese court – as the office of the arbiter, "Kapitan" – in Malacca under the Portuguese (1511–1640) and Dutch (1641–1786) authorities, and second in its construction as a sole corporation under the Cheng Hoon Teng Temple [Incorporation] Ordinance of 1949. Religion was public and engaged to the extent that the Kapitan temple handled the public affairs of the Chinese in Malacca during the colonial period. For centuries, Cheng Hoon Teng remained the political and cultural center of the Chinese in Malacca.[90] To this day, it continues to offer services of paramount concern for Chinese migrants by providing a cemetery and spaces for ancestor tablets.

Christian missionaries who came during the colonial period also pursued their social engagements within ethnic boundaries.[91] Since the treaties between the British and Malay rulers limited Christian evangelization to the non-Malay immigrant population, missionaries pursued their opportunities by founding churches and schools on the west coast of the peninsula (where there were more Chinese) during the late nineteenth and early twentieth centuries. The diverse languages and dialects among the immigrants also encouraged missionaries to structure their work along ethnic and linguistic lines. As a result, education became a crucial field where Christianity could directly express its power to the immigrant non-Malay population. The Catholics and Methodists, the most established and popular congregations for the Chinese in Malacca, were among those denominations that viewed the English-language school as an important means for propagating Christianity.[92]

Since the wave of Chinese immigration in the late nineteenth century, the major charitable organizations for the Chinese had been surname and hometown associations (会馆 or 乡团). They were largely divided by dialect groups: Hokkien, Cantonese, Teochew, Hainan, and Hakka. Li points out

[90] "A Brief History of the Cheng Hoon Teng, Melaka"; Soo, *Studies of the Chinese in Malaysia and Singapore: A Collection of Soo Khin Wah's Works*, 197–217.

[91] Hunt, Lee, and Roxborogh, *Christianity in Malaysia: A Denominational History*.

[92] Lee and Ackerman, *Sacred Tensions*, 115–118.

that the welfare function of hometown associations rapidly declined after the Japanese occupation, and, at the same time, religious philanthropies for all Chinese regardless of hometown, surname, and dialect differences began to be more pronounced.[93] In the early twentieth century temples like the Cheng Hoon Teng continued to provide charitable services and new religious charitable associations began to be established. The Seck Kia Eenh (释迦院), which uses the English name Malacca Buddhist Association, has been the major religious center for Straits-born Chinese or *Peranakan* since its founding in 1920.[94] Like the Cheng Hoon Teng, Seck Kia Eenh provides spaces for ancestral tablets and urns of cremated ashes.

There were also religious associations that catered to the general welfare of the Chinese in Malaysia. The syncretic Che Chiang Khor Moral Uplifting Association, Malacca (德教会紫昌阁), founded in 1954, is part of the international network of the Dejiao Hui (Moral Uplifting Association). This group began as a redemptive society in southern China in the 1930s and, after World War II, spread to Southeast Asia, where it prospered phenomenally as a religious organization.[95] As indicated by its name – literally, "teaching of virtue" – Dejiao aimed at doing good as a means to restore morality and provide a way out of suffering. While Dejiao developed into a distinctive religious institution of its own, the tradition of deity-based benevolent halls (善堂) and redemptive societies from the Chaoshan region of Guangdong in China is well preserved all over Malaysia, including the Seu Teck Sean Tong (修德善堂) Malacca, founded in 1927. Dejiao and similar groups in Malacca typically all do charity work that includes free medical consultation and free (Chinese) medicine, funeral services (donating coffins and funds for burial), and relief work. Charity continues to be an integral part of each organization.[96] And the "good" they subscribe to includes not only these concrete services, but also the "teaching of virtues" to the members, much as we saw in some of the Ming and Qing Dynasty organizations on the mainland.

While Malaysia preserves more of the traditional forms of Chinese religion-based philanthropy, the timing of change there resembles what happened in Taiwan and China. Roughly since the 1980s, we can identify an increasing trend of socially engaged efforts by both old and new religious institutions. This new trend seems to be twofold: old popular local temples began to take

[93] Li, *An Immigrant Town: Life in an Overseas Community in Southern Malaya*.

[94] For a study of Straits Chinese in Malacca, see Tan, *The Baba of Melaka*.

[95] Tan, *Development and Distribution of Dejiao Associations in Malaysia and Singapore*; Formoso, *De Jiao – A Religious Movement in Contemporary China and Overseas*; Freedman and Topley, "Religion and Social Realignment among the Chinese in Singapore"; Duara, "Transnationalism and the Predicament of Sovereignty."

[96] Tan, "Shantang."

Figure 2.2 New Seck Kia Eenh building.

on global and cosmopolitan projects, and new transnational religious philanthropic organizations entered the public sphere of the local Chinese. For example, Cheng Hoon Teng recently opened a public library in a nearby building in the downtown area, and has been showcasing its restoration efforts. By 2006, the already elaborate Seck Kia Eenh had further expanded its assets to a new building across street (see Figure 2.2). It has been increasingly active in welfare provision as well as in Buddhist international sangha organizations. The new building houses a kindergarten and an orphanage. In addition, the group funds a cancer society and a welfare committee for the delivery of charitable relief. Special programs include relief to AIDS patients and delivery of gifts to the elders on Vesak Day each year. Parallel to the older local popular and Buddhist temples, the Catholic church of St. Theresa, which has the highest Chinese constituency, comprising 90 percent of its 9,000 followers, has set up a garbage recycling post in the church, and emphasized the increase of Filipino and other migrant workers' participation.

New transnational religious organizations have also joined in the efforts of social engagement. The Buddhist Lodge (居士林), a network of lay Buddhist associations active across Malaysia and Singapore, founded its Malacca group in 1980, and has been providing distribution of relief annually since 1990. It also donates money to charitable organizations providing medical care (e.g., a Christian dialysis center), and recycles garbage to generate money for charity. The Buddhist Tzu Chi group from Taiwan established its Malacca branch in 1992 and as of 2004 has been the head of seventeen offices across the Malay Peninsula and East Malaysia. Tzu Chi is obviously the most elaborate in its welfare contributions. Their splendid headquarters located in a Malacca industrial park houses a mission complex consisting of two buildings: one is a huge auditorium (seating about 800 people) with a built-in dormitory and offices for administration, publications, and multimedia production, and the other includes a kindergarten, an adult education school, a bookstore café, and a free clinic. Modeled on the mission in Taiwan, Tzu Chi Malacca is active internationally in disaster relief, and offers free clinics from a minivan, garbage recycling, and medical and charity services for both Chinese and other ethnic groups.

These recent changes in the scope and salience of engaged religions of the Chinese in Malacca echo the recent literature on religious changes in the context of Malaysian modernization and globalization. Based on their long-term studies in the Klang Valley, Lee and Ackerman show that secularization never really occurred in Malaysia. Islam, Buddhism, Hinduism, and Christianity each experienced rationalization, institutionalization, and the emerging salience of charismatic movements. The new middle class was a crucial part of these changes, further influenced by the inclusion of transnational religious groups under globalization.[97] The increasing institutionalization and expansion of the scale of such religious groups' social service provision and charitable activities demonstrate what we call industrialized philanthropy.

The cosmopolitan, transnational, and even trans-ethnic trend appearing in Malacca Chinese engaged religion over the past few decades also mirrors broader religious changes among the Chinese in Malaysia. DeBernardi, for example, has shown how in one area the Penang Chinese met the challenge of NEP cultural policies in the 1970s and 1980s in part through a revitalization of earlier traditions, for instance, reworking the annual festival for the hungry ghosts as a symbol of Chinese unity. The same committee that took over the festival also mobilized resources to support provision of public services for the Chinese.[98] Similarly, the committee of Cheng Hoon Teng in Malacca has actively participated in the Chinese New Year festival in the historical district of downtown Malacca, thus responding to the government's multicultural

[97] Lee and Ackerman, *Sacred Tensions*.
[98] DeBernardi, *Rites of Belonging*.

campaign strategy of including different ethnic groups' communal festivals as national holidays.[99]

In her comparative studies of the religions of the Chinese diaspora in Malaysia, Singapore, Indonesia, and Canada, Nagata forcefully argues for the salience of religious identity in fostering and forging a dynamic construction of Chinese ethnicity.[100] She argues that religion, as exemplified by one of the new humanistic Buddhisms from Taiwan (Foguangshan, Buddha Light Mountain), can contribute to a transnational civil society through active engagement in the public sphere of the Chinese diaspora, and provides "rapprochement" between China and Taiwan.[101] In the case of Christianity, Nagata also shows how Christian transnationalism fosters a "subethnic" identity in the global arena.[102]

All of these cases show two broad effects in Malacca that distinguishes it from other Chinese societies studied in this book. First, the Malaysian state's pluralist policies have helped keep Chinese charity limited to the Chinese ethnic world. Second, partly as a result of colonial indirect rule policies, Malaysia has been less influenced by the secularization processes that tried to isolate religion from other aspects of social life in China and Taiwan until the 1980s and 1990s. We thus see a more continuous history of engaged religions in Malacca, as well as the continuation of redemptive societies whose development had been truncated elsewhere.

Conclusion

All three of our cases developed out of a late imperial Chinese cultural world, but placed into very different political circumstances. What has this meant for the legacies of engaged religions as they influenced changes after the 1980s? In many ways the overseas Chinese society of Malacca most resembles the lively engaged religions of late imperial China, partly due to the absence of religious persecutions under such anti-superstition modernizing regimes as the GMD and CCP, and partly due to isolating ethnic policies under the colonial regimes and the modern Malaysian state. Thus, not only is Malacca's seventeenth-century Chinese temple still active in social and political life up to today, but the benevolent halls and redemptive societies founded in the nineteenth century are still actively engaged in public life and providing relief among the Chinese

[99] Cf. Ibid., 223.
[100] Nagata, "The Globalisation of Buddhism and the Emergence of Religious Civil Society"; Nagata, "Christianity among Transnational Chinese."
[101] Nagata, "The Globalisation of Buddhism and the Emergence of Religious Civil Society."
[102] Nagata, "Christianity among Transnational Chinese."

communities. Somewhat counterintuitively, Malaysia's colonial history thus caused the fewest discontinuities from earlier Chinese engaged religions.

Taiwan's path from the late imperial period brought more powerful interruptions to religious engagement. The Japanese colonial regime (1895–1945) separated religion and society and eventually discouraged Chinese popular religions in favor of state Shinto. The GMD continued to pursue their own anti-superstition policies when they entered the island in 1945, and they offered little support (and sometimes active suppression) to god associations, popular temples, and redemptive societies in Taiwan. However, temple associations never fully lost their political roles, and quickly became centers of public life again after democratization, when local government officials hoped to capitalize on temples' abilities to mobilize voters. This changed evaluation of local religious groups (and redemptive societies) further encouraged their active engagement in the provision of relief and other public services. Especially after the lifting of martial law in 1987, we see large-scale Buddhist organizations, such as Tzu Chi, Buddha Light Mountain, and Dharma Drum Mountain engaged in philanthropic activities, providing not only for people in Taiwan, but also worldwide. The former redemptive society Yiguandao, which had been outlawed by the GMD before 1987, has grown into a transnational network of worship sites and charitable societies today. In Taiwan we can thus still see traces of the legacies from late imperial to republican China. The Japanese colonial regime and early years of GMD rule disrupted the continuity, but religions in Taiwan quickly found innovative ways of social engagement and indeed their global impact has by far been the greatest of the three Chinese societies of this book discusses.

In mainland China, the CCP regime was able to carry out the anti-superstition campaign initiated by the GMD in the most thorough fashion. For a span of almost three decades (1950s to 1970s), most religious activities were increasingly stifled. Popular temples and redemptive societies were hit the hardest due to their inability to conform to a definition of religion that resembles the Christian church. However, with the economic reforms since 1978, followed by more relaxed religious policies since 1982, religious groups quickly regained their interest and vitality in social engagement. This started with official religions such as Buddhism and Protestant Christianity in the 1980s. In the 1990s, some former benevolent societies (usually called welfare societies, with the religious identity downplayed) reentered the scene of public good provision, and international religious NGOs such as Tzu Chi were permitted to establish branches in China. As in late imperial China, the state got increasingly involved in religious philanthropies through policies of land, property, and financial supervision.

In all three societies, the mid-1980s constituted an important landmark for engaged religions. In both Taiwan and China, this meant that the state outsourced some of its burden of social welfare to religious groups and religious groups gained increasing legitimacy in providing for the public good. In the case of Malacca, the 1980s meant the increasing transnational connections of such engaged religions. Lastly, in all three Chinese societies, we see that the role of the state figures prominently in religious philanthropies, especially in the post-1980s era, although in very different ways. We turn to the situation after the 1980s in the chapters that follow, and specifically to the role of the state in the next chapter.

3 Political Merit-Making: Religious Philanthropy and the State

In this chapter we begin with the major changes that took place starting in the 1980s. The central question we explore is how the different state systems of China, Taiwan, and Malaysia affect the operation of religious philanthropies. We will begin to answer this question by looking at the land acquisition experiences of one religious nongovernmental organization (NGO), the Buddhist Compassion Relief Tzu Chi Foundation, in Taiwan, China, and Malaysia. Its experiences in all three of our sites provide a glimpse of how relationships between these states and religious philanthropies vary, but can never be completely avoided. We will go on to examine in detail the local patterns of interactions between states and religious philanthropies. We will argue that the states universally play vital roles in the functioning of religious philanthropies, regardless of whether the state is authoritarian (China and pre-democratization Taiwan) or democratic (contemporary Taiwan and Malaysia). The specific forms through which religious philanthropies establish ties to the state differ, but they all assume a relationship with the state that we can call "political merit-making." It is partly due to this particular relationship to the state that the religious philanthropies we see in the three cases take on industrialized forms with a universalizing "goodness."

The Compassion Relief Tzu Chi Merit Society is probably the largest Buddhist NGO in the world. Its members take an insistently apolitical stance, for instance, by refusing to endorse political candidates as other religious groups tend to do in Taiwan. Nevertheless, they have never been able to avoid the political process.[1] Indeed, their very first hospital, which began during Taiwan's authoritarian period, was built on land that was acquired as a result of a personal visit by the president at the time, Chiang Ching-kuo. The state also bestowed numerous awards on Tzu Chi as a model temple.[2] Even with direct state encouragement, however, the hospital met with numerous difficulties, especially conflicting military and civilian interests. The first Tzu Chi hospital

[1] Huang, *Charisma and Compassion*, 2009.
[2] Ibid., 352–354.

was thus built only in 1986, seven years after Master Cheng Yen's initial plan, and only after eliciting personal support from the president's office.

Central government endorsement had thus been crucial for the first Tzu Chi hospital, but by the time Tzu Chi built the second hospital in Dalin County in the 1990s, several years after the democratization of Taiwan, things had completely shifted. Although the patronage of the central government remained prominent, democratization meant that the roles of local legislators became increasingly pertinent in the negotiation process. This was also the first time that the land acquisition process of Tzu Chi showed signs of shaping the government's social policies. Note that democracy does not necessarily result in a favorable position for an NGO like this. The complications during the land acquisition process for the second hospital were no less than those for the first hospital in the authoritarian period. They reflected a new dynamic at play among local legislators, state enterprises, local elites, and government officials, as well as Tzu Chi's growing influence.[3] By this time Tzu Chi membership exceeded that of the Nationalist Party (Guomindang, GMD) and political leaders competed to visit Tzu Chi before elections in order to demonstrate an image of moral righteousness associated with Tzu Chi's work.[4] Tzu Chi's land acquisition in Taiwan shows just how heavily this "apolitical" organization is invested in politics, and how the mechanisms of that investment had to change as the regime itself changed.

In the People's Republic of China (PRC), Tzu Chi began its relief projects in 1991, as part of the function of the United Front Department – the branch of the Communist Party responsible for both religious and cross-Straits policy. At that time the deputy director of the Chinese Communist Party (CCP) Central Committee Office for Taiwan Affairs met with Tzu Chi's vice director via the Association for Relations Across the Taiwan Strait (ARATS) and the Straits Exchange Foundation.[5] Tzu Chi became the first "international" NGO to register officially with the Chinese government in 2008. In 2010, it set up its China headquarters in a historical building in Suzhou, a city with a large concentration of Taiwanese businesspeople. Two years later, the group opened its brand new headquarters, including a medical clinic, comparable in size to the main Tzu Chi headquarters in Taiwan (see Figure 3.1). It sits on the city's most expensive piece of land, a generous gift from the municipal government. Its opening ceremony was attended by central government officials such as the chair of ARATS and deputy director of the State Administration for Religious Affairs (SARA), provincial and municipal ARATS and public health officials, as well as leaders from Tzu Chi. Similar to the land acquisition for the first hospital in Taiwan,

[3] Ibid., 207–210.
[4] Ibid., 201–210.
[5] Laliberté, "The Growth of a Taiwanese Buddhist Association in China."

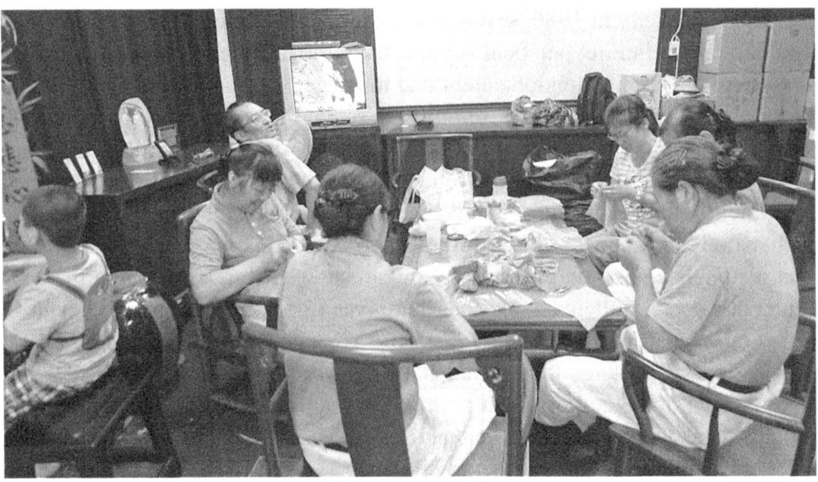

Figure 3.1 Inside Tzu Chi headquarters in Suzhou.

Tzu Chi's entry and expansion in mainland China would have been impossible without this central government endorsement. Even so, they have to follow a "three no" policy (no politics, no religion, and no propaganda).

Moreover, local governments still play crucial roles in accommodating its work, as we can see in Suzhou. One United Front official told us, "Why did Tzu Chi choose to build its headquarters in Suzhou, not Shanghai, not Nanjing?[6] It's because we have the most open-minded (local) government." Other religious philanthropies are not without grudges against Tzu Chi's privileges in Suzhou: "Tzu Chi wants land; the government gives it a gift worth hundreds of millions of yuan; meanwhile the rest of us are starving. It's because Suzhou has the largest Taiwanese business population. They are so powerful that they can influence the government." This accusation is surely oversimplified, but Tzu Chi's crucial role in the United Front work in the eyes of the central and local government plays a major part in the way it fares in Mainland China. Therefore, as in Taiwan, the "no politics" NGO is completely riven with politics, whether it likes it or not.

In Malacca, the first Tzu Chi branch was set up by a Taiwanese business couple inside their garment factory in 1992. The Still Thoughts Hall, the standard name for the main building of the Tzu Chi organization worldwide, was built in 1997 inside an industrial park on land owned by this couple. In comparison to the cases in Taiwan and China, the land acquisition of Tzu Chi in

[6] Shanghai and Nanjing are the two big cities adjacent to Suzhou.

Malacca seems to be the most straightforward and least problematic. These industrial parks maintain relative independence from mainstream Malaysian society, and Tzu Chi's "disembedded" status as a "new foreign religion" ironically helped its growth in Malacca. Similar to the case in China, Tzu Chi in Malacca does not engage in religious propagation, since Malaysian government policy forbids proselytizing toward the Malay majority. Though their charitable work goes beyond the Chinese community, its members are confined to ethnic Chinese, just as with most Tzu Chi branches throughout the world. Most Malacca members are local Chinese who went through Chinese education systems in Malaysia and they often already have a Buddhist background from participating in various Buddhist networks and activities.[7] Indeed, such Chinese religious associations often mediate between the Malay majority government and the ethnic Chinese communities. By taking care of the Chinese communities and beyond and by not proselytizing to the Malay majority, Chinese religious philanthropies such as Tzu Chi provide "safe" alleviation of the welfare burden for the Malaysian government. This creates relative freedom in practicing engaged Buddhism within an ethnic minority community. Of course, the space of freedom the government grants to exercise their philanthropy is quite limited. Chinese religious philanthropies such as Tzu Chi have to learn to walk on thin lines of ethnic politics instead of fully engaging Malaysian civil society at large.

These experiences of Tzu Chi in three different political contexts illustrate how different state systems affect the ways a religious philanthropy can operate and expand. Democracies do not necessarily provide more support for NGOs than authoritarian regimes.[8] Indeed, the generous gift Tzu Chi received from the Suzhou municipal government to build their China headquarters seems to be a luxury that Tzu Chi branches in democratic Taiwan and Malaysia could hardly imagine, despite all sorts of restrictions the group has to endure when doing relief work in China. In all three states, however, this Buddhist NGO cannot avoid a state system that is external to it but heavily intertwined with its growth.

The Interfering State Hypothesis and the State Failure Hypothesis

Even this quick look at Tzu Chi suggests that truisms about the differences between democratic and authoritarian regimes have been overdrawn for religious philanthropies and for NGOs more generally. Here we will briefly consider two further hypotheses regarding the success and failure of religious

[7] Huang, *Charisma and Compassion*, 2009, 240–266.
[8] See also ibid., 210.

philanthropy. The interfering state hypothesis refers mainly to Fuma Susumu's argument mentioned in Chapter 2: whenever the state starts interfering with grassroots philanthropies, those groups start to deteriorate. Fuma holds that historical attempts by the Chinese state to take over charities run by local elites or temples have caused deteriorating conditions for the people receiving aid. This is because bureaucracy and corruption inevitably begin to encroach on these institutions and to create inefficiencies.

While this situation was often true in Chinese history, our evidence suggests that a "neoliberal" state of the sort Fuma seems to favor need not serve as an effective incubator for religious philanthropy either. In the case of both Taiwan and China, we have seen that central state endorsement was crucial for religious NGOs to survive. In the case of Tzu Chi's second hospital construction in Taiwan, local legislators had to interfere in the negotiation process between Tzu Chi and Formosa Sugar, the state-owned enterprise that owned the land. Thus to a certain extent state interference is almost necessary even if, as in this case, the NGO is using one part of the state to influence another. In the case of China, one can say that the Chinese government "interfered" with Tzu Chi's operation by not allowing funds it raises in China to be used outside of China and by forcing it to conduct disaster relief only in places that local governments allocate for them. This does not change the fact, however, that Tzu Chi still remains one of the most efficient and effective relief agencies operating in China. The "interfering state" hypothesis cannot fully explain how religious philanthropy works in both places.

The "state failure" hypothesis typically refers to a proliferation of grassroots charities because the state is unable to provide relief. Taiwan resembles this superficially, since at one point the Taipei city government's social welfare expenditure was well below the relief funding of Tzu Chi alone. However, Taiwan is far from a failed, or even weak state. Instead, Taiwan's authoritarian state (1945–1987) did not make social welfare its priority, in contrast, for instance, to its military expenditures. In this, it more closely resembled the recent retrenchment of some European post-welfare states. However, the state was still powerful enough to veto or permit the functioning of grassroots groups that were willing to shoulder the responsibility.

In the case of Malaysia, the state takes a hard line on its ethno-religious policies, especially through the "Sedition Act," which prevents proselytizing among the Malay majority. Therefore, one can say that the state leaves the Chinese community to take care of itself; this is quite different from a simple inability to take care of the Chinese community. In China, the state has encouraged social organizations to provide social services in recent years, but the timing coincides not with a failed state, but with a state that is growing ever stronger. The state is powerful enough to contain and check religious philanthropies through rules and regulations on accounting and organizational structure and through resources such as land and financial subsidies. The rising number of religious philanthropies is not a result of the state's failure to take care of its people, but a different model of governance in which the state is able to access and better harness grassroots desire to contribute to the public good. State failure does not explain any of the three societies in the current study.

Instead, we propose that in all three states, religious philanthropies make "political merit" with the state. "Merit-making" (做功德) is originally a Buddhist concept. S. J. Tambiah (1968) in his studies of Thai Buddhism has described merit-making as gifts to the sangha, the Buddhist monastic community, that help lay people achieve detachment from their wealth. These gifts can be in material forms, such as food, flowers, and monetary contributions, but they can also be in the form of rituals and paying respect. The monks who are at the receiving end of the merit-making occupy a superior position.[9] In China, lay people's merit-making has come to mean contributions with a specific or generalized return in mind, such as good health, prosperity, or a general well-being of the family. Sometimes viewed as an informal contract, merit-making always involves a relationship. This relationship may be a hierarchical one: similar to what Tambiah described for Thai Buddhism, the Chinese monks, who are the recipients of the gifts, are superior to the lay givers, who make merit through the upward alms-giving.

However, merit-making may sometimes also be reciprocal. In Chinese popular religion, the deities are as reliant on merit-making as the worshipers. If the people stop the merit-making of offerings to the deities, the deities lose their efficacy and are gradually ignored. Merit-making need not be exactly balanced – nobody keeps an account book to track the payment and gain of merit – but there is often a general sense of efficacy that indicates whether the relationship will continue. Here we are using merit-making partly to reflect the common cultural category as it is practiced in Chinese lay Buddhism and popular religion, and partly to develop it into a broader analytic term that might be applied elsewhere.

"Political merit-making" refers to the relationships religious groups cultivate with the state in order to gain more legitimacy, political support, autonomy, or even ways of influencing policy-making. The state, in turn, gets a certain level of legitimacy or endorsement in this process. We suggest that the extent to which religious groups can actively provide social services depends upon how the religious organizations deal with the varying agendas of different levels of governments, regardless of whether they participate in politics in an explicit manner or not. As we explain in the text that follows, political merit-making

[9] Tambiah, "The Ideology of Merit and the Social Correlations of Buddhism in a Thai Village."

takes place in all three societies discussed in this book, with their very different political systems.

While this concept is a transformation of older Chinese ideas, we suggest that political merit-making can be used more generally as an analytical term applicable elsewhere. (Why, after all, should Europe be the only place where indigenous ideas develop into social science theory?) We argue that political merit-making is a kind of state–religion relationship that has been overlooked in the past – one that reflects the mutual dependence of the state and religion and highlights the inventiveness of religions to maximize their growth in partnership with or despite their political counterparts.

As we have seen, even a group like Tzu Chi, which maintains a stance of never participating in formal politics, still practices a form of political merit-making. By staying away from explicit politics and declaring a dedication to share the state's burden of social welfare, Tzu Chi has been able to appeal to very different forms of government. To a certain degree, it made the "deities" (in this case, the state) reliant on them. Therefore, we argue that this political merit-making takes place not only in authoritarian states such as China, but also in democratic states such as contemporary Taiwan and Malaysia. The forms of political merit-making, however, are not all the same. We characterize the political merit-making in China as "defensive," as "collaborative" in Taiwan after democratization, and as "enclaved" in Chinese society in Malaysia. In the following pages, we examine these different forms through ethnographic examples.

China

In the PRC, the state took full responsibility for the social welfare of its citizens during the collective period (roughly 1958–1978). With the economic reforms and opening-up policies in the 1980s, the state gradually allowed very limited space for social organizations to share some of the burdens of social welfare. During the state-initiated "Religious Charity Week" campaign mentioned in Chapter 2, for example, all five official religions joined hands through their separate associations and raised more than 300 million RMB (roughly 48 million USD) in 2013.[10] The Jiangsu provincial Religious Affairs Bureau received a total of 16,797,826 RMB (roughly 2.7 million USD), which they gave to the provincial-level Disabilities Foundation, a government-organized nongovernmental organization (GONGO) of the kind commonly seen in China.[11] This is a

[10] "Annual Report for the State Administration of Religious Affairs 2013" 国家宗教事务局2013年工作情况报告, www.sara.gov.cn//xxgk/ndgzyd/57972.htm (Accessed May 8, 2014).

[11] "A Report on Religious Charity Week in Jiangsu Province" 江苏宗教慈善周活动综述, www.jsmzzj.gov.cn/art/2013/10/17/art_1121_38886.html (Accessed May 8, 2014).

clear example of religious groups making political merit with the state through philanthropy. It certainly is a very different model of state–religious philanthropy dynamic from that of Taiwan after democratization. The difference does not lie in whether the state matters – it does in both cases – but rather in how the state matters.

One way for religious groups to make political merit is to contribute economically and politically to the state agenda. Take Buddhism as an example. China has the largest registered Buddhist population in the world today.[12] In comparison to other religions, Buddhism has often been considered a "favorable" religion by the current Chinese regime, despite rather stringent policies toward religions in general. Important Buddhist temples were among the first religious sites to be restored in the 1980s. The major reason is that Buddhist temples were good sites of domestic and international tourism and can be used as unofficial diplomatic connections with the surrounding Buddhist countries and regions. When China had no formal political exchanges with Taiwan and with Japan, state leaders could still communicate indirectly through informal visits paid to temples in China. These religious sites were earning political merit by paving informal diplomatic relations between states and regions. But this merit-making is defensive in the sense that the temples had little other choice if they wanted to join the reconstruction process; earning this kind of merit by creating revenues for the state through tourism or by easing informal diplomacy was the only way to protect and advance their own religious interests.

During the 1980s most of the funds for temple reconstruction came from overseas Chinese donations and government subsidies. Overseas Chinese businessmen came from southeast China or Taiwan and rebuilt temples, very often with direct invitations from the local governments trying to attract their investment in the newly started industrial enterprises. This obviously had mutual benefits both for religious groups and the local governments. We will see that most of today's larger thriving religious philanthropies were temples that were rebuilt early in the 1980s with funds from overseas, either through locality or kinship ties to overseas China or through tourism. This was true for Protestantism as much as Buddhism. The founding of Amity Foundation in 1985 relied heavily on overseas Protestant donations. It started with Bible printing and arranging to bring English teachers to China, but soon branched out to be the largest NGO with a religious background in the country. The reason why this "foreign and imperialistic" funding was able to come to China was partly because Amity collaborates heavily with all levels of the Chinese government on their projects. Since the 1980s, philanthropy has increasingly

[12] Ashiwa and Wank, *Making Religion, Making the State*, 3.

grown into one of the most important mechanisms for political merit-making for religious groups.

Hanshan Temple[13] offers a good example of such political merit-making. Since its restoration in the early 1980s, the two abbots of Hanshan Temple have occupied important positions in the municipal and provincial governments. Master Xingkong (性空法师, b. 1922) became the abbot in 1984.[14] Having played crucial roles in the temple reconstruction since 1963, he single-handedly built the Puming Pagoda by selling his calligraphy to Japanese tourists. One of his calligraphies dedicated to the sixtieth anniversary of the founding of the People's Republic of China hung at the entrance of the charity office during one of our visits. It read: "Glory to the Chinese Nation, Blessings to the Motherland" (see Figure 3.2).

Besides being the abbot, Master Xingkong was a standing member of the Buddhist Association of China, the vice chair of the Buddhist Associations of Jiangsu Province and Suzhou Municipality, and a standing member of the People's Political Consultative Committee of Suzhou. All of those positions make him a trusted liaison between the state and the religious community, as well as between the Chinese government and other states. Thus Master Xingkong did much to foster unofficial exchanges with Japan and to build diplomatic ties with China's neighbors after years of alienation.

Master Qiushuang (b. 1967), the successor as abbot since 2004, has served as a standing member of the Buddhist Association of China, the vice chair and secretary-in-chief of the Buddhist Association of Jiangsu Province, and a standing member of the People's Political Consultative Committee of Jiangsu Province.[15] These titles and positions demonstrate that the two generations of

[13] A more detailed description of Hanshan Temple and the United Heart Church can be found in Wu, "Negotiating the 'Grey Zone': Buddhist and Protestant Philanthropies in Contemporary Southeast China."

[14] He became the monastic manager of Hanshan Temple in 1963. Subsequently the temple, together with all the other religious sites, was closed down and all the monks were asked to disrobe. However, in 1979, two years after the Cultural Revolution was over, they were invited back to the temple to see to the restoration process.

[15] This is not exceptional. Almost all important leaders from the state-sanctioned five religions have official ties and occupy seats in various levels of the government. Some of them hold those seats to provide protection for their own religious denominations. Some of them do not have actual political power despite their presence, since the state uses their representation to showcase their policy of religious freedom and in the form of the "United Front." The United Front Work Department of the CCP central committee is a special office that was established during the Second World War to unite with those who are outside of the Communist Party in order to fight against the Japanese invasion. After the founding of the PRC, this department has evolved to deal with all the "other" representatives of non-CCP bodies and organizations: other political parties (Bureau One); ethnic and religious affairs (Bureau Two); Hong Kong, Macao, Taiwan, and other overseas Chinese affairs (Bureau Three); non-CCP cadres in the government (Bureau Four); non-state-owned economic bodies (Bureau Five); non-CCP and overseas intellectuals (Bureau Six); and Tibetan Affairs (Bureau Seven).

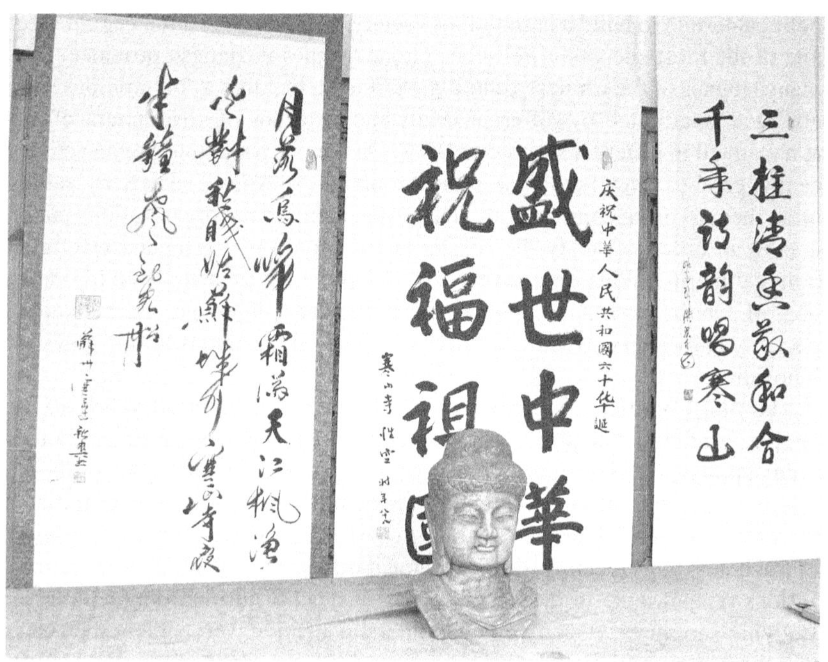

Figure 3.2 Master Xingkong's calligraphy.

Hanshan Temple leadership in the post-Mao era both made political merit with provincial and municipal governments through following state regulations tightly and contributing to national politics and the regional economy.

Hanshan Temple is also a leading Buddhist philanthropy. Master Xingkong donated money, quilts, and winter clothes to government social welfare programs every year since he was made abbot in 1984. In 1996, he established the Hanshan Scholarship Program in Suzhou University to help students from poor families with initial funding of 10,000 RMB. In 1997, he donated 2,000 RMB to a policeman who died on duty. Though piecemeal, all these deeds demonstrate that the early philanthropic acts of the Hanshan Temple were closely related to the needs and desires of the state.[16] Master Qiushuang carried on this legacy and made philanthropy the trademark of Hanshan Temple.

Hanshan Temple established a "Charitable Supermarket" in 2003 when the then president of China, Hu Jintao, announced the central policy for his

[16] Su, "Master Xingkong – Standing Member of Municipal Political Consultative Conference and the Abbot of Hanshan Temple."

political term: "to build a harmonious society."[17] This was just the beginning of one of the most successful religious philanthropies in Jiangsu province. Like many slogans of the Chinese central government, building a "harmonious society" was interpreted by different levels and branches of government offices and resulted in different specific policies. On the one hand, this slogan actively campaigned to funnel political merit through all sectors of society by calling upon them to make contributions. Therefore, many social organizations put on a show in order to satisfy the calling of the central government, performing political merit-making defensively. This is often seen as centralized top-down control. On the other hand, though, this particular political process also unexpectedly allows much room for different social organizations to find ways for innovation.

The first Charitable Supermarket was located in a small alley behind the temple. It offered roughly 250–300 square meters of food staples and household supplies, ranging from rice to soap and plastic containers. According to a senior volunteer at the Charitable Supermarket, Master Xingkong initiated the project after attending a meeting organized by the municipal government of Suzhou. At this meeting, the government officials asked all religious organizations to contribute to the larger society, instead of just building temples or studying scriptures. Poverty alleviation and education were among the issues that the government thought were dragging down the speed of "socialist development." Hanshan Temple then provided each low-income family a voucher worth 60 RMB each month, with which they could purchase goods from the Charitable Supermarket.

In 2004, the national-level religious affairs bureaucracy published a new "Religious Affairs Regulation" (宗教事务条例), to replace the 1994 "Regulations on the Management of Religious Sites" (宗教活动场所管理条例). In the new regulation, which is still in effect today, two features are prominent: the regulation of religious property (Section 5) and the legal responsibilities of religious groups (Section 6). The increasing wealth that religious groups had accumulated and the unclear accounting books of religious charity programs were probably factors that contributed to the rise of such regulations. This rising demand from the state for religious groups to be "accountable" is a central feature of the new regulations and of contemporary interactions between religion and the state in China.

Hanshan Temple is remarkable for having often stayed one step ahead in state–religion interactions. In the same year these regulations were instated,

[17] Hu's collection of essays and speeches, *To Build Socialist Harmonious Society*, was published by the CCP central office in April 2013. This volume includes all his important speeches on this topic, dating back to 2003, when he first moved in this direction.

the Hanshan Temple established its "Charity Center" (慈善中心) to answer questions of accountability. The Charity Center is registered with the Suzhou government as a "Non-profit Social Service Organization," thus gaining its legal status. The Charity Center was the first such initiative made by any religious organization in Jiangsu province and thus completed the transition of Hanshan Temple from just another successful tourist site to a leading religious philanthropy in China.

The Charity Center established separate accounting books for regular temple and charity-related affairs. When one of us visited Hanshan Temple in 2006, there were two separate donation boxes in the main hall – one to the temple, and the other to the Charity Center. The volunteers sitting next to the boxes had to explain very patiently to the tourist/devotee the difference between the two boxes and often added, "The merit is the same no matter which box you put the money in!" Most people ended up putting money in both boxes, because they did not want to miss any opportunity to make merit.

The Charity Center did not rely only on the donation boxes. Companies, and rich devout individuals donated to the charitable enterprise once it became famous. In 2009 one of the largest supermarkets in Jiangsu became partner to the Charitable Supermarket and allowed low-income families to use the vouchers in their supermarkets all over the region. By 2010, more than 422 families in Suzhou benefited from this program and it has extended to various districts of Suzhou and other counties of Jiangsu province since. We can see that both the Charitable Supermarket and the Charity Center were established to make merit with the state, defensively. Unlike the Tzu Chi story in Taiwan, where the religious organization had an agenda first and then sought ways to convince the state into complying with it, the Chinese case often starts with top-down policy changes that result in strategies from religious organizations that try to comply with the state.

The Charity Center in Hanshan Temple remains heavily intertwined with local government. The exchanges go both ways: in 2006, the district level Public Security Bureau donated some rice and cooking oil (worth around 5,000 RMB, about USD 650) to the Charitable Supermarket; in 2009, the Charity Center launched a program in which two lay Buddhists volunteer three days a week in the Public Security Bureau as mediators of civil disputes, occasionally offering counseling services to distressed citizens. This is a direct imitation of Tzu Chi, stemming from when the head of the Public Security Bureau made an official trip to Taiwan, where he was invited to observe the "Tzu Chi Volunteer Mothers" at work. Returning to Suzhou, he approached Hanshan Temple to see if they could do the same. The Buddhist volunteers see this as an opportunity to propagate the dharma or to use Buddhist wisdom to solve mundane problems, but the state still sits at the top as the initiators (and potential terminators) of such activities.

The local government is heavily involved in the decision making of the Charity Center. A number of officials in the Religious Affairs Bureau occupy its administrative positions. Not only are members of the temple and the donors present at Hanshan Charity Center's executive meetings; so are officials of the Religious Affairs Bureau and Civil Affairs Bureau. Government officials have commonly taken roles in religious philanthropies in Chinese societies from imperial times to present-day Taiwan and Malacca. However, the officials taking posts in today's religious philanthropy in China act less as a patron (as in imperial times) or as gentry drawing on the social capital of the religious group. Rather, they act more as supervisors to keep things in line. Thus, allowing or inviting the officials to be board members both seeks protection from and makes merit with the state as a form of self-regulation.

Besides donating to local governments when the country faces disasters, such as the Guizhou blizzard and the Sichuan earthquake of 2008, the Charity Center latches onto development projects initiated by various state organizations. In 1989, the Communist Youth League launched an equal education program for underprivileged children called "Project Hope" to absorb non-governmental and overseas funds. One of the main activities of "Project Hope" was to build schools in rural China. The Charity Center of Hanshan Temple has built many "Hope Schools" in different parts of China. This has become a legitimate and standard practice for secular and religious philanthropies.

To expand the work of the Charity Center, Hanshan Temple founded the Hehe Cultural Foundation (和合文化基金会) in 2011. It is a publically funded organization registered with the Civil Affairs Bureau of Jiangsu Province. This action is partly due to the internal demand of the religious philanthropy to grow and partly due to the increasing pressure and regulations the state imposes on religious philanthropies to be "accountable" (or rather, "auditable"). With this new organization and registration, the temple can collect donations province-wide. The historical diplomatic roles of Hanshan Temple have decreased with the establishment of official diplomatic ties and the rise of other groups that can play these roles better. The other side of the success story of Hanshan Temple is its burgeoning tourism, continuous acquisition of new physical spaces and buildings, and increasingly visible wealth. This conspicuous growth could always arouse suspicion from the state. Therefore, there is more demand for the temple to do merit-making through philanthropy, especially philanthropy well regulated by the state.

However, with this transition to a more industrialized model of philanthropy, new problems emerge. For instance, the state demands that these foundations need to keep their annual operational cost below 10% of their income. This is much easier to accomplish in GONGOs such as the Red Cross, whose staff members are on the government payroll. Hehe Foundation, instead, has to pay staff out of its own income, and so needs to rely heavily on subsidies from

Hanshan Temple's income from tourism. Otherwise it could not meet these criteria. Furthermore, there is sometimes a clash between the Buddhist ideal of the good and state visions of the good. For instance, the abbot plans to build the largest animal-releasing park in the province but he has not been able to obtain land successfully at the time of our writing. In a province where economic growth has led to an acute demand for land, the Buddhist good of compassion in the releasing of animals meets little sympathy. To reach its own goals, therefore, the foundation needs to make further political merit in order to gain space for its growth. Often this means taking on state projects. The state-of-the-art old age home Hehe Foundation built was one such response to relieve the state burden of the aging population. Though its operation still had not fully launched at the time of this writing, the local government has applauded the endeavor.

Hanshan Temple's merit-making history is a telling example of what many religious groups go through: first it played informal diplomatic roles; then it contributed to the local economy by attracting overseas Chinese investment and through tourism; finally, it performed philanthropy to ease the welfare burden of the state.

Christianity, too, needs to make political merit. The Protestant United Heart Church (同心堂), a small congregation on the outskirts of Changzhou, another southern Jiangsu city, was founded in 1946 by a pastor-missionary from Shanghai. It was closed down during the anti-religion campaigns of 1959. In 1994, twelve years after the 1982 religious policy created some space, worship service resumed in several old houses that were purchased by some former church members. The group elected Mr. Wang, the leading devotee, to be their "legal representative" (法人代表). In 1996, the congregation finished a new building, which was immediately filled with believers. A decade later, the church was attended by 200–300 people every Sunday and 400–500 people on holidays such as Christmas and Easter. In 1999, Mr. Wang accumulated some funds to build a two-story apartment building as an old age home at the back of the church and named it the "Gospel Hall" (福音堂). He envisioned two stages for the old age home. In the first stage, it would serve mainly the needs of the believers since "it is easier to manage people with the same faith." Once its operation model matured, they planned to open it up to the general public. With twenty rooms and fifty beds, the old age home was serving twenty-one believers in 2006. Mr. Wang said that they tried to accommodate nonbelievers initially, but they did not get along with believers when the latter went to services and studied the Bible together.[18]

[18] We will see this pattern again later in the book, where religious groups claim an intention to help everyone in need, regardless of belief, but in practice have not extended beyond their own group.

The Gospel Hall charges 250 RMB (38 USD) a month per person, paid in the form of a donation to the church. The fee is waived for those without income. With only one bathroom and no basic medical facilities, the old age home operates in a very modest way. However, there is a prayer room, a small vegetable garden, and a large communal kitchen. Mostly self-sustained, the church hires a little help: one man was paid 200 RMB (30 USD) a month to take care of the vegetable garden and do grocery shopping; there was one cook and one caretaker for 400 RMB (62 USD) a month each. Despite being underpaid, these helpers hoped to provide aid to Christians and they saw their work as half-voluntary.

Despite the modest living conditions, the seniors say they enjoy their residence in the Gospel Hall. They can attend church services without relying on any transportation or assistance. Each day starts with morning exercises followed by prayers before breakfast. After their simple meal of rice congee and pickled vegetables, the residents wash clothes, chat, and help prepare lunch, which normally consists of fresh fruits and vegetables from the garden and meat donated by other church members. The afternoon is dedicated to Bible study and TV-watching after a mid-day nap. On Tuesdays, they join the rest of the congregation in a prayer meeting. On Fridays they participate in choir rehearsals. Through these group activities, some senior residents even learned to read Chinese characters and musical notes.

The government does not offer any financial support to the church or the operation of the old age home. The Three Self Patriotic Movement (TSPM, the official organization for Protestants), where Mr. Wang served as the associate chair at the district level for some time, contributes an annual subsidy of 10,000–15,000 RMB (roughly 1,500–2,300 USD). Because the congregation is composed of mostly elderly members of the nearby villages, college students, and migrant workers, the weekly collection is less than 1,000 RMB (roughly 150 USD). TSPM churches are not allowed to take funding directly from foreign sources, and they can apply for funding only through TSPM. For instance, Mr. Wang related that the Gospel Hall once got a small sum from the United Christian Nethersole Foundation in Hong Kong through TSPM, which allocated the money to specific churches or organizations. In 2012 a new policy that allows the government to "purchase services from social organizations" made it theoretically possible for religious associations to receive government subsidies in their philanthropic endeavors. However, it often favors those more "successful" religious philanthropies that are larger in scale and involves a complicated process of proposal writing and evaluation.

For instance, the local Religious Affairs Bureau, Civil Affairs Bureau, or the United Front can collaborate with a religious group in building an old age home, by providing things such as land or subsidies. In exchange, the management of the old age home will have to conform to state requisites, such as pricing and member eligibility. This might offer opportunities for some religious groups such as the Gospel Hall to get much-needed financial assistance. However, a small operation like the United Heart church is not a priority for the performance-minded government officials. The fact that it serves only believers at this point also poses a problem for government subsidies. Whether it can ride the tide of this new policy is contingent on local government officials, their visions of the new policy, and their attitude toward specific philanthropies. Therefore, political merit-making is crucially important for such religious philanthropies to survive, even on this small a scale.

Sometimes, however, religious philanthropies that are financially sound enough can reject government subsidies. One temple in Jiangsu Province that one of us has studied resisted the local government's funding in order to achieve independence from state interference in the management and operation of its old age home. The abbot's original idea of building an old age home comes out of a situation that most elderly Buddhists face in today's crowded households: a lack of space to chant sutras, keep a vegetarian diet, or burn incense because of the objection of the younger generation who live with them. So he wants to keep the old age home an exclusively Buddhist space, with vegetarian meal plans and ample room for worship. The caretakers and managers are lay Buddhist volunteers who maintain the place with Buddhist-inspired ethics. The "good" here (of maintaining a Buddhist life) certainly diverges from the "good" the state has in mind in promoting society-run old age homes (to meet the needs of an aging population). With government support of land and money, it would have been much faster to build the old age home and much easier to get a license, but the government would also insist that non-Buddhists be able to live there and that they charge a higher fee. At the time of writing, the temple managed to hold off the pressure from the local government, but its independence may not last long because it refuses to perform political merit-making. Since the abbot enjoys high prestige among Buddhist communities internationally and had performed important diplomatic favors for the government earlier, the local government is relatively lenient toward the current temple leadership, but it is doubtful if the situation will last once the abbot passes away. The current managers of the old age home try to be low-key but they also know that further merit-making is necessary for the survival of the old age home.

The situation is different, however, for the Gospel Hall, which is financially much weaker than this Buddhist temple. Despite the fact that the Gospel Hall has been serving the elderly since 1999, the Civil Affairs Bureau did not grant it a license until 2006, although the local United Front and the Religious Affairs Bureau had quietly acquiesced to its existence. In 2002, the Religious Affairs Bureau even awarded the church a plaque reading "Progressive Community in Christian Social Services" (基督教为社会服务先进集体奖状), which, according to Mr. Wang, was related to the Gospel Hall, although it was not clear whether it was awarded this plaque based on this particular endeavor or because it stayed within the state-prescribed limits despite the old age home. One pastor commented on this ambivalence:

> Our [central] government's policy is mostly vague and can be interpreted in different ways. Therefore, the situation of the church is often at the mercy of individuals who are appointed as the head of the local Religious Affairs Bureau. If that person is nice, our lives will be easier. If that person is harsh (不近人情), everything becomes harder and we better watch what we do and what we say.

When pressed further about why there is such a difference, the same pastor remarked, "There is a huge grey area between what is illegal and what is NOT legal on religious issues in China."[19] It is exactly this "grey area" that makes political merit-making so paramount. Like the Calvinists Weber described, religious groups never know exactly if their philanthropy is the ticket to temporary immunity and future development; the only way to gain confidence is to make further political merit with the state. That is why the state almost always has the upper hand despite the existence of the grey area. For example, when the United Heart Church was planning to have a ten-year anniversary celebration for the Gospel Hall, the public security officials got upset at it for not seeking their approval beforehand. As a result, they ordered the church to cancel the celebration. The church immediately stopped all the preparation work and apologized. This way of showing respect to a capricious local government is one way of making merit, albeit a defensive one. For those who struggle to earn political merit, there may be little capacity to pursue their own agenda.

The attitude of the state toward religious philanthropies is influenced by its policy toward both religion and social organizations such as NGOs. Both categories are treated with caution, and sometimes with antagonism. The party-state in China also expects repeated statements of ideological loyalty, which forces religious philanthropies to spend extra energy in ideological work such as reciting mantras of state propaganda (like "Love the Nation, Love the Religion," 爱国爱教, which is heard constantly in public statements from all five religions) in order to gain legitimacy. In this process, the Chinese state always seem to be in control, even though most of the actual work is done by religious philanthropies long before any policy changes are possible. We call political merit-making in the Chinese authoritarian state "defensive," because the state always has the upper hand and religious groups know that earning political merit helps guarantee their safety. Furthermore, this defensive

[19] This echoes Yang Fenggang's article on "The Red, Black, and Gray Markets of Religion in China." What the pastor refers to, however, is not a market at all but rather a grey area between the state and social relations in China.

merit-making has led to a strong sense of self-regulation that not only entails showing respect for government restrictions but also has a shaping effect on the religious philanthropies toward a more industrialized form and a more universalizing sense of the good that is promoted by the state.

Taiwan

The rise of religious philanthropy in Taiwan toward the end of authoritarian rule also took place in relation to the state, as we have seen in the Tzu Chi land acquisition case at the beginning of this chapter. The context, however, was quite different. At the height of the Maoist period, the Chinese state subsumed all aspects of welfare and of social life generally. There was, in principle, no need for NGOs and certainly not for religious-inspired philanthropy. As we have shown, new space opened up in the 1980s as the PRC government began to encourage more social responsibility. Nevertheless, attitudes have changed only gradually, so that it is still difficult to discuss this topic without the state becoming a constant theme.

In contrast, authoritarian Taiwan adopted something like a neoliberal approach to welfare, in the sense that it was willing to take only the very minimum of responsibility, saving its investments instead for the military and the economy. When that regime also began to loosen up politically in the 1980s, they were all too happy to see religious (and other organizations) take on a major role in delivering welfare and other social goods. That is why the Foreign Ministry in the early 1990s took one of us to Tzu Chi's headquarters in Hualian to meet Master Cheng Yen, as we described at the beginning of the book. Tzu Chi was included because its welfare activities so perfectly matched the state's own agenda. Other groups had also begun to move into this newly available social space during the 1980s, including some in Lukang, if not on as large a scale.

The Taiwanese state began to take much more direct responsibility for welfare after democratization, probably in response to the need to compete for votes. This encouraged even further collaboration and cooperation between the state and service-oriented social groups, including religious ones. For example, in interviews with the head and one of the other officials of the Lukang Township government's Society Department (社会科), they described local state programs to provide ad hoc aid for needy poor families. Regulations, however, prevent them from helping some families whom they feel clearly deserve and need aid, for instance, farmers whose net worth is too high because they own land, which they cannot sell. In such cases, they said, they often turn to local temples and other social organizations to help out.

In addition, at the Chinese New Year, many such groups contribute money to the township government (roughly 500,000 TWD [about 15,600 USD] in 2006), which is then distributed to old and poor residents. At other times the township hands out lists of the needy to larger temples (like the Tianhou Temple) and larger charitable NGOs; those groups then distribute rice, oil, and other basic goods. The Tianhou Temple also provides food for local school children from poor families. Local Tzu Chi members (there is no formally organized sub-branch in Lukang) similarly collaborate with township officials to provide aid and other services such as school crossing guards or special classes for "delinquent" children.

We can also see this kind of collaboration with some local community development organizations, such as the Lukang Zijidian Educational Foundation (mentioned in Chapter 2), which branched off from the local community temple (the Zijidian, after which it is named). This small foundation lists all of its donors, which include wealthy individuals, some companies, branches of the Lion's Club and Rotary Club, and the Tianhou Temple. They contributed land for a new community center, and the building itself is being paid for by the township government. Here we see the intimate cooperation that links local government, temples, NGOs, and private individuals. Both state and religious actors perceive a mutual benefit, unlike the more power-laden relationship we saw in China.

These collaborations can cross religious lines as well, as with Guo Xianrong, a Presbyterian church leader who ran the church's kindergarten and their pedicab business (a charity in that it provides jobs for the unemployed) at the time of this research. Guo is also a founding member of the Junior Chamber of Commerce, which does a significant amount of charity work, as well as the Zhicheng Benevolent Association (至诚慈善会), which was probably the first modern charitable NGO (founded in 1977) in Lukang. He explains his activism as the result of his Christian beliefs, but he says that none of the other founders of these groups was Christian.

The need for welfare services during Taiwan's late authoritarian period opened a window for charities run (or at least inspired) by religious groups. After democratization, it also became an arena in which the government wanted to prove its value to voters, leading to many forms of collaboration that served the mutual interests of both politicians and religious activists. Nevertheless, working with the government – not just in Taiwan but anywhere – also brings certain kinds of responsibilities and restrictions. Groups that accept funding or other benefits from the state also have to accept some degree of supervision. Taiwan's restrictions after democratization are primarily financial, setting bars for the registration of different kinds of charitable groups, and requiring financial accounting to retain tax status as nonprofits. Recall that the PRC imposes even more difficult financial restrictions, in addition to political limits, strict rules against religious proselytization, and demands for the expression of ideological loyalty.

Some groups in Taiwan are too small to manage the paperwork, and Changhua County officials (who supervise Lukang Township) in charge of registration told one of us in interviews that there was a constant headache involving groups that did not register or that never managed to follow the rules properly. The Lukang township government also pointed out that probably half the temples in the township are not registered. They think the reason is that registration requires having a transparent accounting system, and most temples are unable or unwilling to supply it. Even the extremely powerful and rich Tianhou Temple has discussed creating its own charitable foundation several times, but has always decided not to take the step. The temple's board members explain that they fear money being siphoned away from ritual activities, but nearly everyone else thinks they do not want their accounting books opened. This opinion was expressed as well by a former representative on their board (信徒代表), who finally created his own personal foundation out of frustration.

Even local temples have felt this kind of pressure to become more like an NGO by global standards. Not only does registration require modern styles of accounting, but temple management is now expected to be "democratic." Rather than choosing management committees through divination, which had been by far the most common method in the past, temples now have to have periodic elections. The awkwardness of this graft onto older roots shows in the very idea of an electorate. Temples now must construct lists of *xintu* or "believers" (信徒) who have the right to vote, usually acquired by paying a fee. This is a drastic departure from the very idea of what it meant to worship in a temple, where being a "believer" in a specific temple was never relevant in the past.

Even as the government has placed restrictions on religious (and other) charitable activity (based on an audit culture very similar to what we just discussed for the mainland), it continues to rely on these groups for help in governance. One can easily see temples making merit with the local state through things like donating fire trucks and garbage trucks, as with the Tianhou Temple, mentioned in the previous chapter, or the smaller and poorer Fengtian Gong, which donated fire hoses. The need is mutual, however. When one of us asked the mayor of Lukang at the time, Wang Huimei, whether it was important for politicians to go to temples, she said,

> Maybe not so much at the level of neighborhood head (里长) or representative to the county legislature [the second lowest-level elected officials, just above neighborhood heads], but for a township mayor like me or a representative to the national legislature, it's absolutely crucial. That's why when the Tianhou Temple Mazu came back from her pilgrimage last week, I marched the entire way with her. Two hours, and it rained the whole time! We have to do this partly to forge ties to the local people, but you also have to remember that the temple leaders themselves are elected now, so they really know how to mobilize votes.

Two officials from the county government echoed this sentiment, saying that being active in religious philanthropy is sometimes just another form of political power for someone running for office. Both officials agreed that all of these philanthropic activists, secular and religious, are somehow involved in politics, even though it might not always be obvious. This point poses a sharp contrast with the situation in China. As we have discussed, involvement in religious philanthropy does not generate political power for the officials. Instead, it is a way government officials there exercise their power over religious groups.

Sometimes the mutual dependence of local state and religious charity affects the ritual itself. A staff member at an earth god temple (福德祠) near the Tianhou Temple explained that they help the local elementary school, for instance by supplying graduation gifts for their students. In return, she said, the school makes sure they have a steady supply of children to take part in their rituals by marching in traditional costumes to accompany a god.

The mutualism of political merit-making in Taiwan, however, leaves room for temples simply to avoid the state if they choose. As we saw in last section, it is almost impossible for temples or churches in China to avoid pressure from the state to conform to its expectations. This is especially true if the group controls significant human or financial resources – only some small, rural temples manage to remain completely beneath the radar, but even they must consider the state in their strategies for remaining out of sight. In Lukang, however, some important temples choose not to play this game. The Longshan Si (龙山寺) is the second most important temple in the township, standing at the opposite side of town from the Tianhou Temple. Both are enormously wealthy, but from different sources. Tianhou Temple relies on its central place in Taiwan's network of Mazu temples, which brings it a steady stream of donations from devotees. The Longshan Si instead relies primarily on extensive landholdings, which began to generate a large income as Lukang's tourist economy developed rapidly in the early 2000s.

Everyone we spoke to, from the mayor to temple management, agreed that the Longshan Si does no charitable activity. In addition, its leaders at the time were all in their sixties and seventies, and thus had little interest in building political careers. They were instead dedicated to a massive reconstruction project that dominated the temple during the time of our fieldwork. Longshan Si thus offers an example of a locally powerful temple that largely avoids the state as well as social engagement, because its sources of income are secure and its leaders hold few political ambitions. In this system of mutual merit-making, some temples can choose to pursue only spiritual merit while ignoring the political kind.

Post-democratization Taiwan has thus developed political merit-making for engaged religions into a mutual art, in which the state's real power consists mostly of the ability to push both NGOs and religious groups into a particular financial and management model (somewhat sketchily enforced). In general, however, each side depends on the other to achieve its own goals, leading to a broadly collaborative relationship. As one final example, when Lukang reconstructed the town's parade to float water lanterns (放水灯) as part of the annual ghost festival, the sponsors included Dizang Temple (地藏王庙), which hosts the ritual; the township and county governments; the Quanzhou Merchants' Association (whose religious aspects were discussed in the previous chapter); the Junior Chamber of Commerce; and Taipower, the state-owned electric company. This is a ritual done partly to ease the suffering of ghosts and partly to keep the tourist trade thriving, but completely representative of the collaborative relationships that have evolved as the core of political merit-making for religious groups in Taiwan.

Malaysia

Religious philanthropy in Malaysia displays what we call "enclaved" political merit-making. It needs to be understood in its historical background of the state's refusal to provide significant welfare benefits across the population. The multiethnic structure of Malaysia and its long history of divide-and-rule shaped how welfare worked. Since the seventeenth century, the multiple colonial governments – Portuguese, Dutch, and British – maintained the multiethnic structure by appointing a leader for each ethnic enclave and almost entirely leaving members of each enclave to look after themselves.

After independence in 1957, the Federation of Malaysia did not follow the older divide-and-rule policies. Rather, divide-and-rule transformed into the *bumiputera* policy, particularly through the New Economy Policy after 1979. It created a new divide along the line between the Islamic and Malay on one side, and the non-Islamic and non-Malay on the other. In the Constitution, all ethnicities and all religions are equal. In practice, however, minorities and non-Muslims coexist with the Malay/Muslim majority peacefully only by respecting the latter's privilege as *bumiputera*. The same conditions apply when we consider how non-Islamic religious groups make merit with the state.

The current governing body for all NGOs is the Registry of Societies (ROS). It was established in 1966, based on the governing regulation for all recognized social organizations, the Societies Act of 1966. Similar to the legal frameworks in China and Taiwan, the Malaysian state developed detailed regulations on how associations should work. All societies are subject to rules concerning membership, organization, meetings, objectives, and audits, for which they must provide annual financial statements. Perhaps slightly more unusual is the specific requirement that forbids any gambling-related activities.[20] Unlike the direct interaction with the state and the local government in China and Taiwan, political merit-making in Malaysia is ethnically "enclaved." The top layer of merit-making with the state for the non-Muslim/non-Malay has to do with being self-regulated within the demarcated ethnic sphere, with full respect given to Islam as the state religion and to the Malays and the aborigines in Sarawak and Saba as the majority. This is explicit in the Societies Act of 1966.[21]

For non-Islamic religious groups, there is an additional caveat: proselytizing can occur only within the limits of pluralism. The Constitution of Malaysia addresses freedom of religion in Article 11, but Clause 4 creates a limit on the ability to propagate religion. In practice, the key is the Sedition Act, which dates back to 1948.[22] After the riots in Kuala Lumpur on May 13, 1969, Section 3(1) was amended "so the constitutionally entrenched special position of the Malays could not be questioned in public (Emergency [Essential Powers] Ordinance No. 45 of 1970)."[23] Section 3 currently states, "A 'seditious tendency' is a tendency – (a) to bring into hatred or contempt or to excite disaffection against any Ruler or against any Government… (e) to promote feelings of ill will and hostility between different races or classes of the population of Malaysia…"[24]

The Sedition Act was originally set up for anti-Communist purposes, but has also been used to arrest missionaries. There was a case in which alleged members of a conversion mission were arrested, although no further information about the alleged "missionaries" was given beyond the place of arrest.[25] In daily life, the constraint operates more or less to foster fear and self-censorship. As a core member of Tzu Chi Malacca explained in an interview about how careful one should be in walking the line of the Sedition Act:

20 Societies Act 1966, www.ros.gov.my/images/Societies_Act.pdf (Accessed July 11, 2014).

21 www.pbs-sabah.org/pbs3/html/party/Akta_Pertubuhan.pdf (Accessed July 11, 2014).

22 Personal communication, Professor Kevin Tan of the National University of Singapore, 17 February 2011. See also "Public Prosecutor v. Ong Kian Cheong and Another" [2009] SGDC 163 (District Court, Singapore). "The accused were convicted under section 4(1) read with section 3(1)9e of the Sedition Act (SA) read with section 34 of the Penal Code for randomly distributing religious tracts which were considered seditious and objectionable to Muslims and being in possession of such publications." Tan and Thio, *Constitutional Law in Malaysia and Singapore*, 1028.

23 Ibid., 1203.

24 "Laws of Malaysia: Act 15 – Sedition Act 1948, Incorporating All Amendments up to 1 January 2006," 5.

25 In July 2010, nine people were arrested by police at Universiti Putra Malaysia (UPM), allegedly on a covert conversion mission for Christianity. It is unclear what happened to these nine people. "Nine Students Arrested at UPM," *The Malaysian Insider*, July 15, 2009. www.themalaysianinsider.com/malaysia/article/Nine-students-arrested-at-UPM/. We thank Lim Sok Swan for helping in collecting the news clippings. www.thejakartapost.com/news/2009/07/15/malaysia-free-9-christians-conversion-mixup.html.

> Even when we discuss Buddhism with [a Malay], we'll be very careful not to mislead him. Oh, for example, if I am talking to a Malay friend, oh, I talk about why Buddhism is good, and he talks about why Islam is good. What if, in the end, he says, oh, what you say about Buddhism sounds really good, I think I'll go with you! Then, you are in trouble. You are in trouble.[26]

He further explained emphatically how it was not just a passive fear for the Buddhists, but also an active protection of the freedom that the non-Muslim religions share: "This is not just about Buddhists. It's also about Catholicism, Protestantism, and Hinduism. If we step across the line, all these religions will also be affected by government's reaction." In other words, staying within one's own ethno-religious enclave is understood as a common good among all the non-Muslim groups. In the framework of merit-making, proselytizing only within the designated sphere bestows political merit on all the non-Islam religions.

Such an understanding, which sees religious freedom within ethnic groups as a common good, also occurs in more advocacy-oriented non-Muslim groups. For example, the Young Buddhists Association, Malaysia (YBAM) has been active since its founding in 1970 in the form of a cross-denominational association of all Buddhist organizations and study clubs in Malaysia. YBAM has always advocated for minority rights, with alliances from Indian and Hindu groups, with the goal of promoting – and protecting – Buddhism. The existence of Buddhism in Malaysia, as well as Hinduism and other non-Islamic religions, is simultaneously an end and a means to the end of protecting multiculturalism.

While the Sedition Act confines religious propagation, Malaysia's version of market-based governmentality opens up a window for social engagement across the limits of pluralism through welfare. Welfare as a path to unblocked religious freedom is signaled by Article 11(3) of the Constitution, which recognizes "the associative dimensions of religious freedom in the right of religious groups to manage their own religious affairs, maintain institutions for religious or charitable purposes and to hold property."[27] In other words, religious groups are more or less confined to bunkers when it comes to proselytizing, but are protected when it comes to "religious or charitable" purposes. While the Sedition Act prevents groups such as Tzu Chi from proselytizing to a person who professes Islam to be his/her faith, Article 11(3) legalizes and even encourages Tzu Chi to invite everyone, including Muslims, to volunteer and to donate for social welfare, in Tzu Chi's terms, "inviting all the benevolent people in the world to cultivate the field of blessings (福田)."

In recent years, Malaysia's policies on social services further encouraged participatory welfare, where primary responsibility came from society rather

[26] Compare with Embong, "The Culture and Practice of Pluralism in Postcolonial Malaysia."
[27] Tan and Thio, *Constitutional Law in Malaysia and Singapore*, 1199.

than the state itself. The government established the Ministry of Women, Family and Community Development (KPWKM) only in 2001. Since 2004 KPWKM has included the governance of welfare NGOs as one of its six missions. In addition, while Malaysia wishes to follow a British model of health care, which would guarantee care for all equally, they have not yet fully managed the transition. The Ministry of Health thus still subsidizes and collaborates with NGOs, both religious and secular, for health care provision and campaigns. Even as late as 2012, the KPWKM was still struggling to set up a complete database of welfare recipients, eKasi. For these reasons, Malaysia continues to rely on the older system of enclaved welfare delivery.

Enclaved merit-making with the state is the most palpable for the Chinese. The Registry of Societies formally traces its history to the British colonial attempt to regulate Chinese traditional associations like huay kuan (会馆) and kongsi (公司), as well as secret societies.[28] In some ways, one can say that the ROS is a result of a long history of dealing with the active associative life of the Chinese as a very substantial minority in Malaysia.

The enclaved field of practice creates two extreme possibilities. One is a near total submission to the state, more or less similar to cases we have described in China. The education system established by Christian and Catholic missionaries in Malaysia is a case in point. Since around the launch of the NEP, the state slowly persuaded, if not coerced, cash-strapped churches to make their schools "public" in exchange for state funding and provision of teachers. The process of becoming public includes, among other things, teaching in Bahasa Malaysia instead of English, replacing the principals and boards of directors with laypersons, and removing religious rituals from the school. When one of us began fieldwork in Malacca in the 2000s, all the schools established by St. Teresa Church, for example, were already completely secular except for the cross that still decorated the façade and the top of the enormous edifices. The pastor at the Methodist church did not even include their schools as a part of their philanthropic efforts. "It's all public now," he said. The Methodists had long moved on to other kinds of welfare, especially programs for the handicapped, although they still donated money to the Chinese schools.

At the other extreme from the heavily controlled religious schools lies the near total freedom from state policy of a case like Cheng Hoon Teng Temple. Ironically, this temple gained its total freedom by preserving the colonial legacy. As mentioned in the previous chapter, the Kapitan Cina (who was also "Teng Choo," temple head, since 1824) presided over the community during colonial times from a base in the Cheng Hoon Teng. They created a Board of Trustees in the early twentieth century. One of the trustees, the legendary philanthropist

[28] The Registry of Societies Malaysia, Ministry of Home Affairs Malaysia. www.ros.gov.my/index.php/en/maklumat-korporat/sejarah-penubuhan (Accessed July 18, 2104).

Tun Sir Tan Cheng Lock, initiated the temple's unique incorporation under an act of Parliament (Cheng Hoon Teng Temple Incorporation Ordinance 1949).

During our fieldwork, almost all the locals agreed that the Cheng Hoon Teng as an organization does not do philanthropy. Their representative, Josephine Chua, adamantly insisted that they do not do conventional philanthropy, for example by distributing relief goods. Rather, the temple is vital to a more traditional form of charity for the Chinese immigrant community, even though it may not be recognized as philanthropy in the current context: it is the one organization that offers the most burial grounds and crematoriums for the Chinese despite Malaysia's changing politics and rapid urbanization. In a sense, the case of Cheng Hoon Teng Temple is very similar to that of Longshan Temple in Lukang. By sitting on its enormous assets it remains immune from the flux of political change and has little need to earn political merit.

The merit generated through charity as a result of religio-political reciprocity takes place mainly in ways similar to how people accumulate social capital in the public sphere. In general, there are two types of relations: One is the most classical Chinese way in which temples invite gentry to occupy leadership positions in order to gain protection and prestige, while the gentry gain the use of the temple as a public stage. This type is common among religious organizations that do not have philanthropy programs of their own. Almost all of Malacca city's more than 300 temples lack their own philanthropy programs. The second type is the NGO type – called *yayasan* in Malay for both religious and secular organizations – in which the religion-inspired philanthropy collaborates with politicians for various purposes. These include gaining the politicians' help in resolving legal issues, providing publicity, and offering donations. The yayasan movement is a recent and ongoing phenomenon, which can be seen, for example, in the way the two largest Chinese language newspapers transformed their role from matching potential donors with needy people to running their own charitable foundations.[29] The two types overlap significantly. However, in the gentry type the politicians always have some kind of formal title at the temple, and the featured events of the gentry type are always reported, and thus publically witnessed, with charity donation as an indispensable performance of political power.

Similar to what we described in Taiwan and late imperial China, politicians build their social capital through associations. For example, Gan Boon Leong of Malacca, who is perhaps the most powerful, and definitely the most flamboyant politician in the State of Malacca, is not only the special aide on Chinese affairs to the prime minister of the State of Malacca, but also the

[29] *Nanyang* claims its charity fund started in 1995, www.yayasan-nanyang.org/support-ngos/, and *Sin Chew* formally launched its fund in 2001, http://news.google.com/newspapers?nid=1309&dat=20010109&id=qywhAAAAIBAJ&sjid=q3gFAAAAIBAJ&pg=6689,4467422.

chair of thirty different groups and associations, ranging from the Hokkien dialect association, to the Malaysia Chinese Association (a political party), to the Boy Scouts and the weight-lifting association. His son, Gan Tin Lok, who is also a senator, is the leader of the alliance of all hometown and surname groups in Malaysia. Gan's son-in-law, Sun Dian Ci, entered politics for the first time in 2008. One of the first steps in his publicity was to campaign against religious fraud.

The Gan family politicians jointly sit on the boards of hundreds of temples. They frequently preside over and deliver speeches at the temples' major events. Both the temples and the politicians benefit from the news coverage. Such news appears in the local pages of the Chinese newspapers more than once a week and at a far greater rate around Chinese holidays and before the elections. The newspapers always report the exact amount of the politicians' donations for charity and the names of the beneficiary organizations or institutions. The coverage usually includes a group photo of the politicians and other board members. For example, all the Gan family attended the Qingshan King's temple as members of the board on the King's birthday celebration in June 2007, during the run-up to the 2008 election. During the event politicians encouraged Daoists to form their own NGOs, and the temple donated RM 3,500 (roughly 1,000 USD) to two Chinese schools, two Chinese charities, and the local police precinct.[30]

The gentry type and the NGO type sometimes overlap. For example, when Wang Naizhi, a member of parliament, was running for reelection in 2008, a newspaper featured a large portrait of him attending the Chinese New Year celebration at the Methodist Beautiful Gate career center for the handicapped. At the event he encouraged handicapped people to contact members of parliament for help such as free wheelchairs. He also announced a gift of RM 2000 to Beautiful Gate.[31] Wang was not reelected in 2008, but he later became Secretary to the Prime Minister. In 2011 Wang took the Prime Minister to visit the Chinese old age home in Sungai Way for the Chinese New Year. The old age home received RM 100,000 (about USD 33,000) funding from the visit.[32]

The NGO type can include an array of relationships, from a politician's direct sponsorship and frequent visits, to sporadic visits and occasional delivery

[30] Zhongguo Xinwen Wang (June 26, 2007), www.taoismdata.org/product_info.php?products_id=2295 (Accessed July 19, 2014). Gan Tin Loc continues his father's gentry style of temple activism. For example, he sits on the committee for the City God Temple and helps with public fundraising for the temple remodeling. The temple also recently donated RM500 to St John's Dialysis Center, *Nanyan wang* (May 6, 2012), www.nanyang.com/node/446133 (Accessed July 22, 2014).

[31] *Sin Chew Daily* (February 27, 2008) http://mykampung.sinchew.com.my/node/5449?tid=8 (Accessed July 22, 2014).

[32] *Nanyang*, www.nanyang.com/node/408406?tid=493 (Accessed July 19, 2014).

of donations or help with fundraising, to specific collaboration and negotiation with the government. In contrast with the gentry type, which tends to be more prominent at the local level such as Malacca city, the NGO model is often used to focus attention on a politician operating at a more urban and national level. Ms. Chew Mei Fun, a former member of parliament from the northern district of Petaling Jaya outside of Kuala Lumpur, was the former deputy Minister of KPWKM, and the vice chairperson of the MCA in 2014. She holds an array of relationships with a variety of religion-inspired philanthropies. The minimum relation is perhaps with the Tri-Ratana Welfare Society, founded and run by a Theravada monk from Sri Lanka, the Most Ven. Datuk K. Sri Dammaratana, who is also the Buddhist Chief High Priest of Malaysia. Tri-Ratana is well-endowed and hosts well-developed welfare programs housing more than 500 residents including 130 orphans, seniors, battered women, and women who suffer from mental disorders, with a plan of building an entire village. Chew wears a bracelet given by the Venerable on her wrist. On the day of our visit in 2012, she appeared to be familiar with the operation, with the manager (who is a Chinese retiree from a high-paid job), and definitely with the Venerable Dammaratana. The monk tied a new knot in the bracelet on her wrist and gave her blessings.

Taman Megah Handicapped and Disabled Children's Home in Petaling Jaya is an example of negotiation. The Children's Home was founded by the late Mr. Manikumar in 1992, who first began as a volunteer through the Sri Sathya Sai Baba Organization. The Megah Home was managed by a Chinese and registered formally in 1997. It is, however, so overly crowded that on our visit the entire first floor of a little more than 1,000 square feet was filled with children, staff, interns, and their medical facilities. Worse still, the appearance of disabled children began to foster hostility from other residents in its suburban, and now affluent, neighborhood. They have received many warnings and fines from the government, and the neighborhood has been going through both formal and informal ways to force them to relocate. According to the manager, Chew helped them find a place for the impending relocation. She reiterated in an interview that it was against the law to keep children beyond its capacity but she nonetheless remained supportive of the Home.[33]

Note that Chew's involvement in Tri-Ratana and Taman Megah to some extent transcends the boundaries of the Chinese enclave that we might expect her to favor. In part this represents her role as a senior official in the Malaysian government's only partially successful attempt to put welfare on a truly

[33] A similar example of "double standards" is the well-established and government-subsidized St. John's Dialysis Center. Recent news discloses that St. John's has been running without a government license for eighteen years, http://mykampung.sinchew.com.my/node/136689 (Accessed July 22, 2014).

national basis, beyond ethnic bunkers. Yet it may also be a misleading impression, because Chew herself says that one of her main goals is to help bring these kinds of welfare benefits to the Chinese, whom she feels have not been able to use the system effectively so far.

We can see this in her support for the Sungai Way Old Age Home, which is located in Chew's precinct and in the now extremely gentrified New Village, Sungai Way.[34] It was originally a shabby place for seniors in the early twentieth century, adjacent to the Nine Emperor Temple (九皇大帝四路灵应殿). It obtained its current parcel of land from the government in 1957 and did not form a formal committee until 1987, when Mr. Foong, a contractor by profession, became the Secretary. Sungai Way appears to be a secular organization. Its relation to the Nine Emperor Temple is more of the gentry type, with the temple remaining an important donor for the old age home.[35]

On the day one of us visited in 2012, Chew was very familiar with the committee and most of the senior residents. Like the case of Megah Home, Chew and Foong were matter-of-fact about working with government regulations: "It's not registered under the *fulibu* (福利部, 'welfare department', here meaning the KPWPM). But it's a registered society and a donation is tax deductible … If you do public fundraising for welfare, you have to get permission from KPWPM. But if you just have a banquet or invite your friends to donate, you don't need permission." Sungai Way has been mainly relying on individual donations, although the government also subsidizes it. Its basic expenses are about RM 20,000 (about USD 6,400) a year: RM 15,000 (about USD 4,800) from donations and RM 5,000 from the government. The government also gives RM 100 (about USD 30) a month to each resident senior.

Sungai Way Old Age Home runs a dialysis center a few blocks away. Chew is again the major sponsor as well as fundraiser for the center. "I have a good friend who will give me the money for the center every year," Chew explained. The center has fourteen units and accommodates fifty-three patients (2012). Sungai Way paid for the rent. The government or the National Kidney Foundation provides the medical staff. The center charges RM 110 (about USD 35) per person per visit (each patient needs three visits a week), compared to

[34] A brief report on Sungai Way Old Age home is here: www.ppbgroup.com/csr/community-festival-2012-1.php. For recent rapid gentrification in Sungai Way, see www.nanyang.com/node/544822, and www.utar.edu.my/dssc/file/SERI%20SETIA,%20SUNGAI%20WAY%202.pdf (Accessed July 22, 2014).

[35] For example, on the gods' birthday celebration and the temple's thirty-seventh anniversary, the temple committee invited politicians, not including Ms. Chew. Each politician gave speeches and an individual donation. The temple announced that it was giving RM 6,000 (about USD 1,800) for charity. The money went to the Sungai Way Old Folks Home, the Dialysis Center, and the Alumni Association for the Sungai Way Chinese School; each received RM 2,000 (about USD 600). *Chew Daily* (November 2, 2010), http://mykampung.sinchew.com.my/node/119860 (Accessed July 22, 2014).

RM 200 (about USD 64) in a private clinic. Out of the RM 110 (about USD 35), the government subsidizes RM 50 (about USD 16). On the day of our visit, the head of the nurses told Chew that they needed money to organize an outing. Chew promised them the money.

In sum, political merit-making in Malaysia is primarily enclaved. The result can be completely free from the government's control if one stays within the designated sphere, such as the Cheng Hoon Teng Temple. It can also move to the other extreme, being completely taken over by the state, when the field of practice violates the boundaries, which is what happened to all the English-language schools established by the Christian and Catholic missionaries. Between the two extremes, we can see two overlapping types of relation between religion and politics: the gentry type, which is more prominent among the popular temples and at the local level such as the city of Malacca, and the NGO type, which covers an array of ways for politicians to be involved in NGO operation. This is reminiscent of the mutualist political merit-making in Taiwan, but with the additional layer of the ethnic minority enclave.

Conclusion

In all three Chinese societies, religious philanthropies perform political merit-making because the state plays such crucial roles in determining the content, form, and parameters for such organizations. In the case of China, we have characterized the political merit-making as primarily defensive. Some religious organizations fulfill their duties to the central or municipal government just enough to stay out of trouble and win an "immunity" ticket, as in the case of the Religious Charity Week donations. Others try actively to collaborate with the state on all fronts of their philanthropic activities, to gain more autonomy to work in areas that the state may not find interesting. Such is the case with Hanshan Temple and its Hehe Cultural Foundation. Defensive political merit-making means that religious philanthropies in China sometimes appear to be "too close" to the state, or sometimes even to be mere extensions of state organizations. Unlike in Taiwan and Malaysia, politicians do not need to participate in religious philanthropy to gain personal influence and power. The authoritarian state often has the upper hand as it is the sole definer of rules and regulations toward religious philanthropies.

In democratized Taiwan, though religious philanthropies have to perform a certain level of political merit-making, the pattern is more based on mutual benefit. On the one hand, just as deities thrive only by having worshippers who want to make merit with them, the state needs social organizations to share its burden of social welfare in Taiwan, and religious groups have been especially large contributors. Besides, temples are reservoirs of social capital that politicians must activate if they want people to vote for them. Politicians need temples and religious philanthropies. On the other hand, those philanthropies must still work under the limits imposed by state policies and legal requirements toward NGOs and foundations. Temples and their charitable work must earn political merit to thrive, but politicians often also rely on temples for their success: it is a mutual arrangement.

The Chinese religious associations in Malacca, however, differ from the other two because of the pattern of enclaved political merit-making in the Malay-majority state. In exchange for relative autonomy, the Chinese religious associations willingly submit to the Malaysian government's legal restrictions on proselytizing and fund-raising. In turn, they take care of their own ethnic group well enough to allow the Malay state to concentrate its efforts elsewhere. Malaysian Chinese religious philanthropies are caught in the enclaves of their own communities through the social webs they create as well as through the state's ethnic and religious policies. This explains further why Malacca's religious philanthropies resemble late imperial China the most. On the other hand, this also seems to be a system that is as much at the mercy of policy changes from the central government as what we saw in the case of contemporary China.

All three cases show the importance of the state in the survival and sustenance of religious philanthropies. They do not, however, support the common suggestion in the China literature that authoritarian states inevitably interfere with the social provision of services by non-state organizations, and so damage their effectiveness.[36] Our cases range from the current raucous democracy in Taiwan, to the more nominal one in Malaysia, to single-party rule in China. If we add a little historical depth, we can also include both British and Japanese colonial regimes as well as the authoritarian periods of rule under the Guomindang in both China and Taiwan. While one might predict a simple correlation between political freedoms and the activities of civil groups, our observations in this chapter have shown a more complex situation. All of these regimes have seen significant welfare activities from non-governmental organizations, including religious ones. The variations across states in our field data relate more to specific local histories than to broad variations in levels of democracy. As we have seen, for example, China's restrictive policies that limit "religious" activities to officially designated religious sites restrict the scope of engaged religions, but democratic Malaysia's laws defining the conversion of Muslims as sedition equally serve to keep religious philanthropy largely confined within ethnic communities.

Neither the "interfering state" nor the "state failure" hypotheses provide sufficient explanations for the proliferation of religious philanthropies in the three

[36] For an example arguing that the imperial Chinese state caused more problems when it tried to exert more control over charitable organizations, see Fuma, *History of Chinese Benevolent Halls and Associations*.

societies. Nor do we exactly have state retrenchment, as in Europe's move away from the welfare state. That term works well enough for mainland China, where the state has stepped back from being the primary guarantor of welfare, but neither Taiwan nor Malaysia (especially in relation to its Chinese population) ever tried to function as a welfare state, and so there has been no retrenchment. On the contrary, Taiwan has actually increased its own welfare provision since democratization.

While states certainly shape charity, our cases show that engaged religions can thrive under various levels of state interference. There is no simple correlation between low levels of interference and effective NGOs. Even the distinction between democratic and authoritarian regimes is far less salient in explaining patterns of religious philanthropy than the unique political conditions in each of our states. Democratization can have a strong effect, as Taiwan shows, but the postcolonial democratization of Malaysia did not have the same kinds of effects on philanthropic groups there, and China has developed similar mechanisms without democratization. This suggests a somewhat different process from what Cammett and Issar found in Lebanon in their study of social benefits provided by sectarian religious political movements. They argue that "when parties prioritize winning votes, they are most likely to distribute services broadly, even across sectarian lines, while nonelectoral mobilization implies that core, in-group activists receive particularly generous and continuous welfare benefits."[37] That is, democratic politics should encourage universalizing philanthropic goals that cross over political and religious divisions.

Our cross-national comparison suggests that this effect may help explain the Taiwan material, but is not very helpful for the other two cases. Democratization itself seems to be a less important variable than we often assume. Malaysian policies make it almost impossible for religions to cross ethnic lines, and the lack of democratic politics in China has not prevented the effective diffusion of universalizing philanthropic values. More important in our cases has been the state's willingness to allow space for non-state groups to provide welfare services – which also helps explain why all these groups are so politically cautious.

The persistence of political merit-making – in its defensive, mutualistic, and enclaved forms – is one of the key conditions that contributed to a converging landscape of religious philanthropy across the three societies in spite of their differences. Furthermore, a more industrialized form of religious philanthropy and a universalizing vision of the good have emerged out of these forms of political merit-making, as shaped by the particular forms of the modern state in China, Malaysia, and Taiwan.

[37] Cammett and Issar, "Bricks and Mortar Clientalism," 416.

4 A (Chinese) Good Person

Consider the following three snapshots of similarities across religions and spaces:

- For half a century, Malacca has displayed a familiar landscape of the splendid St. Teresa Church surrounded by Catholic elementary and middle schools with the Holy Cross on the top. Less expected, however, is that the tranquil Theravada Buddhist temple Seck Kia Eenh (Sakyamuni Monastery) stands adjacent to a three-story modern building with a shiny yellow sign reading "Vesak," meaning commemoration of Gautama Buddha, on the top and with a green banner for the "Seck Kia Eenh Kindergarten" on the ground floor (see Figure 4.1).[1]
- In Taiwan, on entering the Buddhist Tzu Chi Hospital in Hualian, one sees to the left a two-story mosaic portrait of the Buddha caring for a sick monk. To the right stands an array of registration counters and a waiting area with rows of seats filled with patients, families, and migrant caregivers. Men and women wearing dark yellow Tzu Chi volunteer uniform vests approach every stranger with congenial smiles and attentive greetings. Similarly, in the Presbyterian Mackay Hospital in Hsinchu, Taiwan, one enters the red-brick building under the façade arch topped with the Cross and is immediately greeted by volunteers in pink uniform vests offering help and directions, smiling while wishing everyone "peace (*ping'an*)."
- In the Suzhou branch of Tzu Chi in China in 2004, a large number of men and women volunteers in dark blue uniforms were busy rehearsing a sign language musical performance of "The Sutra about the Deep Kindness of Parents and the Difficulty of Repaying It" (父母恩重难报经 *Fumu enzhong nanbao jing*) on the stage. The acting, lighting, and directing are exactly the

[1] Although it may seem unusual for a Buddhist temple to be Theravada in Taiwan and China, Theravada from Thailand and Sri Lanka has a significant Chinese following in Malaysia. The explanation is the early founding of the temple, when Chinese monastics were not available, and its ties to the Straits Chinese community. The monks of Seck Kia Eenh come from Sri Lanka. For studies on Theravada Buddhism among the Chinese in Malaysia, see, for example, Samuels, "Buddhist Temple Networks across the Indian Ocean."

Figure 4.1 Seck Kia Eenh kindergarten.

same as the premier in Taipei back in 1999 and as the performance in Kuala Lumpur by local devotees in 2005.

All three of these snapshots point to a convergence in the transnational currents of religious philanthropy: they show us individuals volunteering for organized (and industrialized) philanthropy. As the first snapshot depicts, there are similarities across religions in evolving programs that cater to a general public. These include running blood donation drives, subsidizing old age homes, providing medical facilities or free medicine and clinics, giving emergency or regular charity funds, building schools or providing scholarships to students, providing disaster relief locally and translocally, sorting garbage for recycling, and even wearing vests in bright colors. A closer look at the growing programs reveals a shared trend of involving active voluntarism, as the second snapshot describes. And, as one zooms in on the third snapshot, a distinctive and yet common trend of embodiment in the form of standardizing emotions has been underway as these organizations expand transnationally.

How do we explain the similarities in organization, voluntarism, and embodiment across religions and in different societies? Why, as the market economy and capitalism rapidly develop in the three societies, and as commodification takes over ever more aspects of social life, from transnational marriage to human organ transplants, do more and more people give out their time and labor for free, in addition to making monetary donations for some stranger's benefit? What do we make of their unabashed expression of affect in the giving?

The previous chapter showed how the interaction between the state and religious groups contributed to the growth of religious philanthropy in the three societies we are studying. Although the timing of contemporary religious philanthropy makes the endeavor appear to be a direct response to the opportunities present in the changing politics of the past few decades, none of the religious philanthropy we discuss was simply created by the state. In fact, most of it began before the political changes, as we have been discussing for all three field sites. These states only increased oversight while encouraging and accelerating the bureaucratization and professionalism that had already been underway as organizations expanded. We concentrated so far on political merit-making; in this chapter we turn to self-making.

We begin by tracing the genealogy of this new doing-good form of religiosity in Chinese societies. We look primarily at how doing good inscribes an individual agency shaped by contributing to a cause through a religious organization that benefits strangers – people beyond one's circles of religion, kinship, locality, and even nationality. We draw from two primary theoretical perspectives: one concerns culture and globalization and the other focuses on voluntarism and civil society.

Inspired by Anthony Giddens' theories of modernity, we view the cultural dimension of globalization as a process of disembedding people, practices, goods, concepts, media, and other cultural subjects from their original place and context, and reembedding the subject in a different place and context, often with a new interpretation and new positioning by riding on an indigenous concept and/or by associating with a social status or a subculture.[2] Similar concepts such as deterritorialization and reterritorialization also capture the shifting relation between culture and place, with reference to the power of the territorially defined nation-state.[3] Two overlapping concepts, with a smaller purview than that of globalization, are also helpful here: transnationalism, meaning the process of forging a social space that straddles two or more countries, and diaspora, referring to a community that spreads across multiple states and whose members hold a shared identity of a place of origin in history or in fiction.

We are particularly interested in how the current form of industrialized religious philanthropy emerged and thrived in different societies around the same

[2] Giddens, *The Consequences of Modernity.*

[3] For discussions on deterritorialization and reterritorialization, see, for example, Appadurai, *Modernity at Large*; Tomlinson, *Globalization and Culture*; Watson, *Golden Arches East.*

time. A genealogy of disembedding and reembedding forms of and concepts for religious philanthropy has unfolded into a social life of goodness. We will argue that the similarities among religious philanthropies come from a diachronically shared heritage of the conceptualization of goodness, such as the idea of merit, and from a synchronically connected mission for goodness. Both the means of doing good and the self who does good have changed under these processes: we now have a mechanism organized under the umbrella of ecumenical religiosity, through a cosmopolitan organization that connects individual volunteers with universal causes. The scope of doing good is disembedded in the process of becoming global, and the unit of organizing shrinks to the size of an individual person.

Inspired by global theories about regional transnational flows,[4] such as the trans-Pacific shuttles for Chinese "flexible citizenship" and capital accumulation[5] and the popularity of Mandopop across the Taiwan Strait[6] and within the Chinese diaspora,[7] this chapter looks in part at the broad flows of Chinese religious philanthropy. These have a smaller purview than the nineteenth-century global flow of philanthropic Christianity, but they are prominent in the Chinese societies we studied. One of these organizations is Tzu Chi, which expanded outside of Taiwan by riding on the wave of increasing Taiwanese transnationalism, and that maps its global expansion onto the Chinese diaspora. In this chapter, we will argue that Tzu Chi is only a representation of a new form of industrialized religious philanthropy that consists of a growing list of "doing-good" programs for universal love, exists as an ecumenical network under charismatic leadership, and promotes a new kind of religiosity by making the follower a volunteer and hence a good person.

We have also benefited from the literatures on faith-based organizations as well as civil society. For instance, to explain the motives of the volunteers she studied at soup kitchens for homeless people in two faith-based organizations in California, the sociologist Rebecca Anne Allahyari proposes the notion of "moral selving," which means "the work of creating oneself as a more virtuous, and often more spiritual person."[8] The idea of moral selving usefully highlights the construction of self through a dynamic process of discourse selection and social interaction, and thus informs and shapes different visions of charity. The self in moral selving is dynamic and malleable. Put in the context of the three societies we studied, we find the new subjects of "doing good" as "doing religion" draw discourses not only from the Chinese heritage of moral concepts

[4] Inda and Rosaldo, *The Anthropology of Globalization.*
[5] Ong, *Flexible Citizenship.*
[6] Yang, "Mass Media and Transnational Subjectivity in Shanghai."
[7] Moskowitz, *Cries of Joy, Songs of Sorrow.*
[8] Allahyari, *Visions of Charity*, 5.

but also from the formation of how that morality should contribute to a broader civic world. We therefore propose "civic selving" for understanding the new subject of doing religion.

This chapter explains the making of the new good person on three levels. First, there is a heritage of notions and concepts in Chinese thought that drives, inspires, encourages, and guides a person to do good. Second, there is a set of flows that contributes to the construction of industrialized philanthropy in the Chinese diaspora. Third, the crafting of a new moral and religious subject draws much discourse from the state's ideology of civility and transforms into an embodied model of a good person through the formation of civil society in Taiwan, China, and Malaysia.

Heritage

In Chapter 2 we examined some of the institutional history of engaged religions in China, and especially its relationship to the state. Here we turn away from institutions toward the conceptual resources underpinning philanthropy, and to more general concepts of the good. The Chinese language has a wealth of words for goodness, good deeds, charity, and philanthropy. *Hao* (好) and *shan* (善) are perhaps the closest to goodness. *Haoren* (好人) and *shanren* (善人) are people who do good deeds and manifest their good or kind heart (好心, 善心). *Zuo haoshi* (做好事), *zuo shanshi* (做善事), *xingshan* (行善), and *weishan* (为善) are doing good; *haoshi* (好事), *shanshi* (善事), *shanxing* (善行), *yiju* (义举) are good deeds. *Leshan haoshi* (乐善好施) means [someone who is] happy to do good and enthusiastic to give. *Cishan* (慈善) is charity or philanthropy. There are plenty of colloquial sayings for the rewards of doing good: "doing good keeps one happy" (为善长乐); "Good begets good, evil begets evil" (恶有恶报, 善有善报), sometimes with the addition, "It's not that there is no response/repayment, it's just a matter of time" (不是不报, 时候未到). Perhaps except in Christian settings, people encourage helping behaviors and contributions as "making merit" (做功德), label donation boxes as "merit boxes" (功德箱), and acknowledge donors as having "immeasurable merit" (功德无量). Even secular nongovernmental organizations (NGOs) in Taiwan use "making-merit" colloquially as a way for mobilization.[9]

The history of these terms already indicates that Chinese culture has long valued goodness. That people should do "good" is so ubiquitous and taken for granted as common sense that one can hardly tell what is religious about it – it seems similar to when people say "bless you" in English when someone sneezes. Indeed, several religious and philosophical lines of thought have

[9] Zeng, "Inescapable Network of Human Emotion (Renqing) and Connection (Guanxi)."

mixed together to construct a variety of motives for doing good in Chinese societies. These traditions have blended to form a shared goodness heritage, which partially explains the modern similarity of religious philanthropy in the three Chinese societies. To better grasp this common-sense notion, let us introduce some key concepts that give moral value and mechanisms for doing good in imperial China. The relevant lines of thought include Confucianism, Buddhism, and Daoism, and the central belief in cosmic retribution that can cross generations and lifetimes, and that is mixed with ideas of karma and an eschatology of merits and demerits. Each of these thoughts and beliefs has inspired an enormous literature, in addition to debates and changes over thousands of years. Thus, a thorough discussion of any of these concepts is beyond the scope of this book. Our concern here is how the assortments of concepts and thoughts connect to the morality and guidelines of doing good, and contribute to the formation of the idea of individual agency for the public and universal goods, which we see carrying so much weight today.

Two ancient concepts in China that still give moral value to goodness are remotely comparable to the European ideas of charity (*caritas*, God's love) and philanthropy (love for humanity): one is *ren* (仁) in Confucianism and the other is Mozi's *jian'ai* (兼爱). Nevertheless, the epistemology as well as the practice of Confucian *ren* is different from the Christian idea of *caritas*. Caritas begins with and is rooted in God's love, and by virtue of the faith in God's love, humans extend that love to other humans. "God is love, and he who abides in love abides in God, and God abides in him."[10] Pope Benedict XVI, in his first encyclical, *Deus Caritas Est* (*God Is Love*), clarifies the multiple layers of love – from ancient Greek *eros*, the love of a man and a woman, connecting to *agape*, a self-sacrificing love, and then to the Latin *caritas*.[11] The practice of *caritas* is "love of neighbor, grounded in love of God, as well as being a responsibility for each individual member of the faith, [it] is also a responsibility for the entire Ecclesial Community, which must reflect Trinitarian love in its charitable activity."[12] It is the duty of the Church to act as a "ministry of love of neighbor … of charity (*diakonia*)."

Ren, "benevolence" or "humanness," is the core of Confucian philosophy. *Ren* is often associated with *ai* (爱, love), to indicate a quality and virtue for dealing with social relations – note that the character *ren* consists of "people" or "human" and the number "two." Today Catholics in Taiwan still name their nursing homes as *ren'ai zhi jia* (仁爱之家, home of benevolent love). This

[10] 1 John 4: 16.

[11] "Summary of *Deus Caritas Est*," *L'Osservatore Romano*, Weekly Edition in English, 26 April 2006. www.ewtn.com/library/Doctrine/sumdeuscarit.htm (Accessed March 28, 2014). See also de Paulo and Rudnytzky, "Introduction."

[12] "Summary of *Deus Caritas Est*."

idea of *ren* was one of the first comparative sources for eighteenth-century European Enlightenment thinkers, who were looking for evidence of a universal moral sentiment. For them "Confucianism confirmed … that [altruism] is possible … without Christianity."[13] *Ren* is acquired through perseverance for Confucius (551–479 BCE) and through cultivation for Mencius (371–289 BCE).[14] In other words, *ren* does not come from God. To activate humaneness, one needs constantly to practice the five qualities: "reverence, tolerance, trustworthiness, quickness, and generosity."[15]

As stated in the *Zhongyong* (Doctrine of the Mean), one of the core Confucian texts, "'Humanity' means 'human': cleaving to one's kin is its foremost element. 'Right' means 'appropriate': honoring the worthy is its foremost element. The degrees that govern cleaving to one's kin and the ranks that govern honoring the worthy are the things that give birth to ritual [*li*]."[16] *Li* (礼, ritual), is a core Chinese idea of how to achieve civility.[17] Thus, *ren* can be said to be a necessary but not a sufficient condition for universal philanthropy: it begins within one's own family, and provides a careful discrimination and ranking among different kin and social relations. Working its way up the entire social-political hierarchy, it eventually sets one up to be a good ruler for the entire state.

Knoblock and Riegel argue that Mozi, a contemporary of Confucius, offers *jian'ai*, "impartial love," as an alternative source for a morality of human relationships.[18] Everyone can and should practice *jian'ai* as a member of society, and as the result of the leader's orders. *Jian'ai* is not exclusively for men of cultivation, *junzi* (君子), as was the realization of *ren* for Confucians. Unlike the Confucian *ren*, which should begin with one's family, *jian'ai* is for everyone, and held equally for all, including strangers; that is, there should be no discrimination among different relationships.

13 Csikszentmihalyi, "Finding Altruism in China," 10.

14 Mencius connects humaneness to innate compassion; compassion is what makes human humane: "All humans have a heart sensitive to the suffering of others."

15 The original text is in the *Analects* 17:6.《論語》陽貨篇：子張問仁於孔子。孔子曰：「能行五者於天下，為仁矣。」請問之。曰：「恭、寬、信、敏、惠。恭則不侮，寬則得眾，信則人任焉，敏則有功，惠則足以使人。」The translation is from Eno, "The Analects of Confucius."

16 《中庸》, chapter 20. The translation is from Eno, "The Great Learning and the Doctrine of the Mean."

17 Weller, *Alternate Civilities*.

18 兼爱is sometimes translated into impartial concerns, even though 爱 in Chinese literally means love. Knoblock and Riegel explain why they choose the word "love," writing in parentheses: "The term *ai* 爱 in the name of the doctrine does not refer to romantic love or sexual attraction. It means something more like "prefer," "covet," "favor," or "care for," nuances that are perhaps best captured in English by "love." Those who object to translating *ai* as "love" fail to appreciate the full breadth of the English word." Knoblock and Riegel, *Mozi*, 139.

If the imperative for *ren* is aspiration for individual virtue and for a ruler's skilled governance, the imperative for *jian'ai* is a divine power, Heaven.[19] Impartial love benefits everyone involved, contributes to mutual or shared interests, and condemns aggression. This is Heaven's intent (天意), or, in Knoblock and Riegel's words, "Heaven's moral blueprint" for all mankind.[20] "Thus those who desire to hold on to their wealth and eminence could not but obey Heaven's intentions. Those who obey Heaven's intentions by impartially loving others and reciprocally benefiting others are certain to be rewarded. Those who oppose Heaven's intentions by selfishly hating others and reciprocally preying upon others are certain to be punished."[21]

The concept of Heaven in Mozi is a slice of the encompassing and essential way through which religion is involved in Chinese goodness: the belief in natural or divine retribution, which is "a deep tradition in Chinese religion," as Lien-sheng Yang observes in his classic study of the Chinese concept of *bao* (报, response, reciprocity).[22] Yang traces this belief back to the classics in the Western Zhou (1121 BCE– 771 BCE). The belief in a supernatural or cosmic retribution, which "has been a fundamental, at times *the* fundamental, belief of Chinese religion since the beginning of recorded history," is defined by Brokaw as

> The faith that some force – either a supernatural force like heaven or the gods, or an automatic cosmic reaction – inevitably recompensed human behavior in a rational manner: it rewarded certain 'good' deeds, be they religious sacrifices, acts of good government, or upright personal conduct, and punished evil ones.[23]

The belief in cosmic retribution, as it appears in concepts such as "hidden virtue" (阴德),[24] "cosmic resonance" (感应), "retribution" (报), and "heaven" (天) or "heavenly mandate" (天命), for instance, is not only the core of the indigenous Chinese religion and political philosophical canons, but also the backbone of the heritage of goodness and an idiom for communicating a habitus, if there is one, for the good Chinese person. Such a habitus draws from a variety of sources of beliefs and has been through many waves of change over several millennia.

The indigenous sources for these ideas include the Classics that all educated people studied. For example, the *Book of Changes* offers a famous and long-lasting maxim for doing good: "A family that accumulates goodness will

[19] Heaven is at times, such as *Mozi* 26:3, "shorthand for God on high, the ghosts, and the spirit," in ibid., 220.

[20] Ibid., 219.

[21] Ibid., 226.

[22] Yang, "The Concept of Pao as a Basis for Social Relations in China," 298.

[23] Brokaw, *The Ledgers of Merit and Demerit*, 28.

[24] Smith, *The Art of Doing Good*, 225.

be sure to have an excess of blessings, but one that accumulates evil will be sure to have an excess of disasters."[25] The individual was thus not the smallest unit in this notion of Chinese personhood and goodness. Indeed, prior to the introduction of Buddhism and its concept of karma early in the common era, Chinese thinkers explained that "fate was shared by members of the same family or clan or by people who lived in the same area."[26] This "sharing of fate" is called "transmission of burden" or "inherited burden" (承负) in the *Taiping Jing* or *Classic of the Great Peace*, a collection from the Later Han (25 BCE–AD 220) that might be considered as one of the founding texts of Daoism. According to the *Taipei Jing*, "Heaven often sends down calamities because it has been angered by wicked deeds of man. ... Such crimes may have been committed by only a few persons of earlier times, but the consequences involved later generations of the offenders' families and their neighborhoods."[27] Some scholars point out such burdens can be from ancestors as well as from heaven and earth and from nature.[28]

This idea of inherited burden explains fate's uncertainties. For example, when disasters happen to someone who does good deeds, it may be a result of the burden inherited from an ancestor's bad deeds and therefore cannot be solely attributed to the individual involved. The concept of inherited burden and its uncertainties implies the necessity of doing good, to balance out one's inherited burdens and/or to accumulate goodness for one's descendants.

The impact of Daoism on charity and philanthropy is nuanced, in part because Daoism consists of different schools and sects that evolved over thousands of years, and in part because Daoism changed after the introduction of Buddhism to China, particularly on the subject of merit and goodness. We rarely if ever heard people outside of the scholarly circle of Daoism speaking of "inherited burden" at our field sites. The influence is instead more indirect and generalized, as well as being filtered through Buddhism.

Compared to early Daoism, Buddhism offers a mechanism of merit that prescribes a list of concrete things to do for the individual while operating in a more complex framework of the cosmos: it spans a much greater timeframe than the several lifetimes of Daoist longevity or even immortality, covers a far larger scope of species than human beings, and refers to universal relations rather than family lineage. The Buddhist merit system works with its currency, karma (业), and is often interpreted in China

[25] Lynn, *The Classic of Changes*, 146. Lien-sheng Yang's translation is as follows: "The family which stores up virtue will have an exuberance of happiness; the family which stores up vice will have an exuberance of calamity," in Yang, "The Concept of Pao as a Basis for Social Relations in China," 298.

[26] Yang, "The Concept of Pao as a Basis for Social Relations in China," 299.

[27] Ibid.

[28] Yuan, "A Research of the Theory of 'Chengfu' of Tai Ping Classic."

through an agricultural metaphor, namely the "field of blessings" (福田).[29] As Kieschnick defines it:

In many early Buddhist texts, the Buddha presents various moral standards … One should not kill or steal or lie, for "a bad deed yields a bad reward," while "good deeds inevitably reap good rewards." This, of course, is the foundation of karma; at some point in the never-ending cycle of life and death, every good deed will be rewarded and every bad one punished. This is a natural, spontaneous process often described with agricultural metaphors: with a good action, one plants a seed in a "field of blessings" (*futian*) and later harvests the "fruits" of these good actions. From comforts or pains in this life, to rebirth in a heaven or hell in the next, one's well-being depends in large measure on the morality of one's actions in this life or a previous one – that is, "fate" depends on one's store of merit.[30]

Although some scholars emphasize that the concepts of goodness related to cosmic retribution such as "hidden virtue" (阴德) and "inherited burden" existed in China prior to the arrival of Buddhism and are therefore not exclusively Buddhist,[31] other scholars argue that the fatalist uncertainty did not have an adequate answer until the introduction of Buddhism.[32] For our purposes, however, it is enough to note that specific associations with Buddhism or Daoism for contemporary Chinese are far less important than the broad attitudes toward goodness that the centuries of interaction of encouraged.

Chinese Buddhism, more than Southeast Asian traditions, invites lay people to model themselves upon the compassion of bodhisattvas. The mechanism of merit has been both the means and the goal for the spread and propagation of Buddhism in China from the outset. For example, the clear promise of merit rewards for copying and reproducing Buddhist texts in the *Diamond Sutra* and the *Lotus Sutra* left a strong impact on book printing, which, directly or indirectly, influenced the Daoist expansion of printed scriptures and, perhaps, the morality books movement in the Ming dynasty, and even the continued production of digital Buddhist books today.[33]

Buddhism is important to the goodness heritage in at least three respects: First, charity or giving is not only omnipresent in Buddhist canons, but also a part of the core of practice. Similar to the status of *zakat* as one of the pillars of Islam or *caritas* in Christianity, the practice of Mahayana Buddhism is to walk on

[29] "The lay person is like a farmer, his or her act is like a seed, the [monastic] Order or immediate recipient of the offering is like the field in which a seed is planted, the resulting merit is like the crop, and the deceased is like the person who benefits from or harvests the crop." Teiser, *The Scripture on the Ten Kings and the Making of Purgatory in Medieval Chinese Buddhism*, 103, n. 5. Cited by Campany, *Signs from the Unseen Realm*, 79, n. 89.

[30] Kieschnick, *The Impact of Buddhism on Chinese Material Culture*, 157.

[31] For example, Brokaw, *The Ledgers of Merit and Demerit*, 28–30; Smith, *The Art of Doing Good*, 225.

[32] For example, Yang, "The Concept of Pao as a Basis for Social Relations in China," 298–299.

[33] Kieschnick, *The Impact of Buddhism on Chinese Material Culture*, 185, n. 101.

the bodhisattva's path by following the six (sometimes ten) perfections. The first perfection is *dāna* in Sanskrit and Pali and *bushi* (布施) in Chinese, whose implications include giving, charity, and generosity. *Dāna* is mandatory for both the clergy and laity. It is here we see the fundamental and cardinal status of *dāna*: it is the first step, the most basic, and the most open for anyone to pursue as they begin on the path toward becoming a bodhisattva by practicing giving.

Second, Buddhism gives a to-do list of concrete and meritorious actions. The list encouraged contributions to specific objects like bridges, wells, paved roads, and planted trees, that benefit people outside of the Buddhist community and hence the public good. For example, one of the key references for merit in China, the *Scripture of the Field of Blessings and Merit* (佛说诸得福田经), which was translated into Chinese by the end of the third century, states that the Buddha lists seven things that would count for the field of blessings:

> The Buddha announced to Indra, "There are seven types of great donations that are termed 'field of blessings,' and those who enact them obtain blessings and are reborn in Brahma Heaven. What are these seven? The first is to construct stupas, monastic quarters, halls and buildings. The second is to provide gardens, orchards, pools, woods and cool places. The third is to donate medicine and treat the infirm. The fourth is to maintain boats to help the people cross rivers. The fifth is to establish bridges so that the ill and the weak can cross rivers. The sixth is to dig wells close to roads so that the thirsty may drink. And the seventh is to make latrines and places of convenience. Through these seven acts one obtains the blessings required for [rebirth in] Brahma Heaven.[34]

Rather like Christian missionaries in the eighteenth and nineteenth centuries, Buddhist monastics did charity to propagate their religion as well to carry out their basic religious practice.[35] Monks could achieve a profile in the *Biographies of Eminent Monks* not only through the knowledge of scriptures or "wisdom," but also *in place* of that knowledge by performing "good works."[36] We have discussed many of these particular acts and institutions in Chapter 2.

In spite of all this, the reputation of Buddhist charity eventually declined, to the extent that in the early twentieth century Buddhist monastics were sometimes stereotyped as "useless" and "dependents," and the reformist monk, Taixu, called for a "Buddhist revolution" to refocus on the Six Perfections.[37] Nevertheless, the Buddhist mechanism of merit has left an impact on contributions to the public good, to the extent that officials in the Qing dynasty and NGO workers in modern times continued to use the terms without any

[34] Ibid., 201.
[35] Quan, "Causes of Charity in Medieval Buddhist Monasteries," 64; Liu, *Medieval Buddhism and Society*.
[36] Kieschnick, *The Impact of Buddhism on Chinese Material Culture*, 161–162; Huang, *Collected Essays on the Song Buddhist Economy*, 148.
[37] Pittman, *Toward a Modern Chinese Buddhism*.

reference to Buddhism. "Buddhist notions of merit, and in particular the idea that one could gain merit through the construction of bridges, had become for such people a common place element of public works and charitable acts; in bridges … the doctrine of merit was well entrenched in the public psyche."[38]

The third long-term impact of Buddhism on Chinese philanthropy is the individual-based notion of personhood for merit. This new personhood went through much interaction with, and was expanded by, Daoism. The issues at stake stemmed from a bigger change wherein Buddhism considerably affected the medieval Daoist eschatology and morality:

> … during the period of the Six Dynasties, a geography of hell takes shape, and previously unanticipated perspectives on the afterlife, such as the theory of rebirth in the Six Realms, are revealed… In the *imaginaire* of death, the 'underground jails' (*diyu*, Skt. *Naraka*) progressively replace the traditional 'yellow springs' hidden within the obscure world (*you*) which the deceased must traverse. As a compensation for these terrifying prospects, rituals for the salvation of the living and the dead develop. One has, by all means, to 'gain merits' (*jian gongde*) and to actively participate in cultivating universal compassion, lest the gates of salvation close before one's eyes. In this way, the new horizon opened by Buddhism on the question of death and the apocalypse, predestination and the world beyond started to transform and to shape the Chinese *imaginaire* for ever after.[39]

This new imagination of an "underground jail" further strengthened the indigenous idea of cosmic retribution. The key question is what allows one to avoid postmortem punishments. While the Buddhist idea of transferable merit – for example, and most commonly, to one's parents – was an adaptation to indigenous Chinese personhood, the idea that karmic causality only rests on individual acts across multiple lifetimes conflicts with the Daoist and Confucian idea of intergenerational responsibility within lineage and family. Mollier shows that some Daoist sects, such as Lingbao Daoism, embraced Buddhism's egocentric implication and preached a "Mahayana Daoism."[40] Other sects, especially the Way of the Celestial Master (天师道), maintained that human destiny is governed by Heaven and one's life span, that is, the chance for immortality is tightly linked to one's ancestors' deeds. By the same token, people's acts will also have positive or negative effects on their descendants' life spans.[41]

With the rising concern about keeping score for the final judgment, a new ideology for goodness began to emerge by the fourth century AD: "a numerical method or organized 'system' of merit accumulation… Such a system appears, albeit in a rudimentary form, in the *Master Who Embraces Simplicity* (抱朴子)

[38] Kieschnick, *The Impact of Buddhism on Chinese Material Culture*, 213.

[39] Mollier, "Karma and the Bonds of Kinship in Medieval Daoism: Reconciling the Irreconcilable," 171–172.

[40] Mollier, "Karma and the Bonds of Kinship in Medieval Daoism: Reconciling the Irreconcilable."

[41] Ibid.

of Ge Hong (c. 283–343), where it is simply one of many different techniques designed to aid in the attainment of immortality."[42] In the late twelfth century, two landmark texts were produced, texts that ultimately served as definitive statements of the numerical system. These were the *Tract of Taishang on Action and Response* (c. 1164) and the *Ledger of Merit and Demerit of the Taiwei Immortal* (1171), which are the first texts "that carried the logic of the system to its natural conclusion by assigning points to the performance of deeds, thereby allowing ledger users to calculate their own store of merit."[43]

The *Tract* and the *Ledger* were not popular when they first appeared. The *Ledger* was originally a text for members of a Daoist cult. Yet, by the late Ming dynasty, the two texts had become popular among the literati. Together the two texts were "the bible of the merit-demerit system" and the prototypes of the then proliferating morality books, turning into what Brokaw calls the "morality books movement" through the seventeenth and eighteenth centuries.

These morality books focusing on divine retribution became important to Confucians as well, even though they were so antagonistic to the concepts of stimulus and response (感应), a law of cause and effect (因果), retribution and response (报应), and to ideas of Buddhist karma and Daoist immortality generally. Sometime during the Ming Dynasty, the use of a ledger of merit and demerit provided guidelines for cultivation that anyone could follow.[44] For some, dutifully following the ledger to scrutinize one's deeds became a way of cultivation in the Confucian sense. The strict and highly calculated ledger provided a sense of control for status advancement and for legitimation of the status quo.

Here the individual has already become the primary unit of action. By the late Ming, the literati, while calculating rewards for good deeds, emphasized doing good as a personal responsibility and as a way to "move from a feeling of compassion to saving lives."[45] In so emphasizing and embodying, "late Ming morality books offered a much needed moral explanation for sudden reversals in social status and wealth and gave men on the margins of the bureaucratic elite a sense of control over their destinies."[46]

Among the complex possibilities in this mixture of heritages, we emphasize two overlapping discourses about the motivation for charity that eventually emerged as the most important and general: the self-cultivation discourse and the karmic discourse. Based on her empirical studies of charity and altruistic behaviors in Taiwan, the cultural psychologist Chu similarly found two core

[42] Brokaw, *The Ledgers of Merit and Demerit*, 31–32.
[43] Ibid., 35.
[44] Ibid., 230.
[45] Smith, *The Art of Doing Good*, 262, 267.
[46] Ibid., 255.

motivations for charity: as fulfilling one's basic obligations and as counting toward karmic cause-and-effect.[47] Her analysis shows that people's specific religious identity is not relevant to how they think about their motivations for charitable behavior. It is, rather, age, urban/rural variation, and education that make the most difference in charity: the younger, urban, and more educated tended to see charity as one's basic responsibility (本分) as an individual (the "cultivational" discourse, in our terms) whereas the older, rural, and less educated tended to see charity as linked to karmic cause-and-effect. The fact that these two discourses do not correlate with the "religion" of the subject seems to suggest that the two discourses have become instilled in the general values and norms of charity rather than being linked to any religious teachings. They have simply become common-sense motivations.

Note that Chu's research took place in the 1980s, before the conspicuous growth in popularity of the new modern Buddhist organizations like Tzu Chi. Her research suggests that at that time religion had become so blended into the goodness heritage that it became barely identifiable. Thus cosmic retribution and the ledger for merit and demerit, as Brokaw reiterates, blended Confucianism, Daoism, and Buddhism, and hardly distinguished one religion from the other.[48] For example, charitable literati in the late Ming dynasty, as Smith points out, were influenced by a cluster of religions and philosophies – from Buddhist elements to the Jesuits, from morality books to Confucianism and Legalism – but would attribute their charity to general feelings of morality and personal responsibility rather than professing any particular faiths.[49]

In sum, the formation of the goodness heritage in imperial China shows two trends: One is hollowing "religion" out of the rhetoric of doing good. This was a gradual process in which secularism was able to reap the products of religion-inspired good deeds while marginalizing religious motivations away from the public sphere. From the foregoing brief review we can see how the richness of the contemporary lexicon for doing good actually stems from religious traditions. This raises the question of how religion has resurfaced as the motivation and guideline for one's moral self in relation to the public good since the 1980s – a topic we continue to address in all that follows.

The second trend is a propensity to emphasize individual agency, with individual personhood as the key unit for merit and the concretization of good deeds. This began with the introduction of Buddhist karmic causality and fields of blessings, and later merged with other traditions to include ideas like the ledger of merit and demerit for calculating the bottom line of a person's daily deeds. Whether the causes and liability are solely a result of individual

47 Chu, "Charity and Altruistic Behavior in Chinese Societies."
48 Brokaw, *The Ledgers of Merit and Demerit*.
49 Smith, *The Art of Doing Good*, 255.

lifetimes or a matter of lineage and family solidarity, individual accountability had become the primary focus in the history of goodness. This slowly emerging individual personhood and deed-based systematic accountability for goodness paved the way for a moral and civic selving of the cosmopolitan Chinese good person in the late twentieth century.

These two trends – the expansion of a secularized discourse of goodness and the propensity for individual accountability – joined with the political factors we discussed in chapter 3 to create pressures for the rationalization of religious goodness. Since the late imperial period, the heritage of goodness first evolved into redemptive societies and benevolent halls, in conjunction with the globalization of Christian missionaries, and later into the global expansion of Taiwan Buddhism. These initiatives share one attribute in common: a translocal and transnational organization and network for universal philanthropy. The idea of an organizational form, in the sense of associating and networking good-hearted, merit-minded, virtue-aspiring, and salvation-driven individuals under one religion, was made available through waves of globalization.

Globalization

The present form of industrialized philanthropy has a few characteristics that were unprecedented in Chinese history and that go beyond the pressures for making political merit that we have already discussed. It generally now combines collective effort by both clergy and lay volunteers organized under one religion, universalism in serving beneficiaries beyond shared localities and kin ties, expansion beyond ad hoc relief, and the tapping and forming of translocal and transnational networks. The combination of ecumenical universalism and organizational networks, we will argue, has to do with two waves of globalization: the first was the Christian ideals of missionaries and the second (with a relatively smaller purview than that of Christianity and primarily within the Chinese diaspora) is a cluster of developments that can be summed up as the global expansion of Taiwan's Buddhism, with the Buddhist Compassion Relief Tzu Chi Foundation as the most iconic and widespread.

The Jesuits already had some influence on doing good in the Ming dynasty,[50] but Christian charity was not introduced into China on a large scale until the nineteenth century. For modern history, we can thus identify a first wave of globalization in the nineteenth-century introduction of Christian models of charity into the three Chinese societies. Although developing at slightly different times and paces, Christian missionary-based charity became established to

[50] Ibid., 253–254.

a certain degree in China, Taiwan, and Malaysia. Even today, Christians and non-Christians still frequently associate Christian missionizing with charity.

As we described in Chapter 2, a lively landscape of engaged religions already existed prior to the arrival of the Christian missionaries, although the Christian model was distinct in some ways. Christianity promoted the ideas of universal love and of charity as an institutional mission with absolute morality (rather than something to be cultivated progressively) more than any of the indigenous traditions. The Christian model focused on, and hence eventually had a powerful influence over education and health. Its charity facilities, especially hospitals and schools, were open to the general public – Christian and non-Christian. This differs, for example, from kinship-based god associations in Lukang and dialect-based "clans" in Malacca, which were organized and functioning institutions and yet limited beneficiaries to their membership. Popular temples in Lukang and Malacca were institutions for a wider general public, and yet they provided minimum charity that was always ad hoc. Benevolent halls in China were perhaps the most comparable in terms of organization, yet they were highly dependent on local assets, and some of them, for example Tongshanshe, deliberately and categorically excluded recipients based on their Confucian moral failings. Redemptive societies were perhaps the most exemplary parallel in terms of their universalism, activism, and transnationalism as many of them branched out from China to Taiwan and Southeast Asia, although they were operating more on the base of lay associations. Redemptive societies, however, are largely in decline in our field sites, with a few important exceptions such as the Yiguandao in Taiwan (and more recently in Southeast Asia and China, where it remains illegal), and the Moral Uplifting Society (providing relief services, free medicine, and funds for burials) or the *Zhenkong jiao* (which continues a long redemptive society tradition of offering opium rehabilitation) in Malacca.[51]

In spite of the Christian model's distinctiveness and accomplishments through the early twentieth century, it had a relatively limited direct impact on engaged religions in our field sites until around the 1980s. The reasons for the limited impact vary across societies. It depends first on the timing, and second on whether the denomination is able to move beyond the role of a demarcated "provider" of social services to the role of a "facilitator," which has become blended into the local context and works through its own social networks.

"Provider" refers to the prototype of "giving" charity, very much as set up by the Christian church and missionaries, by coming in from outside to give materials and services and to establish welfare facilities. "Facilitator" refers to the indirect contribution to charity, such as building up trust and networks for

[51] Luo, "Past and Present of Chinese Religion in the Malay Peninsula."

social capital which then indirectly provide a foundation for forming organized collective acts of charity.[52] An example of a facilitator is the popular Cheng Hoon Teng temple in Malacca. The temple has a very limited and passive role in direct welfare provision. But its existing Buddhist sutra-chanting network facilitates new providers, such as Tzu Chi from Taiwan, in developing charity. Facilitators tend to thicken social ties and merge into the local setting, while providers can avoid pre-existing ties of ascribed status at the risk of lacking embeddedness, as we will discuss in the two chapters that follow.

Becoming a facilitator is the result of localization, in the sense of becoming embedded in the flux of local life and local politics. In China, the most successful historical case of turning a Christian provider to a facilitator was not the one with the most assets. Rather, it was the YMCA in the 1930s. Such a successful localization had much to do with its timely and direct response to the difficulties of life during war time. It responded proactively to the problems of a daily life in turmoil, and its leadership took a clearly political stance. Another example of facilitator is the Catholic village in northern Guangdong, which Lozada calls Little Rome.[53] The church there operates in the local social world in a similar way to a community temple, facilitating philanthropies based especially on community identity, which drove and inspired transnational donations from former village residents who lived overseas.[54]

Christianity in Taiwan offers another example of facilitator/provider dynamics. Presbyterians came to Lukang in 1897.[55] The Presbyterian Church is the largest in Taiwan, and provided charity – especially medical aid – right from the beginning. Nevertheless, they converted only a few percent of the population and the impact was not widespread. In addition, this was right at the beginning of the Japanese colonization, which reduced the possibilities for development, let alone local impact. The Japanese severely limited proselytization especially by the 1930s, when they began trying to promote state Shinto for the entire population. After World War II, however, the GMD regime in Taiwan was relatively friendly toward Christian groups: Chiang Kai-shek and his wife were Methodists, as were many of the mainland-educated leaders who came over after 1945. Moreover, the "Oversight of Temple Regulations," the primary law on religion since 1929 (when the KMT capital was still in Nanjing), continued to exempt Christianity and Catholicism from regulation until 2004. Very large numbers of Protestant and Catholic missionaries left China for Taiwan, built

52 Huang, "Provider and Facilitator: Religion and Social Capital among the Chinese in Malacca, Malaysia."

53 Lozada, *God Aboveground*.

54 Ibid., 170–177.

55 The Presbyterian Church of England came to southern Taiwan in 1865 and the Presbyterian Church of Canada came to northern Taiwan in 1872.

hospitals and orphanages, and established Christian and Catholic schools, seminaries, and a university.

The post-1949 migration of missionaries from China to Taiwan (with some going to Malaysia as well) was only part of the global context wherein a Christian ideal of charity was transplanted to Taiwan. With the outbreak of the Korean War in 1950, the U.S included Taiwan in its Asia-Pacific containment line and restored military and economic aid to Taiwan, marking the beginning of the so-called period of American aid (美援时期), which lasted from 1951 to 1965. This aid brought about a number of sociocultural changes, including the development of Christian churches. Relief goods from the U.S. aid to Taiwan were distributed through Christian World Service (CWS). CWS founded its local branch, the Taiwan Christian Service (TCS), in 1954 and invited thirty-eight denominations, including the Taiwan Presbyterian Church, to help with the distribution of relief goods. With the end of this aid, CWS gradually terminated its relationship with Taiwan from 1968 on. TCS appointed its first Taiwanese director in 1972.[56]

The long-term, large-scale, and state-endorsed provider role of Christianity in post-war Taiwan, however, never made a full transition to facilitator. The major exception is the tie to ethnic minorities in Taiwan – a trajectory reminiscent of the combination of Christianity and the Chinese ethnic minority in Malaysia.[57] While the proportion of Christians in Taiwan remains at around 5 percent of the population, 77 percent of aboriginals are Protestant or Catholic.[58] After World War II, many aboriginals associated the victory with the United States, and this extended to their new religious choices. Among the Ami in eastern Taiwan, for example, the Presbyterian mission group initially defined its god as "the god of the Americans."[59] Catholicism followed in the 1950s. Local politics in Aboriginal settlements is often now divided between the Protestant and Catholic churches.[60] These churches have become facilitators for the aboriginal communities: for example, the Presbyterian Church has been the incubator for the aboriginal rights movement,[61] and instrumental in the choice of which faith-based organizations would provide post-catastrophe village reconstruction after the 2009 typhoon – usually preferring the Christian group World Vision instead of Buddhist organizations.

[56] www.tcnn.org.tw/news-detail.php?nid=5116 (Accessed 29 April 2015).

[57] The aboriginal peoples in Taiwan belong to the Austronesian linguistic family. As of 2015, there are a total of sixteen groups recognized by the Taiwan government. The Aboriginals comprise about 2 percent of the total population of Taiwan.

[58] Tan, *The Paiwan*, 82.

[59] Huang, "Accepting the Best, Revealing the Difference," 263.

[60] Huang, "The Historical Construction and Imagination of Foreigners"; Huang, "Accepting the Best, Revealing the Difference"; Simon, "Negotiating Power."

[61] Simon, "Negotiating Power."

The case of Malacca involves a mixture of timing and Christianity's role as provider. Despite its early colonization, Christian missionaries only began to focus on the education of Chinese and other minorities in the nineteenth century. Such a demarcated goal set off Christianity as a provider more than a facilitator. In Malacca, English education had successfully created a generation of English-speaking and British-identified (and UK-national) elites among the Straits-born Chinese, who were the "superior stratum" in Freedman's terms.[62] These linguistic, national, and class distinctions set the "King's Chinese,"[63] as they called themselves, apart from the new immigrants from China, who had become the majority by the turn of century. Christianity bears a historical association with the King's Chinese. Nevertheless, this group has declined in influence over the twentieth century. This was in part because the British began to privilege the Malay population after the 1920s, and in part because a newer generation of Chinese immigrants has overtaken the old King's Chinese since the turn of the century. The collective identity of the new immigrants is closely tied to the Chinese-speaking school system rather than to English, and much less influenced by Christianity. Ironically, exactly because of its embeddedness in the colonial Chinese elite, Christianity still remains parallel to but separate from the broader Chinese mechanism of engaged religions – provider but not facilitator.

The globalization of Christian ideals of charity therefore did not produce the same patterns of localization in China, Taiwan, and Malaysia: they vary with government attitudes toward religion, relations between state and ethnicity, and the different global experiences especially of postcolonialism and the Cold War. Acting as "provider" is an efficient way for a religious philanthropy to carry out universal ideals and enter a new society. Yet, it may also be a disadvantage as the distinctive and visible provider institution is prone to political pressure. The "facilitator" role requires more thorough localization, and yet, once it is blended in, religious philanthropy becomes enmeshed in all the local politics of place.

One significant feature of this nineteenth-century (and beyond) Christian ideal of charity lies in its global and ecumenical network and the possibility for a para-church network across denominations. Although trans-local charity has not been new in Chinese societies since the Ming benevolent halls, and although transnational religion-inspired charity has its forerunners in redemptive societies, a network of charity under one religion such as the Christian

[62] Freedman, *The Chinese in Southeast Asia*, 11 (cited in Tan, "The Chinese in the Strait Settlements," 198n).

[63] First appears in G. E. Raine, *The Daily Mail* (London), in 1906. Song Ong Siang, "The King's Chinese"; *The Straits Times Annual*, 1936, p. 38 (cited in Tan, "Chinese in the Strait Settlements," 198n).

World Service in Cold War Taiwan is unprecedented in Chinese history. The Christian charity sponsored by the Amity Foundation across China is the latest example of such a Christian para-church charity network.[64]

The Christian model had a definite influence on Chinese charity. To Chinese in the twentieth century, the new, Christian industrialized (large-scale, using corporate management techniques, and disembedded from local society) philanthropy appeared to be novel, even in light of Buddhism's long association with charity. For example, in his survey of Chinese Buddhism from 1900 to 1950, Welch observes that "the proliferation of modern forms of charity during the Republican period was stimulated by the Christian missionaries, whose schools and orphanages reminded Buddhists of their own compassionate principles."[65] For another example, Tzu Chi traced its creation in the 1960s in part to an inspiration from three Catholic nuns who, speaking from the credentials of the CWS establishment, asked its founder, the Venerable Cheng Yen, why Buddhists built no hospitals or schools.

The challenge from Catholicism inspired Cheng Yen to organize donors through women's alternative social capital, and, half a century later, Tzu Chi had grown into one of the largest religious charitable organizations of the Chinese-speaking world. Compared to the state-endorsed CWS in Taiwan, which was more or less a globalization from above, the global expansion of Tzu Chi is from below, has a smaller purview, and presents a case of combined facilitator and provider. It grew out of the grassroots heritage of merit and doing good, and expanded globally not as a result of missionaries or international relations but as a consequence of the transnationalism that had undergone a new wave of development from the 1980s.

The overseas development of Tzu Chi is part and parcel of Taiwanese and Chinese transnationalism.[66] The branches in New York, Boston, Tokyo, Singapore, Penang, Malacca, Shanghai, and Nanjing, among many others, all began with Taiwanese immigrants who were usually already followers of Tzu Chi in Taiwan before migration (for example, Tokyo, Penang, Nanjing, Shanghai), became followers through later contact with Tzu Chi media (audiotapes, videotapes, and books) disseminated through local Buddhist networks (New York, Boston), or through contact with Tzu Chi during a visit back to Taiwan (Malacca).

The first formal contact between Tzu Chi and China was from the headquarters in Taiwan, to deliver relief to the victims of floods in southeastern China in 1991. Nonetheless, unlike the earlier Christian missionizing, the 1991 relief

[64] Liu, "Love and Faith"; Wielander, *Christian Values in Communist China*, 76–77.

[65] Welch, *The Practice of Chinese Buddhism*, 378.

[66] This is based on fieldwork in the United States, Japan, Malaysia, and China, primarily by Huang.

did not result in Tzu Chi's proselytization. The initial development of Tzu Chi in the cities of eastern China typically began instead with economic migration. In Shanghai, for instance, a Taiwanese woman, Ms. Qiu, moved her trading company to China in 1993. Ms. Qiu was already a devout Tzu Chi follower and has become known as "the first *bodhi* seed" in Shanghai, whose "body is filled with Tzu Chi cells," as she described it. She began proselytizing among her employees and through the large Taiwanese network in Shanghai. Although she was able to organize a few charitable services, political pressure meant that Tzu Chi Shanghai remained limited to the Taiwanese diaspora during the 1990s. According to Ms. Yang, who is another of the founding members of Tzu Chi Shanghai, whom we interviewed in 2005, the breakthrough for Tzu Chi Shanghai came from two major changes. One was a new cause, "starting from the village," for education in rural areas, beginning with scholarships for 2,000 students in Shanxi in 1997, followed by a series of relief programs with or without help from the headquarters in Taiwan; this continues today. Moving away from the city seems to have freed Tzu Chi from earlier political pressure and created some space for development, especially because such programs fit well with the agenda the government was promoting at the time. The other change comes from inside the Taiwanese diaspora: because of the increasing practice of intermarriage, and because of the spread of Tzu Chi ideals through other kinds of networks (as we will discuss in Chapter 6), participants gradually expanded beyond the Taiwanese to include locals.[67] The change in Tzu Chi Shanghai's constituency is a part of a broader shift in Taiwanese cross-Strait transnationalism: reembedding through intermarriage and personal contacts with the locals, and eventually expanding on its own in the local population.[68] Tzu Chi in China had moved far enough along the road to becoming a facilitator by 2014 that locals already outnumbered Taiwanese in some major cities, such as Nanjing.

Similar to the pioneer efforts in China, the development of Tzu Chi Malaysia is an example of transnationalism, but with a very different format. The earliest branch, Penang, began with a devout Taiwanese woman who was sent to Malaysia by her company. She then began proselytizing among her local colleagues and networks. The Malacca branch began with the economic migration of a Taiwanese couple, the Lius, who moved their textile factory to Malaysia. As we will discuss in more detail in Chapters 5 and 6, the Malacca case is similar to that of Shanghai in stemming from an initial economic migration and localization, but has gone well beyond Shanghai or other Chinese cities in how thoroughly it has become embedded among the locals.

[67] Yang, "The Funeral Pattern of Tzu Chi Shanghai."
[68] Shen, " 'The First Taiwanese Wives' and 'The Chinese Mistresses'."

The somewhat happenstance nature of Tzu Chi transnational practice eventually resembled that of some Catholic models, where each of the overseas branches began at the grass roots and then went through a process of standardization under the supervision and approval of the headquarters. This is why we call it an organizational network rather than a religious diaspora. Standardization includes the formal recognition of the local branch, which usually requires a certain number of titled core members ("commissioners" in Tzu Chi terms); a model for the development or perpetuation of multiple programs (the Four Mission model or the Eight Footprints in Tzu Chi) with standard operating procedures specified for each practice; and a globally uniformed presentation that includes a logo, standardized terminologies, architecture, the uniquely Tzu Chi set of three statues for the Buddha Hall, interior design, and personal embodiment in uniforms, hairstyles, emotional expression, etiquette, and bodily discipline.

Note that Tzu Chi's transnationalism is only part of a broader trend of the global expansion of Taiwan Buddhism. All of the groups involved feature a particular form of Buddhism that involves a modern organization with socially engaged programs, and has a propensity for industrialized and transnational networks of religious philanthropy that overlap with the Chinese diaspora. In addition to Tzu Chi, the major carriers for the global expansion are the other two major Taiwan-originated, modernist Buddhist organizations: Foguang Shan (佛光山, Buddha Light Mountain) and Fagu Shan (法鼓山, Dharma Drum Mountain).

These three organizations have several characteristics in common. First, all three are similar in leadership and organization. Each group is founded and led by a charismatic leader: Tzu Chi was founded by the Venerable Cheng Yen (b. 1937), Foguang Shan was founded and led by the Venerable Hsing Yun (b. 1927), and Fagu Shan by the late Venerable Sheng Yen (1930–2009). Each group runs a large-scale modern organizational network consisting of monasteries, secular institutions including universities, and nonprofit foundations, and is supported by a large lay following in Taiwan and globally. All of the three charismatic figures maintained their leadership of the widely spread branches as the spiritual authority and CEO.

Second, all three organizations are socially engaged, each as an example of "Humanistic Buddhism" (人间佛教, or "Buddhism for the Human World"). Humanistic Buddhism is a this-worldly path first traced by the Venerable Taixu (1890–1947) around the 1920s in China, and significantly articulated and propagated by the Venerable Yinshun (1906–2005) in China and Taiwan. Taixu was one of the first reformist monks who wanted to "rescue" Buddhism from providing primarily death rituals, and to bring Buddhism to compete with the philosophies of the world. He was also active at the time when Christianity began to attract a significant following in China and established a reputation for doing charity. According to Pittman, Taixu was particularly impressed by Christianity for its organization of people under one coherent religion. Taixu made efforts to build Buddhist seminaries and to bring Buddhism into non-funerary rites of passage, such as weddings. Taixu also resisted sectarianism among the sangha and readvocated the bodhisattva's path for the laity. Yinshun continued these two legacies.[69]

Third, the three groups are similar in the timing, scale, and ethnic constituency of their global development. Foguang and Fagu have in common their globe-trotting leadership and an increasingly international sangha system, which supports resident monastics in their overseas temples or meditation centers. All three organizations have a worldwide distribution of branches and lay members. Outside of Taiwan, Foguang Shan oversaw 208 temples, Chan centers, and Buddhist culture centers in a total of 30 countries (2010); Fagu Shan oversaw 39 temples, Dharma associations, chapters, and contact offices, in a total of 8 countries (2010); and Tzu Chi has branches in 67 countries around the world (2011).[70]

The global expansion of these three organizations features millions of followers who primarily speak Chinese and have strong links to Chinese heritage. All three organizations are working relentlessly to shift from being diasporic to ecumenical in their own distinctive approaches. For example, Foguang has native non-Chinese converts and graduates from their seminaries who worked for their mission in South Africa and Tanzania.[71] Fagu Shan has succeeded in attracting non-Chinese students to their Chan meditation retreats, like the meditation workshops conducted in English in the San Francisco Bay area, and has created an endowed professorship in Chinese Buddhism at Columbia University.

Peripatetic monks are not new in Chinese history and neither is institution building in a non-Chinese host society. For example, since the 1960s the Venerable Xuanhua (Hsuan Hua) (1918–1995) had established monasteries and a translation institute in California, and his legacy continues to be an importance face of American Buddhism today. Border crossing notwithstanding, a distinctive global network with its headquarters in one place (in this case, Taiwan), reminiscent of Roman Catholicism with a holy center in Vatican, we would argue, is unprecedented in Chinese Buddhism. Foguang and Fagu – and, Tzu Chi, although with a relatively smaller monastic order – form

[69] There were important differences between the two monks as well, including Taixu's greater skill at public activism, and Yinshun's more developed attempt to remove all traces of divinity worship from Buddhism and emphasize the human origins of buddhas. See Pittman, *Toward a Modern Chinese Buddhism*.

[70] See www.fgs.org.tw (Accessed November 15, 2010), and www.ddm.org.tw (Accessed November 23, 2010).

[71] Chandler, *Establishing a Pure Land on Earth*, 297–298.

a combination of cenobitic communities and peripatetic practice. The combination simultaneously represents two ongoing and related trends: Chinese transnationalism and religious organizational networks on a vast scale.

The propensity for organizational network building has been under way in both Taiwan and China. In her discussion of the Buddhist ecology in post-Mao China, Yanfei Sun proposes three developmental patterns: the hollowing-out of the dominant groups there; the vigorous growth of legally ambiguous groups; and the success of those on the fringes of institutional Buddhism.[72] The three Buddhist groups from Taiwan (as well as other Buddhist groups such as the followers of the monk Jingkong) are the most representative of her second type, which is laity oriented and emphasizes "doctrinal teachings and practices, the internalization of the religious messages, and the enactment of the religious teachings in daily life."[73] Sun predicts that this type of Buddhism "as a whole will likely become a more active and greater force in the Buddhist ecology."[74]

The importance of organizational networks lies in their ability to disseminate both content and new structural forms across geographical boundaries. Just as McDonald's brought the world not just hamburgers but also a new way of organizing dining itself (from how food is ordered to cleaning up your own trash), these new Buddhist groups brought in new structures for organizing philanthropy, not just the philanthropy itself.[75] They featured a new propensity for differentiated philanthropic programs and for pipelined building plans – forms of industrialized philanthropy. In a nutshell, making merit is no longer limited to the Seven Fields of Blessings. Rather, the list has been expanded in a way that is both a cause and a result of a new image of unlimited goodness, a point we will discuss in later chapters. Here, we emphasize how the model of industrialized philanthropy by virtue of an ecumenical universalism is being disseminated through the organizational networks of successful iconic groups like Tzu Chi.

Contact and competition have been the primary mechanisms creating convergences in industrialized philanthropy across space and religion. In the three societies we studied, the phenomenal success of the Buddhist Tzu Chi foundation, especially since around 1990, seems to have encouraged or propelled other groups – Buddhist or non-Buddhist – to follow suit. In Taiwan since the early 1990s, all other large Buddhist groups, even though they proclaimed themselves to be more sangha-centered, began to put out plans, blueprints, or visions of building large-scale secular educational and medical institutions in the style of Tzu Chi: Foguang Shan first purchased a private college and

72 Sun, "The Chinese Buddhist Ecology in Post-Mao China."
73 Ibid., 503.
74 Ibid., 508.
75 On McDonald's, see Watson, *Golden Arches East*.

then opened up a university of its own; Fagu Shan has been pushing for a full-fledged university in addition to its Buddhist seminary; and even the most sangha-centered Zhongtai Chan temple runs elementary and middle boarding schools.

In Lukang, the competition brought about by Tzu Chi is even more palpable, because a clearly expanded religious interest in philanthropy emerged only after Tzu Chi's success became so well known in Taiwan in the 1980s. The Catholics opened a school for severely mentally handicapped children in 1988, for example. The Presbyterians began to open to the wider community around the same time. The leader of a nearby Yiguandao branch explained in an interview that Tzu Chi gained so much positive publicity after delivering aid to victims of the terrible Taiwan earthquake of September 21, 1999, that Yiguandao had been forced to publish a book trumpeting their own relief work.

One of Tzu Chi's innovations in religious philanthropy is sorting garbage for recycling, which takes place on a much more elaborate scale than paper-collecting (惜字) practices in the Ming Dynasty.[76] In Taiwan, Tzu Chi was all alone, and somewhat laughable, when they pioneered recycling in the 1990s. By 2000, however, with government support for environmental facilities, garbage recycling had become mandatory in every school and workplace, and something of a national pastime.

Jiangsu's Lingshan Cishan Foundation carries out environmental projects very similar to what Tzu Chi has done. When interviewed in 2006, they were still named Lingshan Ciji (Tzu Chi) Foundation, and the volunteers there were very open about their admiration and emulation of what Tzu Chi was doing in China. This Foundation has since grown much more elaborate in its activities and massive in influence. However, the similarity with Tzu Chi is still palpable in spite of the name change.

We can see something similar again in Malacca. There, a local Buddhist group, Jushilin, has a taskforce for garbage recycling, and its name is "Tzu Chi Team" (慈济组). The manager claims it has nothing to do with the arrival of Tzu Chi in Malacca. The Chinese Catholic church, St. Teresa, also has garbage recycling. Father Huang initiated the program and made no reference to Tzu Chi in our interview. His reason for recycling is to turn trash into money. He was educated in Taiwan and retuned directly to Malacca around 2000. Most of these groups deny emulating a Tzu Chi model, just as intellectual property defendants deny copying patented techniques, but the evidence seems convincing that groups are carefully watching each other and borrowing anything that looks successful.

[76] Smith, *The Art of Doing Good.*

In Malacca, both the oldest and the relatively new engaged religions face pressure from competition. The Chinese Methodist Church located in downtown Jonker Street was founded in 1895 and was the first Chinese (Hokkien)-speaking church in the Malay Peninsula. Throughout most of the twentieth century, the Methodists enjoyed and took pride in their complete school system. However, such a solid accomplishment came to an end when the government slowly took over Christian schools, made them public, and eventually discontinued the Church's involvement. The church remained committed to education by contributing a tent at the Chinese independent school's fundraising bazaar annually. Such an effort does little to change their historical image as the "King's Chinese" – and therefore not part of local Chinese politics. Another effort the Methodist church has been making is the "Beautiful Gate" (美门) training center for the handicapped, named after one of the gates to the Temple in Jerusalem, in front of which a handicapped man was miraculously healed, according to the Bible.[77] The branch in Malacca was the fifth Beautiful Gates branch established by the Methodists in Malaysia. The Center received attention from the local Chinese newspaper upon its opening, and further publicity came when the Malaysia Chinese Association (MCA, the major political party for the Chinese ethnic community) candidate campaigning for the Parliament of the State of Malacca donated money to the Center. As of 2004, the Center housed just one resident trainee, who converted when she first joined the Center in Kampar four years ago. In addition to the efforts in finding a new welfare niche in lieu of education, the Methodist church is obviously under pressure from its loss of followers. On a Sunday in 2004, the service in Malacca had only about ten participants. The Pastor had been so concerned that he asked the anthropologist to introduce him to the coordinator of Tzu Chi Malacca. During the visit, he listened attentively to Tzu Chi's procedures for charity case investigation and the coordinator's personal testimonial. He was particularly interested in Tzu Chi's fundraising for relief and the operation of the Still Thought bookstore café.

Very similarly, religious charitable organizations in China actually have more contact with one another across religious denominations than what we might think. On the one hand, the Religious Affairs Bureaus and various religious associations host regular meetings in which leaders of different religious denominations are required to present their reports on social services. During our fieldwork, we found that religious leaders know remarkably well what other religious groups are doing. As a result, some of them take on actions to launch similar projects. Some religious charities arrange "research tours" among themselves on their own budgets to learn from one another. Amity

[77] Acts 3: 1–7.

Foundation, for instance, receives these research groups from all religious denominations as well as secular NGOs. The Hehe Foundation from Hanshan Temple made conscious efforts to research and learn how other religious philanthropies, such as Amity, Tzu Chi, and Lingshan, operate. These are obvious results of similarities brought about through direct contact.

In all three of our sites we can see the kinds of pressures reported by a group called Humanistic Buddhism of Malacca, which was founded in 1976 as a "new" Buddhist group. It was an offshoot of the Young Buddhist Association of Malaysia (YBAM). Mr. Kim, the founder and leader, feels that the "golden era" of Buddhism in Malaysia was the 1980s, when he and other fellow activists of the YBAM were leading all of Malaysia toward studying humanistic Buddhism instead of sutra chanting, and before strong competition had entered the field. As he said in an interview:

> It was spectacular [in the 1980s]. Then in the 1990s, many foreign Buddhisms came from Taiwan … Many different thoughts and ideas came in. YBAM became no longer the head of Buddhism in Malaysia. People go wherever they like. They have different thinking. Tantric also came in. This and that, and even heterodoxy (邪教) came in. Haha! … We no longer hold 'one heart' (一条心) like we did in the 1980s. … You see, Foguang Shan and Tzu Chi are also influential now.

He was very concerned about a rapidly aging constituency without new blood. He was frank about having no participants under the age of forty-four, and the majority of core members are over fifty. He said, "Maybe we are traditional, and not interesting the young people. By contrast, Tzu Chi and Foguang Shan have a lot of young people … . They are mostly in their 20s and 30s." While the Center has always been running blood donation drives, raising funds for emergency relief, and giving cash to senior homes and to children of needy families, he is now thinking of "reform" (改革), so as to attract new affiliates. One of the new efforts has been using their worship hall for karaoke for both Buddhist and popular songs. He said in the interview, "As long as they sing in front of the statue of Buddha, they'll have a contact with Buddha. Eventually they'll become Buddhist."

What Mr. Kim imagined is a combination of a variation of Foguang Shan's (and more recently China's Shaolin Monastery's) Buddhist music composition tournaments and an imagination of Tzu Chi's popular approach to the laity. What Mr. Kim perceived to be the appeal of the new and foreign groups, especially Tzu Chi and Foguang Shan, is a combination of a few things: a laity-oriented, popular, modern, and participatory spirit of activity. As a non-follower described it, attending a Tzu Chi event is totally "different from worshipping the Buddha (拜佛) in Malaysia." How is this experience distinctive? And, what is the subjectivity for such experience-seeking religious participation?

A New Subjectivity

This new appeal overlaps with the making of a new religious subjectivity. A new kind of Buddhist carried the global expansion of Taiwanese Buddhism and especially that of the Tzu Chi model. These people are professional, middle class, transnational, and even globe-trotting; savvy in organizational skills; and well-versed in cosmopolitan idioms and self-presentation. Above all, such a person identifies herself as a volunteer for her organization wherein doing good is the same as doing religion: she supports her organization's causes by donating money and by participating at ground zero with other uniform-clad and cellphone-swiping follower-volunteers.

This new personhood has become even more pronounced in the recent wave of transnational Buddhism. The actor-centered perception of charity practice indicated in Chu's studies two decades ago was perhaps an early indicator of a much larger and more general movement of Humanistic Buddhism, with its focus on working for and building a Pure Land in this world rather than the one after death. To provide a source for individual agency, it offers a new personhood model through emulating a bodhisattva. This bodhisattva personhood complements – and perhaps gives rise to – what we observe as a new subjectivity. As Pacey writes:

> In the Buddhism articulated by Taixu, Yinshun, Xingyun, Zhengyan, and Shengyan, the average individual could essentially become like Dharmākara. Rather than an idealized, divine figure from whom people could only hope to seek succor and aid in times of distress, or who would welcome the faithful into an other-worldly Pure Land after death, the bodhisattva became a model person – the peak of evolution, and the ideal human being. Furthermore, such individuals could, also like Dharmākara, create a Pure Land, although this time within the world of human beings. Just as the Pure Lands became models for society, the bodhisattva became a model for its inhabitants.[78]

Tzu Chi is perhaps the best summary of the reworking of the concepts of the field of blessings, goodness, and bodhisattva personhood: they have turned the medieval field of blessings into modern and international relief, mobilizing followers as bodhisattva-volunteers. We can see this in the maxim that appears ubiquitously in Tzu Chi buildings and publications: "inviting all benevolent people to the field of blessings, building a Tzu Chi world through thousands of heart-lotus flowers" (福田一方邀天下善士, 心连万蕊共造慈济世界).

This new personhood has moved out of the passive deterrence of bad conduct so characteristic of the morality books movement in the Ming and Qing dynasties. Subjective benevolence is not an end in itself. Rather, it must be put into action. People must actively pursue causes and get things done to construct a Pure Land here and now. This active, collective, and organized pursuit

[78] Pacey, "From Taixu to Shengyan," 274–275.

of causes distinguishes the latest wave of industrialized philanthropies from what came before. By "building" collectively, one embodies the abstract religious idea of the bodhisattva by becoming a deployable agent for a cause. We observed the volunteer as a new form of subjectivity across all three societies.

China, Taiwan, and Malaysia have witnessed several important concomitant and overlapping changes: the increasing importance of the laity, a rise in actor-centered pursuits, and a pursuit of reembedding religious life in a global context. As in many places around the globe, the laity in all three societies has become the driving force and even the trendsetter for different religions, rather than the clergy or religious specialists.[79] The increasing importance of the laity combines with a more general shift in modern consciousness – a quest for identity in the face of the "homeless mind,"[80] which reworks tradition to address current concerns and remakes locality in the global. We can see this in the pervasive new fad of volunteering. It appears again in the appeal of cosmopolitanism in keeping up with the larger world outside of face-to-face everyday life. One way to describe these trends is to invoke Peter Berger's notion of "Protestantized religiosity" as a kind of "voluntary imperative," "an increasingly assertive laity and the transformation of the church into a de facto denomination."[81] We would add a "cosmopolitan imperative" as well, an increasing awareness of the translocal world and the transformation of temple or church into a de facto field for reembedding on a global stage.

The Chinese translation of the term volunteer (志愿者) or volunteer worker (志愿工作者) in religious contexts has several distinctive genealogies. The idea was once commonly expressed as "obliged worker" (义工), a term strongly promoted by the the Nationalist Party (Guomindang, GMD) state apparatus and ideology in Taiwan and Malaysia, arguably until Tzu Chi's proclaimed new invention of "willed worker" (志工). In other words, similar to the term "believer" (信徒), "volunteer" appears not to be an indigenous term in Chinese religious life. It has become essential, however, for industrialized philanthropy to describe its participants this way by virtue of their piety and devotion in a new modern and cosmopolitan context. At the same time, it is also a secular and modern term with a cosmopolitan image of doing religion that could attract new blood to an old idea of religious charity.

In China, the fad of volunteerism can be said to be relatively new, at least in an important sense. Certainly all Red Guards and participants in other Chinese Communist Party (CCP) campaigns were "volunteers." However, the new kind of volunteer culture builds on a post-Mao subjectivity. One has a choice of

[79] Hefner, Robert W., "Multiple Modernities: Christianity, Islam and Hinduism in a Globalizing Age."

[80] Berger, Berger, and Kellner, *The Homeless Mind*.

[81] Berger, "Pluralism, Protestantization, and the Voluntary Principle," 25.

organizations or causes, albeit limited, just like the free and yet limited choices in consumerism. A hallmark for the new trend of volunteer culture would be around 2008, when a large number of aspiring youth came to volunteer for the Beijing Olympics, and when the catastrophe of the Sichuan earthquake moved people and especially the youth nationwide to volunteer at ground zero.[82]

The existence of professional and institutionalized philanthropic religious groups further kindles and fosters a volunteer culture among the younger generation of Chinese, religiously or nonreligiously minded. It provides a channel through which the young and the educated can express their altruistic sentiments and universalistic ideals in what they often describe as an "increasingly materialistic and selfish world." One university student who volunteered for Amity said, "Nowadays people, like my classmates, only care about making money. Therefore, they become more and more selfish. I want to help others but there are not many places where I can go. Amity really does philanthropy for the public good (公益) and they are really well organized. I meet many people who are like-minded." The majority of their volunteers are university students or other young professionals. Charity and philanthropy, promoted by the government and propagated by international NGOs, have increasingly become part of urban middle-class ethics in today's China.

Urban middle-class "Protestanized" religiosity, together with its voluntary imperative, has become the selected ethics that people consider compatible with modern religious charity or philanthropy. What used to be "doing good deeds," "contributing to the Socialist enterprise," or "meeting the needs of my own people" has been replaced by a globalized discourse of charity and philanthropy, and modern social service provision is now increasingly dominated by bureaucratic concepts of professional management and accountability. This voluntary imperative did not grow in a vacuum. It is embedded in local political contexts and may not be able to opt out or escape from the demands of political merit-making.

Just as we saw for religious groups that are pushed to rework themselves as public philanthropies, individual followers may not be as autonomous as the term "volunteer" implies.[83] It is common now in China to hear the aptly coined term "to become volunteered" (被志愿) or even "to become modeled upon Lei Feng" (被学雷锋, referring to the high socialist epitome of the volunteer as propaganda hero). During our research with the YMCA in Jiangsu and Zhejiang provinces, for instance, we learned that the pool of their volunteers came from universities nearby. The YMCA often has close contact with

[82] David Palmer, personal communication.

[83] Gareth Fisher found that the new Buddhist volunteers in Beijing are more interested in self-fulfillment than in sacrificing for others, unlike in Maoist discourse. See Fisher, *From Comrades to Bodhisattvas*, 71–72.

the Student Union and the Young Communist League (团委), who organize volunteers as part of their regular activities. During the World Expo 2013 in Shanghai, similarly, many university students were called upon to be volunteers. In exchange, they automatically got grades of A for the classes they missed. The fact that these students had "been volunteered" led YMCA leaders and other supervisors to have some concerns over recurring quality problems. Reminiscent of the socialist past, the state has tapped into the rise of this voluntary imperative, as we see in this kind of volunteering in the passive voice.[84]

Similar to China, a shift in the concept of what it means to "do good" took place in Taiwan. This shift occurred in part as a result of democratization since the 1980s, which brought about a thriving civil society, with a burgeoning number of associations and foundations that connected the individual to the larger social world and the general public. In part, it reflects a new appreciation of the traditional and the local in a rapidly modernized and global world. The campaign for "total community construction" (社区总体营造) in the 1980s created a solid foundation for organizational practice and for rekindling a local-cosmopolitan and volunteer culture among the young, urban, and educated. The success of Tzu Chi brought about an even wider impact on volunteer culture across the generations, which can be seen even in the widespread adoption of its invented term for "volunteer" (志工, willed worker). All of Taiwan's major Buddhist organizations emphasized their participation and recognition by international organizations, such as the United Nations. New groups have arisen that also capitalize on this new form of cosmopolitan volunteer culture, such as the Fuzhi Buddhist Foundation, which focuses on college student volunteer training and on the promotion of organic whole foods, or an old Catholic missionary who became active in bringing college students to volunteer in Tanzania. Old temples sometimes do similar things, such as Xingtian Gong, which built a free library and set up a cultural and education foundation. Even Mazu has her own general hospital, and some of the temples promote pilgrimage as a cultural learning experience for the young and the international.

Our field site in Lukang is filled with volunteers of both the new and old types. The Tianhou temple uses volunteers much as it has for a long time – to carry out simple jobs in the temple such as cleaning or selling incense, to manage the tens of thousands of pilgrims, or to take part in the temple's huge processions. Roughly 100 people volunteer in the temple in an ordinary week, with 500 being mobilized for a large procession. Newer conceptions of the volunteer, in which people are deployed to help others in ways more like NGOs, are just as widespread. The Presbyterians began sending volunteers into the community, for instance, to help with old age and medical care for needy

[84] Complaints about *bei zhiyuan* are also common in southern universities. See Sum, "'Therefore I Am Made Indifferent'."

people. Even their credit union has very few paid staff; the director himself is an unpaid volunteer. Again, this was not a continuation of an early missionary tradition but instead began only in the late 1980s as this kind of cosmopolitan volunteering spread across Taiwan. Similarly, everyone in the Zijidian Cultural Foundation and all but a single secretary in the Zhongyi Charitable Society (both of which branched off from local temples, as we discussed) is a volunteer. These groups also date from just the last few decades. Finally, of course, Tzu Chi has its own corps of volunteers in Lukang, serving as school crossing guards, taking pulses, and recycling garbage.

In Malaysia a similar trend of volunteer culture is found in the appeal of Tzu Chi to members of sutra chanting clubs. Many of the local participants of Tzu Chi said that Tzu Chi is more "practical" and it is the only place where they can practice how to "walk" on the bodhisattva path. Local followers spoke forcefully about how Tzu Chi provides a meritorious field for them to cultivate, a way to realize the meaning of Buddhist texts they have studied, and embodies "walking or practicing scripture" (行经). The local followers can be divided into roughly three groups according to their occupations and livelihoods: (Chinese language) educators/college graduates, professionals, and retired working-class craftsmen. All three groups spoke about the importance of Tzu Chi's practice, yet in slightly different ways. An example of the first group is a core follower and staff member who came to Tzu Chi when she was a member of the Buddhist Study Club at college. She initiated volunteer services to the New Villages, and, owing to a lack of practical experience, she contacted Tzu Chi and invited a few followers to train her club members in how to carry out social work. Tzu Chi's presentation made her feel that she suddenly understood what she had been reading about Buddhism. An example of the second group is a self-employed computer dealer, who described how he emerged in Tzu Chi's mission: "I am busy for Tzu Chi, but when you are busy, you have that dharma joy (法喜)! … I like participating in these activities … when we give we feel that it's meaningful. It's not just for one's own livelihood." Devotees with a working-class background, the third group, expressed a strong commitment to doing good as complementary to sutra chanting. As a seventy-three-year-old former seamstress said about Tzu Chi's distinctive appeal in comparison to her experience of decades of sutra chanting: "I can see what Tzu Chi has been doing. I said to myself, worshipping and chanting I can do, but in charity I have done nothing."

The voluntary imperative is not exclusive to foreign groups in Malaysia such as Tzu Chi. Being a substantial minority, the Chinese in Malaysia share a long tradition of activism. In fact, the entire Chinese diaspora is built on associations, which are predominantly religion based, from the pioneers of hometown and surname associations, to the Moral Uplifting Society, to the postwar groups such as YBAM. Of course, Christian churches such as the Catholics have long been running St. Vincent de Paul. Tzu Chi's distinction is that it offers an opportunity to participate in a niche that is simultaneously religious or religion-based in the Chinese tradition *and* not political about the Chinese, namely, not overlapping with the politics of the enclaved. Religion here provides an arena for the new bodhisattvas.

Closely related to the voluntary imperative is the surfacing of a cosmopolitan imperative, which is also found in both foreign and local groups. At Tzu Chi's art exhibition of the journey of Xuanzang, the Chinese Buddhist monk who went to India to obtain scriptures in the seventh century, inside Time Square, a bustling shopping mall in the heart of Kuala Lumpur, a visitor in his thirties said excitedly: "You know, these new [Buddhist] groups from Taiwan are different. Like Foguang Shan, like Tzu Chi, they all run activities (办活动)! They make you feel cool about being a Buddhist." The other Taiwan-based Buddhist group he mentioned, Foguang Shan, had been organizing mega-ceremonies of taking refuge (皈依) in gigantic auditoriums near Kuala Lumpur[85] as well as running frequent tournaments for the composition of Buddhist music. All of these events are highly publicized.

In addition to the appeal of "out-and-about" Buddhist cultural events, as opposed to the tranquil and secluded appearance of sutra chanting, a young man from the YBAM said he comes to Tzu Chi to indulge himself in the books, herbal teas, and air conditioning at its bookstore café, Still Thoughts Book Pavilion (静思书轩), which is similar to a Barnes & Noble, with open shelves and free Wi-Fi, yet surrounded by Buddhist statues and art works. It creates a meditative and mindful ambiance with soothing music, soft lighting, incense burning, and features Chinese-language books and media (predominantly Tzu Chi publications), garnished with amiable service from the smiling and soft-spoken Tzu Chi volunteer wait staff.

Many older temples now also emulate the cosmopolitan aspirations of the new Buddhist groups. The 500-year-old Cheng Hoon Teng Temple, for example, decided to go through a tremendous and expensive project of restoration. Its effort was recognized in global terms: the UNESCO Merit Award for Restoration in the Asia-Pacific Heritage Conservation Awards 2002.[86] The other relatively traditional Buddhist temple, Seck Kia Eenh, also expanded its transnational networks in ways that extended from an international sangha conference to fund-raising for the HIV-positive. As another example, YBAM in recent years has also shifted its more politically oriented advocacy to a new focus on (and more new-aged approach to) wellness, training volunteers to provide individual counseling. The counseling center is located upstairs in the

[85] For example, there were 80,000 participants in 1996 and again in 2012. *Nanyang wangbao* (November 25, 2012), www.nanyang.com/node/493725?tid=460 (Accessed July 22, 2014).

[86] We discuss this in more detail in Chapter 7.

YBAM's newly completed gallery-style main hall in its Malacca branch office. Perhaps paralleling the state tapping into the voluntary imperative in China, the Malaysian government also sees new resources in the cosmopolitan imperative. For example, the Bureau of Tourism announced that the Mazu Temple in Kuala Lumpur, which also houses the Hainan native place association (会馆), would be one of the official sites for international conventions in 2012.[87]

In sum, the new fad of volunteering combined with cosmopolitanism is a dual process in which doing religion means volunteering, and volunteerism finds its arena in religious practice. On the one hand, new and often young volunteers find an outlet for voluntary and cosmopolitan imperatives in religious philanthropy. On the other hand, the traditional followers are now doing religion in the form of or in the name of volunteering. For example, an elderly woman in Jiayi, Taiwan, who came to boil water at the construction site of Tzu Chi Dalin Hospital every morning at dawn, explained the source of her commitment: she had vowed to boil water for the bodhisattva Guanyin. She resembles the old type of volunteer for Tianhou Temple's daily maintenance, yet now placed in the very different context of an international nonprofit organization. She is ostensibly a volunteer in a secular sense and yet with traditional religious motivation. For another example, one of the local temples in southern Jiangsu is practically run by lay volunteers. When asked what motivates them to volunteer here, an old lady said, "Don't you watch TV? Nowadays everybody volunteers. Even the Hollywood movie stars volunteer!"

This idea that some stranger's action on a different continent has anything to do with what has essentially been practiced for hundreds of years in local temples in China shows that the cosmopolitan imperative is now genuinely motivating people. For yet another example, Josephine Cua, the English-speaking and highly articulate woman who was behind the restoration project of Cheng Hoon Teng Temple in Malacca, responded matter-of-factly to a question about her position at the temple in an interview: "I am a volunteer." Such a statement places her squarely in the realm of the new cosmopolitan volunteer, although her history with the temple is in fact as traditional as possible: she is from one of the few prominent Kapitan lineages whose descendants have continued to control the temple committee and its assets over centuries. In other words, this is traditional power phrased in the new terms of volunteering. At the same time, the old type of elite membership has been reembedded in the global context of heritage restoration. When she was complimented on her accomplishment in pushing for the temple's restoration against all odds, Josephine Cua smiled humbly, saying "I am just a busybody."

[87] www.hainannet.com.my/NewInfo/Y2012/2012_SuaraHainan39b.pdf (Accessed July 22, 2014).

Ms. Cua's self-effacing joke about being a "busybody" – a busy body – ironically brings up another side to the new way of living religion and the new subjectivity: embodiment. The emphasis on embodiment includes both bodily presentation and emotional expression, as well as the need to keep the body busy doing good works. Religious volunteers are expected not only to get their hands dirty, so to speak, but also to "look" a certain way: from uniforms to hairstyle, from greeting gestures to etiquette, everything enters into an orderly collectivism. Moreover, people use emotional terms to give expression to their volunteering for religious philanthropy. They describe how they feel about the suffering of disaster victims, for example. Doing good is a result and an expression of having a "loving heart" (有爱心).

Tzu Chi has been conspicuous in fleshing out the embodiment of doing religion. All their follower-volunteers wear uniforms in group contexts. On every such occasion, one sees Tzu Chi followers acting in unison, as an orderly collective. Followers not only follow the appropriate hair template for their gender and age group, but also abide by an etiquette of daily life. For instance, they state that at the table one should hold the bowl like a dragon holding a pearl with his mouth, and hold the chopsticks like a phoenix bending over to sip water with her mouth (龙口要含珠 凤口要饮水). They regulate the postures of daily life just as much, walking like the wind and sitting like a bell. Moreover, Tzu Chi followers are expected to control their tempers through mindful training, in their words, by wearing the Tzu Chi "facial cream" of four ingredients: contentedness, gratitude, generous understanding, and inclusiveness (知足、感恩、善解、包容).

Recent decades have brought a new emphasis on love across religions. This is easy to see in two of the largest, most modern and transnational (and so most cosmopolitan) groups we looked at: the Buddhist Tzu Chi Foundation and the (Protestant-inspired) Amity Foundation in China. Bishop K. H. Ting (Ding Guangxun) of Amity, according to Wielander,[88] put love at the center of Chinese Christian theology: "The central tenet of [Ding's] theology was the move to a non-denominational Chinese church built on the core message that God is Love (*shangdi shi ai*)."[89] Parallel to Ding, Tzu Chi's Cheng Yen has since around the year 2000 been promoting "Spreading Love" (*aisa*) and naming all the group's large-scale missions as "Da'ai" (great love), such as the Tzu Chi television station and the villages they built for disaster victims in Indonesia, Haiti, and other places. Her teaching of love is, in a nutshell, to go

[88] Wielander, *Christian Values in Communist China*.

[89] Ibid., 49. Wielander further shows the elaborate list of the CCP's official writings on harmonious society which refer to Western civilization and Christian universal love as being among the many sources of the idea, and reinterpreting Confucian *ren* as *airen* "loving people." Ibid., 51–53.

beyond love, namely, to transcend the limitations and the bonds of familial and personal love. In other words, she ties it to the Buddhist idea of the perfection of generosity by virtue of freeing oneself from the suffering of attachment. As she recounted how her father's death ultimately drove her to Buddhism, Cheng Yen explained that love always involves the suffering of separation and loss (爱别离苦), one of the eight sufferings in Buddhism.[90] She said, "No matter how close you are with your loving family, you will still be parted one day .... So, instead of confining one's love to a small circle of people, one should extend the love to all living beings."[91] This discourse of love has become dominant across religious and national lines since the 1980s.

This surge of love in religious discourse is intriguing. In some ways, the word "love" was more or less hypo-cognized in the Chinese world through much of the twentieth century, yet had become hyper-cognized by the millennium. Up until the 1990s, children in Taiwan, for example, were taught to show filial piety toward their parents and were never told to love their parents or to say that they love their parents; parents rarely expressed love to their children in so many words. In this sense, it matters that the new way of doing religion included an expressive and emotive aspect. For example, when one of us participated in a summer camp for college students at Tzu Chi, one of the first classes shamed students for not appreciating their parents and eventually drove every student to rush to call his or her parents, tearfully screaming to the receiver: "Mom, I love you!"

In other ways, "love" has always been there but it was compartmentalized or regulated into higher abstractions, especially the expression of patriotism in both Taiwan and China – love of one's country (爱国家). This was broadly sloganized in China as "Love the Nation and Love the Party" (爱国爱党), and in Taiwan as "Loyalty to the Party and Love for the Nation" (忠党爱国). In this sense, the latest religious popular usage of "love" can be seen as rescuing the emotion of love from the state. Religious philanthropy released love from its limited usage for the nation-state and for romance and reapplied it as a love that is secular, neutral, generic, and universal – just like the volunteers themselves.

Civic Selving

In sum, the new subjectivity brought three roughly simultaneous changes across our field sites: a new image of volunteers as deployable agents of civic love,

[90] This list appears in "Nirvana Sutra," 103. The Nirvana Sutra discusses the idea at some length.

[91] The Tzu Chi Foundation, "Ai bie li ku," April 15, 2012. www.us.tzuchi.org/us/index.php?option=com_content&view=article&id=3089:tzuchi-2012-04-12-07-37-59&catid=59:2010-08-30-08-46-53&Itemid=266

an active embrace of cosmopolitanism, and new forms of embodiment. These new philanthropic volunteers do not share the subjectivity of earlier Chinese literati who wrote down memories and reflections on their good works, such as those figures in the Ming and Qing dynasties described by Johanna Handlin Smith. He or she does not work alone, and is part of a membership or at least a regular donor on the roster of a religious group that has an open membership across gender, hometown, surname, or occupation, and that runs a program of charity. He or she may wear a uniform or carry a name tag when acting as part of the group, not only to participate in rituals, but also – and perhaps mainly – to volunteer in the organization, receive and give training, and deliver social services. He or she is reachable by cellphone, familiar with social media, apt to pack up and move for a mission, and enthusiastic in speaking for and of the group – be it for proselytizing, fund-raising, or "sharing" her personal transformation with fellow devotees. Such a person is compassionate in delivering services and goods to recipients, and acts and moves with a certain body language of gestures, emotional expressions, and even dietary constraints and hairstyles that are considered attributes of the group's identity. In a subtle and yet noticeable way, these features contribute to the feeling that she or he is a "better" person.

We have been showing how and why religion blended into the genealogies of goodness. Both the cultivational and the karmic discourses suggest that doing good concerns the self and that the preference for one discourse or the other could vary sociologically. These new "good" people have adapted to the two waves of globalization we have discussed. The Christian ideal of charity and the transnational expansion of Taiwan's Buddhism highlighted ideals of universalism in doing good, and at the same time reembedded those good deeds in a global context. This occurred through new organizational networks as well as through competition between groups for their cause-driven and program-differentiating ways of doing religion. In the era of globalization, doing good now brings the possibility of and the propensity for a form of industrialized philanthropy. Doing good as a way of living religion is experience-seeking, action-centered, and participatory in spirit, and it relies on the crafting of a new subjectivity. For many people this new subjectivity came from a view of bodhisattva personhood that bestows religious individuals with deployable agency, and such an agency is expressed in a "Protestanized" voluntary imperative combined with cosmopolitanism. The new fad for volunteer-cosmopolitans has brought a new emphasis on embodiment. To put it bluntly, the rise of the industrialized philanthropy we see in China, Taiwan, and Malaysia grows from the collectively organized embodiment of "loving hearts."

The embodiment trend in this new subjectivity under industrialized philanthropy directs our consciousness to look outward rather than inward. One becomes a better person by engaging the collective, by being out and about to bring philanthropy to complete strangers. One speaks of one's love and works on one's mind in an organized and collective context. A good person crafts rational action to contribute to the public good. What brings the public to the religious self and vice versa?

The meanings and the processes of the resacralization of the self through public activity differ in China, Taiwan, and Malaysia. Here, we tentatively suggest an explanation of the differences with the term "civic selving," to highlight the uneasy combination between the public and a good individual, between secular civil society and religious goodness.[92] We hope also to capture how a shared set of heritages, reworked through waves of globalization, would eventually be transformed into a new good person who contributes as a member of a broader civic collective.

The new subjectivity in the three societies invokes a sense of moral mission for their philanthropic way of living religion. One frequently hears in China and Taiwan about the goal of transforming society and hence the world by transforming individuals from the inside out – purifying human hearts (淨化人心). For example, "Spread Charity Culture, Purify the Way of the World and Human Hearts" (弘扬慈善文化，净化世道人心) is the slogan for the Lingshan Charitable Foundation in China. In other words, charity culture is perceived to be a partial antidote to concerns about a rising moral crisis. For another example, Tzu Chi settings and media in Taiwan ubiquitously offer a vision of social change that starts from the human heart and extends to the surrounding society and ultimately the whole world: Tzu Chi followers collectively utter the vow, "Purify human hearts, harmonize society, toward a world without catastrophe (净化人心 祥和社会 天下无灾难)." This perception of social change that starts from the person and reaches to the world assumes a causal relation from center to circumference, a concentric zone mode of movement. Indeed, the latest Tzu Chi organizational reform is named the Concentric Zone of Unified Hearts (同心圆). Such a concentric vision of social dynamics recalls the Confucian ripple effect of social relations and its related cultivational discourse: one begins from cultivation of the individual, to complete the family, to govern the country, and to rule all under heaven (修身 齐家 治国 平天下). Tzu Chi's Buddhist version of cultivational discourse does not share the political agenda of the Confucian version. It is nonetheless a kind of civic selving that puts individual goodness in the perspective of the larger society and hence the greater world. Civic selving thus empowers the new good person with a vision of a better world. Many Tzu Chi followers in Taiwan explained proselytizing as a moral process of social change through the aggregation of

[92] As we pointed out earlier, we borrow loosely from the concept of "moral selving," as developed by Allahyari, *Visions of Charity*.

goodness: "One more Tzu Chi person means one more good person and one less bad person (多一个慈济人，就多一个好人，少一个坏人)."

Morality notwithstanding, the new subjectivity in these three societies indicates deployable agency that places one's self in the social context of organized philanthropy. By engaging the common good, one is not only morally correct but also socially and politically competent. It is in this sense that we use civic selving instead of the more psychological analysis of moral selving. It is here – in the mechanism placing the individual into society, allowing a person to "feel something larger than him/herself," in a new embodiment mechanism formed through participation in religious philanthropies – that we can see differences across China, Taiwan, and Malaysia. Certainly, as we have explained, the three societies share heritages, experiences of globalization, and the formation of a new subjectivity. The formation of a new subjectivity through narrating a self who does good draws on more global discourses such as the cosmopolitan idea of being related to strangers beyond face-to-face local settings, and, at the same time, relies on more local discourses such as genealogies of civility. Here, we will mention only a few examples of our observations on the differences among the three genealogies so as to illustrate the proposed concept of civic selving for further research.

Civic selving in China embraces a distinctive discourse of socialist morality and discipline in collectivity. Espousing the rise of individuality in the post-Mao era, individuals who were socialized into socialist forms of embodiment have been left alone to search for a new sense of order for the self. A former member of the Chinese military, for example, explained why she came to volunteer for Tzu Chi: "I need to do something to help people! You know, doing good deeds, using up my remaining heat (发挥余热)![93] … Unlike other places, [Tzu Chi] is very institutionalized (制度化) and organized. There are very clear rules. … Each uniform speaks of the person's role. … You know this is a trustworthy organization … very professional."

Civic selving in Taiwan harkens back to the KMT's civility campaigns since the New Life Movement (which began on the mainland in the 1930s) and its subsequent revisions in Taiwan such as "public virtue heart" (公德心) and just "lining up," as ways of creating discipline in collectivity.[94] Somewhat like the assumption of "teachable bodies" in the state-engineered civility campaigns, one of the distinctive discourses of civic selving in Taiwan is a sense of education through doing good. This is reminiscent of the cultivational discourse for doing good, and yet with a much clearer sense of the self in society. Much like what cultural psychologist Heidi Fung (1999) calls "opportunity education" (机会教育) in the socialization of children in Taiwan, one commonly hears

[93] This is a very socialist expression as well, meaning to make better use of old age.

[94] Weller, *Alternate Civilities*; Lee, "Subway as a Space of Cultural Intimacy."

about the obligation to be taught through doing good.[95] Most representative is Tzu Chi's founding motto: "relief for the poor and instruction for the rich" (济贫教富), namely, the rich should learn about themselves and about life and Buddhism through encountering poverty. In recent years one of the most common narratives in Tzu Chi is that "I am a recycled resource. Thanks to [the Buddhist doctrine of] skillful means, I can be a useful person."

A public morality is not as important in Malaysia as in China or Taiwan. As a substantial minority with a discrepancy between their economic dominance and their political demarcation, civic selving among Malaysian Chinese has adopted a distinctive discourse for going beyond the ethnic enclave of the Chinese and thus breaking away from the ghettoization of purely Chinese associational lives. For example, the Moral Uplifting Society's free medicine was for the public, but no non-Chinese came forward to receive it. Members attributed the unintended ghettoization to a rumor that Chinese medicine uses alcohol, which thus put off prospective Muslims recipients. The newer form of civic selving draws instead on a distinctive discourse that allows Chinese to help the non-Chinese and hence move one step closer to equal civic participation. For example, the coordinator of YBAM, who has been a pious Buddhist since college and was an outspoken veteran activist in Chinese and minority issues, had to think about it when asked, "What welfare or charity programs is YBAM currently running?" He hesitated before saying, "We do blood donation drives … and recently we started counseling services." After the interview he called on the phone and spoke excitingly: "We are part of creating the slogan of "Malaysia, Truly Asian." By making it all Asian, all races can be just Malaysian. This is very important. All of us. All!" That is, he had great difficulties moving between the very standard, enclaved practice of things like blood donation drives and the vague abstractions of a generic Asian identity, but he knew how important it was to establish the group's contribution to this new form of civic selving.

We have seen in the previous chapters how the idea of political merit-making spread through the region even as it took different forms in China, Malaysia, and Taiwan. Here we can see a similar process in the creation of new kinds of subjectivity, where certain tendencies have been widespread in all of our field sites, but the local realizations vary significantly. In spite of these local adaptations, we have tried to show how the contemporary process of civic selving has highlighted an individual self who chooses to become an active volunteer, who accepts the wider authority of religious organization and discipline, who seeks cultivation and fulfillment through a broader civic responsibility to society and humanity, who sees herself as a cosmopolitan even though she may never have

[95] Fung, "Becoming a Moral Child."

left home, and who achieves these ends by accepting new forms of embodied action. Note that this is not simply the spread of what some have described as a "neoliberal" self. While it does indeed relate to the broad economic and political changes of the end of the twentieth century and beyond, it also grows out of China's own complex heritage of multiple ways of doing good and of thinking about that good. Above all, we have identified how cultivational and karmic discourses helped shape the reception of Christian and other important ideas of charity and the good, and how they helped give birth to the regional forms – especially the new Buddhisms that have spread out of Taiwan – that are now so influential transnationally.

Placed in the comparative context of humanitarian services, the rise of civic selving resonates with (and perhaps mutually reinforces) an ongoing trend: an increasing emphasis on the suffering of the victims of manmade and natural disasters. The formation of suffering victimhood has much to do with the recognition of the commonness and the universality of the category of trauma – something that began only in the nineteenth century and expanded rapidly in the past few decades, much like the concept of a civic self that we have been discussing.[96] The production of victimhood as a new subject for humanitarian and human rights has further developed to the extent that local victims learned to perform "suffering narratives" so as to become eligible for aid through the "bureaucraft" of international NGOs.[97] In an ironic way and almost like two sides of one coin, the rise of civic selving that we observed in the Chinese contexts works hand-in-hand with the rise of suffering victimhood around the globe. The very wording of "loving hearts" that feel and empathize with the suffering of the recipients puts the new subjectivity of a Chinese good person in a critical position in a double sense: the civic selving of volunteers is an embodiment that echoes or resonates with the traumatizing self the victims; and, in so echoing, civic selving emerges in accordance with what Joel Robbins rightly observes as the coming of age of the "suffering slot" for anthropology in the last two decades.[98] The next step, as Robbins and other anthropologists have already suggested, would be to develop of an anthropology of the good.[99] That is the project to which we now turn.

[96] Fassin and Rechtman, *The Empire of Trauma*.
[97] James, *Democratic Insecurities*; James, "Haiti, Insecurity, and the Politics of Asylum."
[98] Robbins, "Beyond the Suffering Subject."
[99] Ibid.; Faubion, *An Anthropology of Ethics*; Laidlaw, *The Subject of Virtue*.

5 Gifts, Groups, and Goodness

In our previous chapters we have discussed the multiple forces that have fostered a new understanding of "doing good" that has become increasingly important over the past few decades. Promoted by changes in governance, communication, economy, and mobility, this new goodness rests on a conception of selfhood as universal, cosmopolitan, and fundamentally individual, and on an industrialized social organization of philanthropy mediated by the state. In this chapter and the next, we ask how people create and socially reproduce such notions of goodness, including both the industrialized form and its alternatives. What fosters various images of the good? What are the shapes of the social ties that make organized philanthropy possible and how do they relate to the good?

These questions lead us to reconsider the ways that philanthropy is a particular form of the gift economy. This has been a core topic in the social sciences since Marcel Mauss wrote his essay on the gift almost a century ago.[1] His work inspired a long line of research examining how gift exchange creates ties of social solidarity and expands an individual's social capital. These processes enmesh people in ties of reciprocity that can compel, provoke, or encourage them to help their neighbors. Philanthropy, even in its most industrialized forms where gift-giving is no longer face to face, also fosters such ties.

This observation, however, also conceals a dilemma: the creation of social solidarity (in part through the gift economy) tends to be conservative, leaving those who benefit from it with little reason to innovate. In the language of the previous chapter, the move from provider to facilitator may offer many advantages, but tends to leave structures of social and cultural power untouched. By enmeshing people in webs of reciprocal ties, social capital can easily become a brake on innovation, helping to maintain the status quo and working to diminish innovative trends that might threaten existing networks. That is, there is a tension between the creation of new social constructions of goodness and older systems of social capital. Even successful innovations do not resolve

[1] Mauss, *The Gift*.

the problem in the long run, because they create their own structures of social capital. This chapter focuses especially on how ties of social solidarity both promote and are promoted by philanthropy, and on the advantages and limits of this process. The next chapter concentrates more directly on the problem of innovation.

Our goal in these chapters is to understand what seem like several of the most significant innovative directions for engaged religions. In particular, we will undertake (1) a reconsideration of the role of women in charity, in which women have taken on much wider leadership roles and the appropriate space of action for women extends far beyond the family and neighborhood; and (2) the redefinition of what counts as a worthy charitable cause, toward one that accepts a more universal conception of the "good." In the current chapter, however, we begin with the ways that older patterns of engaged religions were effective in delivering certain kinds of social goods, and certain images of goodness, but also resistant to more innovative changes.

Gifts and Groups

No matter how deeply implicated modern philanthropy may be in the market, and no matter how much it borrows from the industrial management techniques of corporations, it remains ultimately an aspect of the gift economy. The source of funds may be primarily from the market, but its use as philanthropy redirects that money to solve problems that the market has not successfully addressed, from emergency relief to education or medical care in poor areas. Anthropology has a long history of writing about how gifts create communities, and of course a long set of arguments that grew out of that literature. In this chapter, we extend those lines of thought to religious philanthropy: how do gifts make religious groups in Chinese societies, and how do religious groups make gifts?

A series of influential books on Chinese gifting appeared in the mid-1990s.[2] They differed significantly from each other in theoretical and methodological approaches, but all pointed us to how significant the gift remains in contemporary Chinese life. Following Yunxiang Yan, we can somewhat simplify broader themes in the literature into an argument between those who see the gift primarily as a way of creating long-lasting social networks and thus building the basic infrastructure of society (often associated with Mauss), and those who see the gift as one move in an attempt to accumulate individual troves of social capital, which can potentially be converted into other forms of capital (most closely associated with Bourdieu).[3] As Yan shows, neither view adequately

[2] Kipnis, *Producing Guanxi*; Yan, *The Flow of Gifts*; Yang, *Gifts, Favors, and Banquets*.
[3] Mauss, *The Gift*; Bourdieu, "The Forms of Capital."

describes the situation for most Chinese, who draw on both. We can thus see gift practices that range from the purely utilitarian (like bribes phrased as gifts) to the purely communitarian (like socially required forms of gifting at village weddings or funerals), from calculation of interests to expressions of interpersonal emotion (人情). They also create different kinds of social organizations, from ego-centered networks to solidary groups.

For purposes of this book, there is no need to enter this literature in detail. We note, however, that none of it discussed philanthropy, and none of it discussed religion. This has been true as well for the sociological literature on social connections, *guanxi* (关系), in China – relationships that are, in part, both created by and reflected in gifts. This literature's lack of interest in either philanthropy or religion probably stems from a shared cause: both philanthropic and religious gifts tend to be mediated by a third party. In contrast, the gifts studied in the literature on guanxi tend to be direct and unmediated; that is, the gift materializes a social tie directly between the giver and the recipient. While certain kinds of charity can be unmediated, such as a handout to a beggar, the larger forms in both contemporary and earlier Chinese societies often take place with no direct contact between giver and recipient. With religion, every financial exchange is mediated: spiritually by some notion of karma, or by the gods, or by God's Love; most are also mediated by the religious institution itself, which collects and redistributes the funds.

Religious gifts, even if they are earmarked for quite mundane uses such as construction or poverty relief, are still visible to the eyes of the gods. Sometimes they are visible *only* to those eyes, for instance when people drop cash into a large donation box. In Chinese religious contexts, it might be most useful to distinguish two broad forms of gifts. One is given directly to the spirit world, most frequently in the form of paper objects or "spirit money," which people transfer to the invisible realm by burning (see Figure 5.1). Even incense might be considered in this category. Such gifts occur primarily in popular religious practice and Daoism. The temple may profit by selling those objects to people, but that is merely a commercial transaction; the gift is from the worshipper to the invisible world. Like other forms of Chinese gifts (as Yan in particular discusses), this one creates hierarchy as well as community, with the donor in the inferior position – often literally as he or she kneels in front of an altar or grave.[4]

The other form of donation goes directly to the church, temple, or mosque, and occurs across all traditions. Religious institutions in Chinese societies have historically relied on three broad sources of funding: rent from landholdings (which generally began as gifts from wealthy patrons), direct gifts

[4] Wagner, "Fate's Gift Economy"; Yan, *The Flow of Gifts*.

Figure 5.1 Spirit money for sale, Nanjing, 2014.

of cash (which could vary from a few anonymous coins in a collection box to huge donations where the donor's name is inscribed in stone), and something like religious taxation (in which the temple demands a payment from each household at certain times of year, or the church expects the equivalent of a tithe). We will return to this in the following chapter, but it is worth noting here that the land reforms and political changes of the twentieth century greatly weakened two of these mechanisms. Beginning in the Republican period and continuing through today, those wealthy temples, mosques, and churches that gained significant income from rent lost control of all their land except for the site of worship itself (which was often greatly reduced). They also lost the ability to compel people to pay annual fees. The overwhelming importance of the voluntary gift in religious finance is thus primarily a twentieth-century development, needed to replace lost income from rent and compulsory fee collection.

While some of these donations are earmarked for particular projects – often construction – many more are simply given with the confidence that religious leaders will make the best use of the money. Even in the absence of such confidence, a gift might still be made in the knowledge that the deities know a good deed has been performed, even though the humans involved may be less than upright. Such gifts refer to what we have called in the previous chapter the "karmic" discourse of charity. In all of our contemporary cases, uses of that money often include some form of philanthropy, as well as providing other forms of "goodness" such as spiritual protection.

Giving in these mediated ways can help build institutions, from temples to secular philanthropies. It also builds treasuries of social capital that allow people to trust that having given also gives them the right to receive gifts – from divine interventions to philanthropic aid should they ever need it. The aspect of human emotional connection (人情) between donor and recipient, which Yan, Yang, and Kipnis all emphasized in their books on the creation of social relationships, is thus less important here than ties to deities, or prestige-creating ties to important temples.

The Qualities and Limits of Social Capital

In the classic anthropological portrait of how gift-based reciprocity creates social relations, givers do not expect compensation or even the return of an identical gift – that would simply balance the books. There would be no lasting social tie because there is no debt. The return of a different gift, however, does create such ties. If you give someone chocolate and she gives you a scarf, the books are not balanced. Instead, both people owe each other and a social relationship has been created. If I buy the drinks today, you will buy them next time. If I buy them every single time, however, the relationship takes on a more hierarchical quality.

More communitarian versions of social capital have tended to emphasize how such ties can create horizontally integrated communities characterized by interlocking ties of trust and exchange.[5] Anthropologists, however, have grown increasingly uncomfortable with the imagination of a unified and egalitarian community, and recognize that strong community ties tend also to reinforce community inequalities of gender, age, and wealth, among others. Perhaps most influentially, Pierre Bourdieu greatly complicated this image by showing how gifts could be used strategically to advance particular interests within the community.[6] The timing of a return gift, he pointed out, carries all kinds of implications beyond simple reciprocity and trust. Even the early works of Mauss and Malinowski recognized the importance of vertical ties in the gift economy.[7]

This is true for the specialized gift economy of religious philanthropy as well, as we will describe. Carving a donor's name onto a stone stele in front of a temple, or onto its walls, creates and reinforces an obvious hierarchy of prestige. Gifts to gods, even anonymous ones, also establish hierarchy between deity and supplicant. The forms of social capital that religion produces can

[5] This tradition goes back to Tocqueville, *Democracy in America*. More recently, it has been popularized by works like Putnam, *Making Democracy Work*.

[6] Pierre Bourdieu, *Outline of a Theory of Practice*.

[7] Mauss, *The Gift*; Malinowski, *Argonauts of the Western Pacific*.

certainly include an important aspect of horizontal community. Yet as we shall see in the following chapter, the vertical aspect – the power of the deity, the charisma of a leader, the clout of a wealthy patron – remains central. In particular, our focus on religion leads us to look especially at charismatic ties, which always have a vertical character. Given our attention to the possibilities of innovation in engaged religion, charisma seems like a logical place to look, because the charismatic leader's direct inspiration makes it possible to challenge received authority.

In addition to distinguishing between the horizontal and vertical ties that religious gifting and social capital create, we have also found it useful to distinguish between different qualities of ties that can be created, especially whether such ties can be considered strong or weak. Here we have been inspired by the early work of Mark Granovetter, who suggested that strong ties characterize tightly knit groups of people in cliques.[8] Bonds of this type can be very useful in fostering group solidarity and collective action, but Granovetter also suggested that they might limit potential innovation. The ties that connect individuals to people in other cliques may be much weaker, but they can also form bridges between groups and thus become pathways for new ideas to flow. He refers to this effect as the "strength of weak ties."[9] Granovetter's own case was built on evidence that people who succeeded in the American job market tended to be able to invoke weak ties that cross-cut various networks of stronger ties.

Yanjie Bian, who has pursued some of these ideas in the Chinese context, pointed out in a book review that Yunxiang Yan's and Mayfair Yang's books on social connections actually illustrate this difference.[10] Yan's village study shows how gifts create tight, densely knit ties of community, while Yang's more urban study involves looser, more disconnected ties that create ego-centered networks. At least in these two studies, the village ties appear to be stronger and the urban ones weaker.

For our purposes, Granovetter's idea suggests the interesting possibility that innovation may be most difficult in tightly knit groups united through ties of reciprocity and trust – exactly the kinds of groups most emphasized by the concept of social capital – and may instead occur more often when those very ties of social capital can be challenged or superseded. The idea of the strength of weak ties points us toward the innovative potential of breaking out of close-knit groups by combining the resources of different kinds of social capital, or by reworking the social structures that stand behind social capital. The material

[8] Granovetter, "The Strength of Weak Ties."

[9] Note that there is some connection here to Putnam's suggestion of a distinction between bridging and bonding social capital, although he does not cite Granovetter. See Putnam, *Bowling Alone*, 23–24.

[10] Bian, "Review of *The Flow of Gifts*, by Yunxiang Yan," 475.

we will discuss in this chapter and the next reinforces the idea that weak ties may be just as crucial as strong ties in the operation of religious philanthropy, and may indeed be more conducive to innovation, as Granovetter suggested.

This discussion indicates some of the limitations as well as the strengths in the kinds of social communities created through gifts. Alejandro Portes had already pointed to a number of these in his important review article on social capital.[11] For example, increasing social solidarity and trust does not always work in the broader social interest: gangsters depend on social capital as much as church groups do, and corruption requires thick ties of trust as much as the extension of credit in the market does. Social capital may thus work in ways that are inherently unfair, and sometimes not even civil.

Portes points out that one of the implications of strong ties is that people find it very difficult to break out of the tight communities they create, in addition to the ways such ties can make it difficult to deal civilly with people outside the group. He is thinking particularly of the limitations strong ties can create for social mobility, but we can extend the insight to apply more generally to the issue of innovation. The point in either case is that such tightly knit systems tend to establish and reproduce a status quo, making fundamental change difficult.

Our findings suggest that social networks created and supported at least in part through the gift economy are in fact vital in building some forms of community and supporting certain kinds of engaged religion. Yet those same ties have also tended to limit innovation and to reinforce a status quo that includes unequal power and status as much as ties of trust and reciprocity. In this chapter we will be looking at these dynamics. In most cases, these processes are clearest in religious institutions that have the strongest continuities with past practices. We can thus see it especially clearly in the Lukang and Malacca cases that we will discuss, but ties of local social capital and community temples are again becoming important in parts of the Chinese mainland as well. We will turn in the following chapter to "weak" ties and the mechanisms of innovation.

Local Temples and Social Capital

"Social capital" – in the sense of networks that connect people through multistranded ties of reciprocity and trust – has long characterized many temples across Chinese societies. Most Chinese temple worship has little large-scale institutional life. Its social organization is almost entirely local, based in villages and towns, with temples run by local committees. Such temples will

[11] Portes, "Social Capital."

hire outside priests (Buddhists, Daoists, and similar specialists) as needed to conduct their rituals, but these are simply contracted employees, not temple leaders or managers. In areas where temple worship is strong, temple leadership often interlocks with other forms of local leadership and temples integrate tightly with their communities. Local elite men typically lead temples; they include political leaders, the wealthy, and often retired school principals and teachers. This is part of the vertical aspect of such social capital.

As an example, the leaders of the main temple in the township of Sanhsia, Taiwan, for more than three decades after the end of Japanese rule were a handful of local elite men. The most important were a doctor and an artist who had earned higher degrees in Japan – two of the only fields in which Taiwanese were allowed to pursue post–high school education during the colonial period. The artist Li Meishu became particularly important as the leader of the massive temple reconstruction project that lasted for forty years. He had also served briefly as acting township head at the very end of the colonial period, and held various other political posts, including representing the town in the County Assembly. Both he and the physician were among the most respected members of the community in the 1960s and 1970s. In addition, Li Meishu's son-in-law, a retired school principal, did much day-to-day temple management. The temple provided a base for one of the township's two political factions (locally called the "temple faction"), further confirming its importance as a node for local social capital.[12]

When one of us asked one of these old leaders in 1978 why he devoted so much energy and money to the temple, he replied that deities embody positive moral messages, including a sense of loyalty to the community.[13] Nearly everyone else in town, however, said it was because he credited the god with having saved his son's life during World War II. These answers are not at all inconsistent; each one is just incomplete. That is, the gifts of time and money from the leadership went to the temple directly, but the crucial intermediary was the god himself; these gifts helped balance the karmic books. At the same time, they solidified the community by creating an economic engine, a symbolic center, and a node of political power. The process of temple reconstruction that these men led also meant constantly soliciting a stream of gifts from the people, well beyond what was needed for the maintenance and ritual function of any temple. While none of this was used for "philanthropy" in the usual senses of the term, everyone saw it as creating a crucial kind of goodness that included both the social organization centered on the temple and the cosmic protection provided by the god.

[12] Weller, *Unities and Diversities in Chinese Religion*.

[13] This took place in 1978. That generation of leaders has now passed away.

Far away in China's northwest, we can see something similar in Adam Chau's ethnography of the Temple of the Black Dragon King, whose leader was an ex-cadre, school teacher, and entrepreneur.[14] His experience, connections, and flair had been crucial in allowing the temple to flourish. He had also built a local school, which was a way for him to accrue political merit and strengthen local support. As both this case and the Sanhsia temple suggest, political merit-making of the kind we discussed in previous chapters can intertwine with local social capital. Indeed, one of the main political benefits local temples like this can offer is local support built on the thick social ties of the temple leaders.

Yongning Temple and Wuling Temple in southern Jiangsu Province again illustrate the kinds of strong ties that religion can create, the way those ties tend to be limited in geographic extent, and the role of vertical connections as well as horizontal ones. Both began as village temples, though now both sit in the middle of suburban industrial zones as a result of the expansion of nearby cities. Both have become Buddhist sites that adhere to the teachings of Master Jingkong [Chin Kong] – a monk from Taiwan who has been enormously influential among lay Buddhists in China, though with very little formal institutional structure. Both temples have female lay leaders who had close ties with the local government, just as we saw in the Temple of the Black Dragon King. Both also operate old age homes offering services to older people who used to live in the neighboring villages and towns, which are disappearing fast. Though the two temples have moved toward Buddhism because of the influence of Jingkong's teachings, their ties with Master Jingkong were actually mostly only through his books, tapes, and videos. Lay Buddhist volunteers – primarily women from the former surrounding villages (now urbanized), towns, and city neighborhoods – run most of their daily operations. In both temples, local social capital is very important. Without the extended social networks of each lay leader, the temples' obtaining of licenses, construction, and sources of funding would have been impossible.

One of the temple leaders was a former village doctor and women's affairs cadre. She depended on her former ties with government officials to obtain protection for the autonomy of the temple, used her entrepreneur son's business ties with other entrepreneurs to secure funding for the temple construction, and relied on her socialist cadre skills to mobilize and manage the lay believers who had mostly gone through a socialist education. Exactly because she relied so heavily on local social capital, the temple's influence is almost exclusively local, with only occasional visitors from other temples in the region (such as Jiangsu and Anhui Provinces) through their shared connections to

[14] Chau, *Miraculous Response*, 2005.

Master Jingkong's teachings. The old age home they operate also caters mostly to local residents.

The organizational base for temples like these is almost always exclusively local. Sometimes the gods on their altars are known across the Chinese world, but even then we do not see a significant national or international organization. Many other deities are not known at all beyond their local areas. Small numbers of temples may connect in networks, sometimes when there has been a historical alliance between two communities, and more often when one temple has branched off from another. No independent social institution holds such networks together, however, and they exist socially primarily only when renewed through occasional pilgrimages.

Even the Mazu cult, which extends from China's southeast coast to Taiwan and many overseas communities, has no effective larger organization, although it has evolved into the most important religious connection on Taiwan. Temple worship thus intertwines deeply with local ties of social capital, but has little institutional presence on a larger scale. This effect was made stronger by its lack of legal recognition as a religion in Taiwan until after democratization and still today in the People's Republic.

As we will discuss, religion at this level was often socially engaged in charity, but its goals were almost entirely parochial – designed to benefit the local neighborhood or other local social groups defined by the temple. As we saw in Chapter 2, not all late imperial charity was this inward-looking. Some of the benevolent halls of the period, for example, had cross-provincial operations. Lukang still preserves a famous "half-well," which also suggests a more generous vision of charity. This is a well that was built for an elite family's house, which was surrounded by a wall that cut directly across the middle of the well – this charitable act gave anyone access to the water, even total strangers. Nevertheless, this kind of more universal commitment was never the most common pattern (and even the half-well in practice would have served only local people), and it declined greatly over the twentieth century, especially during the war years and beyond. Neither Taiwan nor the mainland had many such activities from the 1950s until late in the twentieth century.

The examples of local temples that we have been giving show a pattern of parochial ties to social capital that has long been described in the ethnographic literature, though usually with little attention to charity. Urban neighborhood temples are considerably more unusual in mainland China – after the great disruptions of religion during the first decades of communist rule, and with the enormous transformations of urban neighborhoods through migration and urban renewal, most urban temples there now have less clear ties to these forms of neighborhood-based social capital; they have been replaced in part by extremely large religious sites (involving all of the five recognized religions) that attract thousands of worshippers on important occasions, but with few neighborhood ties.

Such urban temples in China construct networks that are based more in ties to unrelated individuals than to local communities. Rather than the multistranded ties of the more rural pattern or older urban neighborhood pattern as seen more clearly in Lukang and Malacca, these dyadic ties usually involve only religion and connect leading clergy directly to individual followers. Obviously, some of the most important such ties are between religious and local political leaders, as we have discussed. It is thus not at all unusual in contemporary southern Jiangsu for the mayors of major cities to offer the first stick of incense at important Buddhist temples at midnight as the Chinese New Year begins. The other crucial ties are to entrepreneurs who have been willing to make very large donations to such temples in recent years. Even ordinary followers, however, tend to have only their ties to the temple in common. Unlike the rural temples we just mentioned, multistranded ties of reciprocity do not connect their communities.

The main exceptions are some Christians, especially in the small house churches that regularly bring people together and form a sense of tight community quite different from what can be found in urban Buddhist and Daoist temples. As with more traditional temples, Christian congregations in China – especially small, house-based groups – develop multistranded ties among members that are often mobilized for purposes that go beyond religion proper, such as mutual aid. We will return to these groups at the end of the chapter, although it is worth noting that much official Christianity in urban China now also takes place in mega-churches with few neighborhood ties to unite congregants.

Lukang's Temples

Let us return to Lukang as an example of how religion, gifts, and social capital intertwine, and what this means for engaged religious activities. Temple religion in Taiwan has been tremendously active, having enjoyed a wide resurgence as the island grew wealthy in the 1970s and beyond. Even in comparison with other Taiwanese communities of comparable size, however, Lukang's temple life has a reputation for being extraordinarily active and elaborated. The small township was home to ninety-five active temples in 1995.[15] Of these, about half a dozen attract worshippers from the township as a whole, while the rest are based in neighborhoods. Even those local temples, however, are quite large and elaborate in comparison to other towns of comparable size. In

[15] This is based on an unpublished and uncirculated list collected by the township government. It does not include all the very small shrines, like most of those for ghosts or earth gods.

the more urban part of the township, most neighborhoods had originally been dominated by one surname and each had one temple. The temples were crucial reservoirs of social capital for leaders at that local scale, and the pattern largely continues today.

One reason why Lukang has preserved these structures relatively intact is that the town was left behind by much of Taiwan's economic growth for roughly a century. Lukang had been one of the three major port cities of Taiwan in the mid-nineteenth century, but the gradual silting up of Lukang's harbor that began at the end of the century caused serious economic stagnation. Matters became worse when the railroad bypassed the township. Perhaps it is no wonder that it looks back so fondly on its past history. The advantage, however, is that a weak economy led to the preservation of much of the town, both architecturally and socially. Tourism and the closely linked religious economy – primarily owing to the fame of the Tianhou Temple – have now breathed new life into the town.

We can begin to see the intertwining of social capital, charity, and religion first by looking back at how some earlier social institutions survived these changes. We have already mentioned the various merchant associations, all organized as god-worshipping societies, which were so important in the nineteenth century. The town's economic decline badly undermined both the purpose and the economic base of these associations in the early twentieth century. The Quanzhou Association, however, continues to thrive because it owned enough land that rental income allowed the group to survive. Their original business function ended completely in 1937, when Japan's war with China ended trade with Quanzhou. The next year they registered with the Japanese government as an "association for the benefit of the neighborhood" (善邻会) as a way of continuing some charitable activity.

In practice, they had become a corporate group of fourteen surviving shareholders benefitting from their communal income and using some of it for charity. The current group consists of the descendants of those fourteen families. The corporate property enabled them to function as a pure god worshipping society focused around the altar created by the original founders of the group. They registered again with the new GMD government in 1948, returning to their old name as the Quanzhou Merchants Association. They first experimented with new forms of charity the next year, when they opened a small clinic with a nurse in the front of their old association hall. As one of the current directors explained it, however, managing the clinic eventually became more than they could handle, and they gave it up after a couple of decades. It had deteriorated to a drugstore in the 1960s.[16] In

[16] DeGlopper, *Lukang*, 165.

1976 they reincorporated under yet another new name, as the Quanzhou Merchants Association for Benevolent Love (泉郊仁爱之家); they dropped Benevolent Love in 1984 in favor of Compassionate Good Association (慈善会). As the legal framework evolved, they finally incorporated as a foundation in 1986. The name kept evolving, but the strong ties of social capital behind it remained constant.

In part, their activities reflected the value of real estate in Lukang – the recent tourist boom has greatly increased their rental income. In part, it shows an experiment with a broader idea of charity in the 1950s, which they ultimately could not manage. Their current activities do not look so very different from what they did in the nineteenth century, but with the business functions removed: they help the poor and give emergency relief (in cooperation with the township government), and they contribute to important temple festivals. The group continues primarily as a tightly knit network of wealthy men, quite visible in the community and doing some charity on the side. God associations continue today mostly on a small and informal scale, either for historical reasons (like the Quanzhou Merchants Association) or for small and relatively informal groups like rotating credit associations.

At a very different scale, Tianhou Temple – the same one that had accepted the Mazu image from Admiral Shi Lang in the seventeenth century – has become one of the half dozen most important temples in Taiwan. Its leaders are all powerful men – only the powerful can be chosen to lead such a temple, and leading Tianhou Temple itself conveys power. Just as an example, one of the temple committee members became wealthy running a well-known fabric store in Taipei. His father had been on the temple committee before him, and it is also typical that a few important families dominate – hierarchy and social capital intertwine.

The temple is the most important economic engine in the town, and one of the most important in the entire county, attracting enormous donations and probably hundreds of thousands of visitors each year. There is a constant stream of visiting deities and their followers, with each group paying its respects (often through performances by the visiting gods themselves via the bodies of their possessed followers) in the front courtyard before entering the temple.

The scale of social capital such an institution can mobilize becomes tangible during large festivals, especially in the days around Mazu's birthday when tens of thousands of people visit the temple each day. Even small rural temples can celebrate their festivals with massive parades in which the gods are brought out of their temples to tour their territories (绕境). Staging these events at such small rural temples may involve hundreds of people, including sedan chair bearers to carry the images of gods, performers of lion dances and a vast array of other folk performance genres, costumed people to accompany the god, and Western and Chinese musical groups as well as more people to secure the route.

At a really important temple like the Tianhou Temple in Lukang, the scale is far greater. A group from the temple had gone on a pilgrimage to the mother temple in Meizhou in 2006. They returned one hot summer evening in a huge parade. It included hundreds of pilgrims returning from the mainland, 108 middle-aged women dressed as the arhats of the Buddha, performing groups from neighboring temples, dozens of children dressed as Ming Dynasty soldiers, the mayor, and many more, plus the thousands who lined the parade route. In a town of just 20,000 people, it showed the tremendous ability of the temple to mobilize people. In some cases, groups practiced all year for occasions like this. None of this is directly philanthropic, but it does show how deeply embedded temples are in the thick ties of local social life, and how effectively they can mobilize those ties. We can clearly see the power of social capital in events like this. No other temple in Lukang can do anything on this scale, but all of the town's "neighborhood temples" (Hoklo: *khak-thau biou* 角头庙) feature smaller versions of similar events.

Religious activity has thus long intertwined with the broader processes of social capital in Taiwan (as in other Chinese societies), and the present situation is not so different from the case of Lukang in the nineteenth century. Not everything about this process is positive: strong social capital opens up possibilities for abuse as well as benefit. We can see this, for example, in the rampant rumors about the powerful Tianhou Temple. When one of us interviewed the head of the Civil Affairs section of the township government about charitable activities of temples, he mentioned that Tianhou Temple had purchased 6,000 *ping* (just under 5 acres) of land to build an old age home. The government approved the purchase, but unfortunately, he told me, internal disputes among the temple leaders had stalled the project. A later informant, however, scoffed at this story. He insisted that the temple had never intended to build an old age home, but that it was just an excuse to get the government to allow its land purchase. Yet another informant said they had discovered that the land was actually not registered in the temple's name, but rather as the personal property of the previous head of the temple committee. These implications of corruption may be untrue – we made no attempt to investigate further – but they do indicate a widespread suspicion of an old boy network tending to its own. Such complaints also occur around some other important Taiwanese temples.

Looking at Lukang's neighborhood temples makes it easier to trace networks of social capital than for Tianhou Temple, which was reticent about disclosing its details. Taiwanese sometimes characterize their business practices by saying that "it's better to be a chicken's beak than a cow's rear end." This logic that people would prefer to be the boss of something tiny than a drone in something huge works just as well for the world of social organizations (including temples), at least in Lukang. The mayor at one point joked to one of us that whenever she forgets someone's name, she just calls them "director" (会长), because everyone important is the boss of some group. It never fails, she said.

This first became clear during a serendipitous interview with a man who ran a handsomely reconstructed old elite house as a tourist site. Built in the late Qing dynasty, it was home to one of the last *jinshi* (进士, the most advanced degree in the imperial civil examination system) degree-holders in Lukang. The façade facing the main business street had been rebuilt during the Japanese period when the Japanese widened the street, but the rest of the architecture dated back to the nineteenth century. It had housed dozens of members of the family early in the twentieth century, but with the town's economic decline, they gradually abandoned it. The building was badly damaged during Taiwan's huge earthquake on September 21, 1999, but this is what eventually saved it. Because the government had already recognized the historical significance of the house, they gave TWD 30 million (roughly 1 million USD) to rebuild it. Mr. Ding Zhenxiang, a descendant of the original owner, oversaw the reconstruction, and turned the site into a tourist attraction that included a coffee shop at the front, a small museum in the center, and some small traditional shops (such as a fortune teller) at the back.

In addition to taking care of the rebuilt house, Ding had been a director of one of Lukang's four Kiwanis Clubs, which had a typical range of charitable activities, such as a blood drive and emergency relief for local families. At the same time, he was an official in one of the neighborhood temples. He was chosen every year as either the incense pot master or another leading post in the temple. "I don't actually burn incense there," he added, "although my wife sometimes does. I sort of half believe and half doubt. But you just have to do things like this to meet your responsibilities to the community."[17] In addition, he pointed out that these leadership positions, including the secular ones, come with the expectation of making significant donations.

A leader of a larger temple elaborated further on how one becomes a member of the temple committee. Many temples in Taiwan have moved away from the traditional system in which people put their names forward and are then chosen by the god through divination. Now there are official lists of "believers" (a status usually achieved by paying a fee to the temple, another form of gift) who vote for the leaders. When asked how one gets elected, this man said, "It's easy! It's guaranteed! Because it's all based in local communities, sometimes it's enough just to get all your relatives to vote for you. Or you can just buy the votes." These are, of course, exactly the techniques of local politicians; even

[17] Interview of July 9, 2006.

vote buying is usually phrased as gift. As another informant said when asked how he was continually elected to such leadership roles under both the divination and election systems, "We had our ways under the old system, and we have our ways under the new system too."

This pattern of interlocking local leadership positions recurred frequently. A presbyter of the local church was a founding member of the earliest modern, secular medical philanthropy group in Lukang, the Zhicheng Charitable Society (至诚慈善会), and helped found one of the two Junior Chamber of Commerce branches in the town. As another example, a former director of the Zhongyi Charitable Society had also been the director of the Zhicheng Charitable Society, chair of one of the three local Lions Clubs, an elected neighborhood head (里长), and committee chair of both the Xinzu Gong and Nanjing Gong neighborhood temples.

This evidence suggests that while specific organizational forms have changed significantly since the Qing Dynasty, we see a great reintegration of religious leadership into broader forms of social capital over the past few decades. Local business and political leaders recognize and act on the principle that they need to appear across the range of community activities, creating enormous overlaps among temple committee membership, philanthropic nongovernmental organization (NGO) leadership, business club membership, and sometimes political office. In the late Qing, we saw this primarily through god associations, merchant associations, and temple leadership by serving as "incense pot master" for a year. All of these forms have been largely replaced by the late twentieth century, with even temples taking on democratic and NGO characteristics with boards of directors elected by the community of "believers." In spite of these modern, legally empowered forms, however, the general principle that religious and secular leaderships overlap to form a web of community-based social capital has not changed, and neither have the gifts of time and money that help to cement and create those webs.

The model of charity based in this sort of social capital is generally particularistic and ad hoc. Help in the late Qing tended to go only to people within the network of the god-worshipping association (including merchant associations), kinship association (again often structured as god worshipping groups in Lukang), or temple/neighborhood. It was usually not generalized to all the needy of the world, or even of the broader community. In the present, most of these groups in Lukang still provide charity only for their own neighborhoods (for temples) or members of their groups. Furthermore, it tends to be one-time aid when needed (a scholarship or an emergency food donation) rather than an ongoing commitment to changing lives.[18] This is a strictly local image of the

[18] Large cities on the mainland did have some groups with broader philanthropic goals in the nineteenth century, but this does not seem to have been the pattern in small towns like Lukang.

good, reinforced by the gifts and accumulated social capital of an established leadership.

The foundation that grew out of Ziji Dian Temple, for instance, devotes all its money to neighborhood improvement. It has published two volumes of old photographs of the area, was building an activity center during our fieldwork, and provided scholarships for young people in the neighborhood. Fengtian Gong, a neighborhood temple just across from the huge Tianhou Temple, also gives scholarships, but only to the children of registered believers. For instance, in 2004 they gave TWD 93,000 to thirty-one college students, and TWD 18,000 to high school students. Tianhou Temple also offers such scholarships, claiming to spend roughly TWD 1 million per term on the program, but again only for the children of registered believers.

When temples offer aid more broadly, they tend (rather like late imperial elites) to work through the government. Many temples thus give cash gifts to the poor at the Chinese New Year or to the elderly at the Chongyang festival in the ninth lunar month, but they often funnel the money through the township government. The reverse is also true – local neighborhood heads and the township government will approach temples with specific cases of families needing emergency relief.

In each of these cases, the leaders share some obvious characteristics – they are relatively wealthy, middle-aged or older, and almost always male.[19] This is especially true of temple committees, where we almost never see women taking management roles in temple activities. As we mentioned, the gods in much of China traditionally chose temple committees – that is, an essentially randomizing divination process selected among a potential pool made up, in principle, of the entire community. In practice, however, it is extremely rare to see a single woman (or young person, or poor person) on these committees. While the divination process itself is not subject to control, there is significant self-selection in who becomes a candidate. Women, the young, and the poor are almost always ruled out at this stage. Little has changed in practice even though most larger Taiwanese temples now elect their committees democratically. The same groups of middle-aged, wealthy men still run temples. It is worth noting that men also almost always run local churches, although the majority of members are women.

See Katz, "The Religious Life of a Renowned Shanghai Businessman and Philanthropist, Wang Yiting."

19 Not entirely always, however. The mayor of Lukang was a woman at the time of this research, and she was also active in many of these same social organizations, although apparently not temples. She explained that there was no other way to succeed in local politics. She was also helped, however, by the fact that her father had been a very popular mayor earlier. Older webs of social capital were still crucial.

That is, community leadership, very much including temple management in a place like Lukang, remains the province of a group of similar individuals, tied to each other and to their neighborhood. We can also see how limiting such ties can be for a community and for any kind of social innovation that might challenge the status quo. There is certainly engaged religion occurring through these mechanisms, but it has seen little innovation.

Cheng Hoon Teng and the Chinese Community in Malaysia

Lukang is by no means unusual in the ways that temples, gifts, and conservative hierarchies of social capital intertwine. In Malacca, for example, in spite of its very different political history from Lukang, we can see some important similarities. Cheng Hoon Teng, as we discussed in Chapters 2 and 3, has been a central node of social capital for the Chinese community since it housed the Kapitan under colonial rule. It was the colonial state's primary connection for indirect rule over the Chinese community. For centuries, Cheng Hoon Teng served as the political and cultural center of the Straits Chinese in Malacca.[20]

The temple has taken some nominal steps to move beyond its original forms of ethnic connections by responding in some ways to the government's recent multicultural campaign strategy of including different ethnic groups' communal festivals as national holidays.[21] Nevertheless, to this day, the temple continues to work primarily within the confines of its network of social capital. For instance, it offers services of paramount concern for Chinese migrants by providing a cemetery and spaces for ancestral altars. It serves primarily as a facilitator for social capital, sitting on its well-endowed land (the cemetery Bukit China and assets in the expensive downtown district). By being a hub, it provides a platform for various levels of engaged initiatives, such as the charity fund and the library organized by its nun, or the charitable tour organized by the sutra-chanting group that meets in the temple once a week. Both the nun's charity efforts and the old age homes the charitable tour visits are technically open to all ethnic groups. Nevertheless, in these activities the temple in practice sheds its multiethnic character and once again appears as a purely Chinese organization benefitting primarily the Chinese community.

The intertwining of leadership is as clear here as in Lukang. For instance, the Cheng Hoon Teng is the center for the Chinese New Year street fairs, which were initiated by the leading Chinese politician in Malacca, Datuk Gan. The

20 "A Brief History of the Cheng Hoon Teng, Melaka"; Soo, *Studies of the Chinese in Malaysia and Singapore*.

21 DeBernardi, *Rites of Belonging: Memory, Modernity, and Identity in a Malaysian Chinese Community*, 223.

very first street fair in 2004 would not have been possible without the collaboration between him and the temple. Its public face shows a full array of foreign and local groups, including veiled Muslim Malay girls, who frequent and enjoy the festive events of the Chinese New Year. Nevertheless, it remains closely tied to Chinese social capital, and largely involved in a very traditional set of activities; its multiethnic face is primarily superficial and intended to make political merit only.

A few elites dominate the temple management of the Cheng Hoon Teng. Its management board had long been known as the Four Great Managers, although they increased the number to six in 2008. The method of selection for the Great Managers has never been transparent. The only thing that is clear is that the board consists of Straits-born Chinese, who are Malay- and English-speaking, and who mostly operate separately from what Malaysians usually call the "Chinese social world" (*huashe*, 华社, literally, Chinese society or Chinese associations).

The historical foundation for *huashe* is the lively associative sphere consisting of hometown and surname associations mainly formed by and for the more recent wave of Chinese immigrants, those who arrived during the twentieth century. Politically, this Chinese social world supports a political party, the Malaysian Chinese Association (MCA), founded in 1949, and has been one of the three components for the ruling coalition, the National Front. The cultural glue for *huashe* has been Chinese language education (华教 or 华文教育). Chinese language education has been one of the most mobilizable issues for the Chinese social world to the extent that the former president of New Era College, a higher-learning institution founded and supported by Chinese, remarked that "*huajiao* (华教) is in many ways the 'religion' for Chinese Malaysians" – punning on the possibility that *jiao* could refer to either education or religion.

Such an important role of Chinese language in local politics draws an invisible line between the *huashe* world and the Straits Chinese or Peranakan, who are descendants of the Chinese immigrants between the fifteenth and seventeenth centuries and who control the Cheng Hoon Teng. While members of both groups are non-*bumiputera* Malaysians, the board of the temple continues to be viewed by local Chinese politicians and businessmen as operating separately from the political goals and social instruments of the broader Chinese world. In an indirect way, Cheng Hoon Teng does not argue with this perceived division from the majority Chinese social world, although the board would proclaim that the primary difference is because they are a religious rather than political organization. Perhaps as a result of this demarcated self-identity, Cheng Hoon Teng, at least from the perspective of its lay management, focuses on the social capital of the elite Straits Chinese in particular.

Christian Cases

Protestants in most of the Chinese world have a very different kind of relationship to local communities than the temples we have been discussing so far in this chapter. In contrast to those temples, churches are rarely the key nodes of social capital for a village or neighborhood (except in the small minority of Christian-dominated villages). In some cases, churches draw instead on people who may live scattered over a wider area, and who may not have had many preexisting ties that united them in networks of reciprocity. In others, they capitalize on existing social networks to create a new kind of tie. In either case, small churches in particular tend to become centers for new modes of social capital that are less based in neighborhood.

For example, in a study of a rural church in Anhui Province, Zhou Dian'en shows how it initially spread through the success of its charismatic healing.[22] This group achieved a rapid rate of growth by building on the social networks of their initial small core. When a church member had a friend with health problems, the person would be brought in and healed. After growing to several thousand members and increasing the size of their church building several times, however, the congregation eventually stopped growing. As Zhou analyzes it, people's personal networks were exhausted, and the departure of old members (through migration or sometimes simply lack of interest) reached equilibrium with new converts. The networks of social connections that allowed the church to grow were not identical to the village itself, and certainly not everyone in the networks joined the church. The result was a new nexus of social capital, not quite identical to anything that had existed before.

Some urban examples from China show similar patterns of systematic engagement, but primarily within the immediate community. The Kaile Church (恺乐堂) in Changzhou, for instance, has regularly paid visits to older members of the church when they get too old to participate in Sunday services, bringing them gifts on important occasions such as the Chongyang Festival (a traditional holiday for honoring the old), Christmas, and the Chinese New Year. In Suzhou, many churches are organized by neighborhoods, mostly because different missionaries were building churches in different parts of the city in the early twentieth century. This pattern was later sustained and even migrant workers after they arrive in Suzhou start identifying with their neighborhood churches.

One of the oldest churches in Suzhou, St. John's, has a clothing drive for the poor families in the congregation. The donors and the beneficiaries are mostly from the same neighborhood. Since Suzhou is relatively well to do and most people feel they might lose face if they take charity directly, the church

[22] Zhou, "Experiential Belief, Habitual Ritual and Social Capital."

receives clothing companies' donations of new clothes and the needy members of the church can "purchase" them at extremely low prices. The income is used for Sunday school and other church expenses. Of course, most residents of these neighborhoods are not Christians, but these patterns also create new, locally based forms of social capital that tie the Christian portion of the population together.

As another example, a Christian nursing home outside of Hangzhou was open to any Christian in the city and its neighboring towns. They were willing in principle to extend their services to non-Christians, they said, but they had limited capacity owing to financial constraints. Perhaps more importantly, considering that Christian donations had to cover all of their expenses, they also had to respond to the donors' requests to keep their charity within the church. The pastor we interviewed also cited "easier management" with people of the same faith as a reason to serve only the Christian community. Many of the communal activities in the nursing home center on religious rituals and practices. In this case, even though this nursing home is not bound in principle by one church or one neighborhood, its services are in fact limited to a locality and to its own people.

Lukang's Presbyterian Church has a much longer continuous history – about 120 years – but we can still see how its network of social capital pushed it to traditional patterns of charity very similar to what we see in temples. In 2006 their membership consisted of about 200 households, not counting a branch in the more rural part of the township. Perhaps 200 people attend on a typical Sunday, and maybe 300 on a holiday like Christmas. Like many churches, they also have special interest groups (for young people, old people, couples, women, children) to further strengthen ties within the congregation.

This church had actively instituted a large list of "engaged" activities. Until recently, however, these activities served almost exclusively to benefit the congregation itself. Just like most of the temples we have discussed, they had an idea of charity that did not extend beyond their lines of social capital. For instance, they started the first credit union in Lukang, back in the 1980s.[23] Most credit unions in Taiwan are church related, the director explained, because relationships of trust are so important. Each new member has to be introduced by an existing member. It is thus not surprising that the original membership was almost 90 percent Christian, and Christians still constitute more than half the members. In a distant echo of Weber's argument about trust, dentists, and churches, the church itself has created the bonds of trust that allow its more engaged side to function.[24] But those very bonds also kept its activities limited mostly to the small congregation itself until recently.

[23] Interview with Mr. Huang Zhenbin, Director of the Aizhu Credit Union, 12 July 2006.

[24] Weber, "The Protestant Sects and the Spirit of Capitalism."

The change to a different vision of charity for the Presbyterians and many other groups began to happen only around the turn of the twenty-first century. On the mainland, at much the same time, some churches have also broken out of this pattern to become active on a national scale; these recent changes are part of a much broader pattern across religions that we will take up in the following chapter.

Conclusion

All these examples point to a robust and long-lasting pattern in which a group of (usually) men constructs a complex, interlocking social network that is materialized in all kinds of local social institutions – temples and churches, NGOs, business associations and clubs, and sometimes political office. Note that donations of time and cash are critical parts of this process, and are expected from leaders in all these roles.[25] Social clout grows out of such people's ability to mobilize these institutions, whether to mount a parade to welcome pilgrims back home, to provide aid for the needy, or to mobilize votes. The engagement of religious institutions with broader social needs grows naturally from this kind of social capital, where locally important men act through a wide variety of social forms to solidify their own positions while also providing public goods for their communities.

This is, of course, not simply a communitarian world tied together through horizontal ties of reciprocity and mutual trust; as we have seen, it reinforces hierarchies of class, gender, and sometimes ethnicity. Such a completely horizontal world may not in fact exist anywhere. Nevertheless, we can see how these strong ties of social capital foster community engagement by these leaders, in addition to helping them secure their own status. Although many things have changed over the twentieth century in the three places we are examining – revolution, the end of colonialism, economic transformation, multiple regime changes – the patterns we have identified have managed to adjust to the changing times. Cheng Hoon Teng preserves and protects Straits Chinese ethnic identity in ways not so different from when it was founded 400 years ago. Lukang's temples provide both local aid and bases for local leaders much as they did during the Qing dynasty. To some extent and in some areas, Chinese mainland temples are again taking on these roles as well. Social capital, leadership, religion, and engagement with the community's social needs remain intertwined.

[25] "Gifts" many not always be the most appropriate designation in politics, where vote-buying is common. On the other hand, even those transfers of cash can sometimes work in more subtle and complex ways than simple bribes.

Note that this pattern is not entirely the same as the political merit-making we discussed in earlier chapters. We still see political merit-making, of course, as when these temples work with local officials to identify and help the deserving poor. Because local officials in Taiwan are democratically elected, however, they are overwhelmingly local people. That is, temples have close relations with the township government because both local and temple officials have long been part of the same interlocking ties of reciprocity and trust, rather than because they have to defend themselves by cooperating with the state. We can see this even in mainland China, where defensive merit-making is more common: successful local temple managers often have preexisting ties to local political leaders. In addition, these forms of social capital have lasted much longer than the current patterns of political merit-making. That is why we can trace families that continue to dominate local temples and civic organizations in Lukang back to degree-holders in the late Qing, as they constantly reinforce their connection through gifts of time and money.

As we suggested at the beginning of this chapter, however, recent decades have also brought significant innovations in forms of engaged religion. The patterns of social capital and associated gifting that we have been talking about here have been robust and relatively stable for a long period of time, and they have been effective at delivering some social goods to their local communities. They have not, however, been among the innovators creating any of the new charitable practices. This may not be surprising: the relevant leaders are more tied to maintaining the status quo than nearly anyone else in the community. While they have adjusted rapidly to changing economies and political organizations (like the constant reinvention of the Quanzhou Merchants Association, or the change to elected temple committees), they have had little to gain from breaking out of the patterns of very local engagement that tie them directly to their followers. Their mediated religious gifts cement their positions in local networks, but give them little interest in breaking out of those networks. In the following chapter we will explore some of the alternate visions of religious engagement that have emerged over the past several decades, and the ways they often bypass the older forms of social capital that we have described here.

6 Innovating Goodness

Previous chapters have addressed some of the reasons for the rapid pace of innovation and reshuffling of priorities in engaged religions over the past few decades. These include especially the opening of greater political space (though very differently in each of our field sites), which combined with increased state influence over philanthropy. At the same time we have seen the evolution of new ideas of cosmopolitan, globally oriented subjectivities, where even a villager with a cell phone could feel just as connected to the broader world as anyone in Shanghai or Paris.

Here we turn to the group dynamics of innovation. What processes have allowed groups to overcome the inertia of the strong ties of social capital (and its related forms of religious gift-giving and social engagement) that we discussed in the preceding chapter? How can religious groups challenge the status quo to develop new forms of mobilization and engagement? At the same time, we need to recall that successful innovations themselves construct new webs of social capital, which in turn tend to discourage further innovation.

Two changes will particularly concern us here. The first is the increasingly visible role of women, who have emerged as leaders of some of the most important organizations, and as core activists in many of them. Second, there is a redefinition of what counts as "the good," from the dominance (but not total monopoly) of older community-based forms of charity to a far stronger insistence that everyone deserves help equally, even utter strangers. This change ties directly to the processes of disembedding from earlier social structures that we have been discussing throughout. It is realized specifically here in a reworking of the nature of the gift, almost entirely downplaying its role in establishing the personal emotional ties (人情) that earlier authors had emphasized. Or perhaps it is more accurate to say that such gifts spread those emotional bonds so far that they are as thin as possible – tying the donor to the entire universe of potentially needy people rather than to any specific individuals or communities. They also work in important ways on the self, becoming visible signs of the generous and enlightened heart of the individual donor. Such discourse of changing the heart has become increasingly dominant across the religious spectrum.

The cases we will discuss accomplish these changes at the institutional level by combining different forms of social capital that might otherwise have had little interaction with each other, by increasing the scale of organization far beyond what we discussed in the previous chapter, or by using charismatic ties that make vertical instead of horizontal connections. The innovations in gender roles and the idea of the good itself have their origins in the strength of these weak ties.

One of the organizational innovations that we will address activates connections that had largely been dormant previously. This could include class, gender, or other ties of common interest, where people can be induced to act around shared issues by using informal networks that had never been put to such use before. The Buddhist group Tzu Chi offers one example of an association that mobilized mostly middle-class women in very new ways. Old forms of associative life can be used for new causes, and new forms of association can be created by inspiring people to see themselves as sharing common ties that they had not been aware of before.

Another innovative drive, as Granovetter's work suggests, comes from capitalizing on the weak ties that may link people in one strong network to those in another. The result can be new forms of social capital that can be mobilized for new kinds of purposes. This mechanism may be particularly important in urban areas whose social connections rarely match the strength of multistranded ties in rural areas. This process of forging new, more single-stranded kinds of ties is especially important in China (and to a lesser extent in Taiwan and Malaysia), where cities have experienced a large and rapid influx of new migrants over just the period we are talking about, along with a destruction of established urban neighborhoods through urban renewal. That is, this process is part of a general disembedding of people from older social forms.

One result that we will discuss is the creation of organizations on a scale much larger than is usually found in rural areas, and this alone helps to create new possibilities because such an increase in scale always involves a challenge to existing ties of social capital. Many large-scale organizations thus exhibit less of the kind of personal and local networking (mediated through temples), based on gifts of time and money, than what we saw in the previous chapter. Think, for example, of something like the International Red Cross or Doctors Without Borders, where someone might be a contributor, but the person's neighbors would be unlikely to know.

The religious groups we are discussing here, however, tend to function differently from that model. In many cases, they maintain or create smaller groupings (local congregations, for example) that continue to foster strong face-to-face ties even within their larger institutional structures. Both Christian and Buddhist versions of this model create local reservoirs of social capital that work differently from what existed before. The entire range – from Christian congregations that sprout up in Chinese villages to Tzu Chi branches in large cities – fosters new forms of social capital, networked in ways that no longer directly reflect local geographical communities.

At larger scales, religious groups may also involve charismatic relationships that allow adherents to feel directly tied to a leader they may never have met and that allow people to transcend many more purely local ties. This is a very different dynamic from long-lasting, gift-based networks, and shows how some vertical connections can still make innovative social contributions. Several of our examples show the particular power that an individual can exert to create new networks, often exactly because – like all charismatics – he or she stands in part outside of existing networks.

Connecting across different networks of multistranded, "strong" social ties can thus take several forms. Scaling up can sometimes accomplish this by uniting similar networks that are geographically separated, like pulling together local temples of different towns into a broader organization. In other cases, different kinds of networks of social connections might be brought together, as when wealthy Buddhist volunteers make regular visits to an old age home. Still others may activate dormant ties that are reinvigorated for a new purpose. Charismatic leaders can sometimes bring people together in ways that would not have happened otherwise. Each of these ways of constructing new ties, however, carries some tension with it because it challenges the status quo of existing social capital. Even if they can successfully overcome such problems, of course, they establish new networks of social capital, which in turn discourages further innovation. The cases that follow bring out the innovative potential in these processes, but also detail the problems that can develop.

The close ties between social capital, the power of communal leadership, and local temples have long been important in keeping religions socially engaged. Yet because these relationships rely on an effective status quo, they have not tended to lead the innovations that have characterized religious charity over the past few decades. We need to examine other kinds of social processes that explain the important changes in gender roles and in what counts as charity, as the "good" or the civil virtue to which religions urge us.

We will suggest that thinning out, transcending or transforming local social capital is exactly what has made the change possible. As something inherently tied to local social structures, including the structures of power and authority that communitarian thinkers sometimes downplay, the strong ties of local social capital limit some kinds of change, no matter how powerful they may be in some ways, as we have been discussing. In this chapter we will see instead the kind of strength of "weak" ties that Granovetter identified. To some extent such processes had always existed (for example, in the charismatic sectarian leaders who sometimes appeared), but the displacements and disembeddings of recent years, and the rapid mobility of both people and information that has accompanied them, have greatly enhanced the prospects for innovation.

Catalyzing Dormant Ties and Repurposing Networks

One way in which this occurs is when organizations can give new life and meaning to social ties that have lain dormant or that have never been used for a particular purpose. In this section we briefly examine a number of cases of this sort from all of our field sites. Beginning in the mid-1980s in Taiwan, for instance, a number of local temples mobilized followers to take part in environmental protection movements. Some temples had long been bases for political factions in ways that fit more traditional uses of social capital; they were part of broader networks used to capture votes. Under the one-party rule of the Guomindang (GMD) these factions always had patronage connections to higher levels of the state; all factions had strong ties to the GMD, even though they competed with each other for votes. Now, for the first time since the end of colonial rule, temples began to take part in civil action for goals that departed from the government agenda.

One of the first and most influential of these cases occurred in Lukang in 1986, when the community successfully fought off an attempt to construct a titanium dioxide plant there.[1] Temples continued to be active in environmental protection movements and in civil action generally throughout the period. For instance, one local temple in Kaohsiung effectively mobilized the neighborhood against construction of a naphtha cracker. Temple leaders were not especially enthusiastic about using the temple in this way – they were tied to the status quo just as we have described for Lukang.[2] Nevertheless, other religious leaders were able to repurpose the temple network.

A spirit medium played a crucial role as the protest reached a peak. A goddess possessed her on the night before a crucial referendum on whether to compromise with the construction project. The deity, speaking through the medium's body, denounced the naphtha cracker as a threat to people's health and livelihoods. Many people credited this event for turning the tide of the referendum against construction. Spirit mediums wield a power independent from temple committees because they speak directly with the voice of the god. We will discuss the role of charisma in a later section, but this is already an example of how charismatic power can create new possibilities by disrupting and redirecting social capital, in this case creating a new religious alliance that helped sway the vote the next day, and that existed beyond the social capital of the temple committee.

1 Reardon-Anderson, *Pollution, Politics, and Foreign Investment in Taiwan*, 17.
2 Weller, *Discovering Nature*.

We can sometimes see similar developments on the mainland as well. Jun Jing gives the example of some goddess temples that specialize in childbirth, which organized an environmental protest in Gansu, for instance.[3] As in the Kaohsiung case, spirit mediums were important. It is also significant that these mediums were women, in contrast to the historical pattern in that part of China. These environmental examples show how religion could serve as a reservoir of social ties that are suddenly put to an unprecedented use in organizing social protest. One could say that in both cases there was no activist community until a few leaders and spirit mediums were able to repurpose existing ties that had never been used this way before.

In many other cases, the religion itself is instead creating new possibilities out of nonreligious ties that had previously been dormant, which we can see from the example of the Buddhist Tzu Chi movement. We analyze the case of Tzu Chi in Malacca in some detail later in this chapter, because it shows all the processes we discuss here. For now, however, let us make some general observations about how the group organizes locally. Even though Tzu Chi is a global movement with millions of adherents, its primary method for interacting with followers is through local branches. The group appears to be about 70 percent women, more or less across all the branches we have visited in our field sites and well beyond. In addition, most branches attract women who are educated, relatively well off financially, and in many cases not working. They are quite clear about taking their understanding of proper domestic women's roles – nurturance and love – as core virtues, which can be spread beyond the family to the world at large. The bodhisattva ideal they espouse, of helping everyone in need to create a this-worldly Pure Land, takes this traditional female model but adds the radical Buddhist step of moving it out of the household into the world as a whole. It repackages family values as cosmopolitan values.

These cosmopolitan values include a broad effort toward rationalization of action and consistency across all aspects of life, a kind of post-Enlightenment humanistic universalism that extends to everyone equally, an insistence on the acceptance of respectable convention, and an embrace of the entire globe as their stage. We see these things not just in Tzu Chi's broad agenda of philanthropy but also in its members' everyday practice, as we discussed in Chapter 4: details of body posture like the admonitions to "sit like a bell" and to wear seatbelts; the uniformly practical, modern, and respectable dress (dark blue conservative dresses for commissioners, unisex white shirts and gray pants for volunteers); the ubiquitous smiles that greet everyone in all circumstances; and so on.[4]

[3] Jing, "Environmental Protests in Rural China."
[4] See also Huang and Weller, "Merit and Mothering."

The members of any branch quite likely knew only a few of the other members before. Many people's tales of becoming committed to the group are about individual experiences with Cheng Yen, especially through watching her on video. Networks are hardly irrelevant, but they tend to bring together small groups of friends or relatives who often had no previous connection with other such groups. At a large public meeting of the Nanjing branch in 2013, in which they were celebrating their accomplishments for the year, it was clear that several quite different networks were involved even in recruiting the core members. There were (as usual with this group) Taiwanese expats who knew each other because they (or more typically their husbands) worked in Nanjing. There was a group of Chinese medical doctors from a local hospital. There were kinship groups (for instance, a middle-aged man along with his wife and younger sister, both of whom were newly anointed commissioners). There were people who had initially become involved while college students, through the youth organization.

The earliest local volunteers in the Nanjing branch were recruited mostly in similar fashion, with a few coming in because of strong ties to a spouse or sibling, but never in large groups. Instead, small, incidental, weak ties crossed these mini-networks to bring new people in. For instance, the first physician to become involved was introduced to Tzu Chi by a Taiwanese patient; she eventually brought in a small group of medical colleagues.[5] In another case, a kindergarten teacher learned of the group through the parents of a student, and she later also brought in one of her aunts. We will not go on, but it is enough to note that none of these networks was very large, and in most cases the new intimate ties through Tzu Chi were more important than the ties that originally brought these people in. This was a mobilization of weak ties very much in the way that Granovetter suggests.

In part, Tzu Chi is able to build on dormant ties of class and gender, but we should also recall that the group actively promotes a view of the world with roots in particular cosmopolitan and gendered values. It is no coincidence that some of these same values – especially rationalization and universalization – fit precisely with the impulse coming from the all three governments we are talking about here as they try to "modernize" the philanthropic sector. This is especially clear for China, as we discussed in Chapter 3.

Christians provide a far more complex set of variations. In some cases in Mainland China, villages have been almost entirely Catholic for many centuries, or Protestant for over a century.[6] Church and local social capital in such cases tends to overlap, much as we described in the previous chapter.

5 These cases come from Zhong, *Contemporary Buddhist Philanthropic Organizations and Their Activities*, 52.

6 See Menegon, *Ancestors, Virgins, & Friars*; Harrison, *The Missionary's Curse*.

Nevertheless, much of the growth in Christianity on the mainland has been far more recent and tends to challenge rather than reinforce local social capital.

Sometimes the patterns are similar to what we have just discussed for Tzu Chi. As we mentioned in the preceding chapter, Zhou Dian'en's research in Anhui shows the spread of a kind of charismatic Protestantism through multiple rural networks.[7] As with Tzu Chi, we can see how recruitment in this congregation (and many others) indicates the kinds of dormant ties that are being mobilized. In his case the people involved are mostly middle-aged and older women. Nevertheless, the particular attraction of this group is quite different from Tzu Chi – it shows a desire for embodied experience rather than rationalized humanism, and an appeal to women as people who suffer more than as people who nurture. Both groups are mobilizing dormant ties, but the specific ties are quite different.

We can see a very different kind of Christian repurposing underway in the Chinese Catholic-affiliated Jinde Charities (进德基金会). Founded by a priest in 1997, Jinde resembles other national religious charitable groups in being registered as a purely civil association.[8] Even though Chinese law has made it very difficult for religious groups to run nongovernmental organizations (NGOs) directly, Jinde again resembles others in making the ties to the religion very clear on its website and in other media. They also engage in a typical range of activities for such groups: disaster relief, AIDS prevention, rural development and education, help for the elderly and disabled, and similar activities. Except for a few more directly religious activities such as help with rural church construction or provision of missals for poor Catholic communities, their range of activities looks very much like other large NGOs in China, including both purely secular and religious-affiliated groups (e.g., the Protestant Amity Foundation or the Buddhist Ren'ai Foundation). Their beneficiaries are not limited to only Catholics.

One of their most interesting characteristics, however, is the way they have repurposed the Catholic infrastructure toward these projects. The "backbone" of their activities, as Susan McCarthy describes it, consists of Catholic nuns.[9] These nuns are probably best known for fund-raising by taking part in the Beijing Marathon, which always attracts media coverage. They are also, however, the people actually running the old age homes, helping earthquake victims, and generally carrying out the activities of the organization. These are religious women whose calling has been reworked through the opportunity

[7] Zhou, "Experiential Belief, Habitual Ritual and Social Capital."

[8] Their original name was Beifang Jinde (北方进德). They changed their name in 2006, when they were able to register as an NGO for the first time. For details on this group, see McCarthy, "Serving Society, Repurposing the State."

[9] Ibid., 58.

of Jinde Charities. As one nun reported on the group's website after having volunteered to help people hurt in the 2008 Wenchuan earthquake, "I suddenly felt they were like the incarnation of Jesus, and that taking care of them would be like taking care of Jesus ... when I am with them, I am with Jesus."[10] She is describing a new combination for her, which brings together religious devotion and universal charity, and thus creates a new kind of experience.

Sometimes innovation can be achieved by repurposing an existing network through new kinds of knowledge and expertise. Suzhou's official Protestant organization, for example, launched a social enterprise project in Yunnan.[11] It was initiated by a group of lay Christians who work in high management positions in international firms. They decided that poverty relief in the traditional sense of money donation (which had been the practice until then) was not sustainable. They went on to build roads and subsidize sheep farming directly. After repeated visits at their own expense, they have finally concentrated on the growth and marketing of gastrodiae rhizome (天麻), a locally grown medicinal herb, as the main product for the social enterprise they would help the local farmers build. They insist that the farmers themselves must control the largest share in the enterprise, and provide small-credit loans to help them. The aim is to build a replicable model that can be used elsewhere to alleviate poverty and stimulate local economy. The leader of this group is a highly successful female business executive; she is also a devout Christian who had theological training overseas and donated all her wedding gifts to the church. One of her duties is to keep this social enterprise under the leadership of the church, although anyone, believer or not, can participate in this enterprise. In this case, Christians from outside the organizational core of the Protestant leadership were able to redirect resources to innovative programs; purely religious ties were catalyzed for secular philanthropic purposes. As in most of the cases we have been discussing, this one features innovation in both the greater role for women and in a more universalistic vision of what should count as the charitable good.

Connecting across Networks

We have been emphasizing the way some innovative religious activity works by repurposing or reinvigorating social ties that had previously been only latent or passive. As we have seen with Tzu Chi or some of the Christians, the new networks that result both build on and construct feelings of a shared community through gender, cosmopolitan aspirations, or other issues. In this section we emphasize an aspect of that process that we have already seen in the earlier

[10] Quoted in McCarthy, ibid., 61.

[11] This is the Two Committees – the Three Self Protestant Movement and the Christian Association.

examples: the way thin social ties (a doctor speaking to a patient in a hospital, a teacher meeting with parents of a pupil) can allow a group to jump from one mini-network to another, eventually constructing a new kind of group on a scale potentially much larger than any of the original networks.

Urbanization can encourage scaling up of ties by stitching together tiny networks, and thus helps break through more established forms of social capital. This process may be especially important in large cities with many new migrants, which has become typical in mainland China, Taiwan, and Malaysia over the past few decades. The kinds of multistranded ties that characterize small communities – where people are linked simultaneously through kinship, neighborhood, economic relations, and so on – do not transport well to cities. Earlier generations of urban migrants in Chinese regions often replaced those multistranded ties with new ones of common surname or place of origin associations, but those groups have in general not fared well recently. The dialect, surname, and native place ("clan") associations that were once very important in Malacca, for instance, have declined since independence. In the cities of the People's Republic of China, such groups were among the first targets to be attacked as cities were reorganized in the 1950s, and they have generally not recovered. Such disembedding of people from multistranded, place-based ties has created an opening for them to build innovative structures out of single-stranded ties, or by uniting across the weak ties that connect small groups.

There is no absolute difference between urban and rural in this, and the main cities of our study vary significantly in what kinds of ties exist. Lukang is the closest to an earlier pattern of local temples with strong neighborhood ties. This is unsurprising given that it is by far the smallest of the cities we examined, and also the one that was most bypassed by the economic and transportation changes of the twentieth century. This may also help explain why many larger-scale religious groups, from redemptive societies to Christians, report that Lukang has been a difficult place for them to develop – with less disembedding it has been more difficult for innovations to develop. In Malacca, on the other hand, the decline of the "clan" associations that had been so important in taking care of the social needs of the Chinese community coincided with the rise of new kinds of association that worked on much larger scales, such as the Malaysia Buddhist Association and the Young Buddhist Association of Malaysia.

In Jiangsu, older neighborhoods in established cities often had local temples, even in the 1950s, much as we have seen is still the case in Lukang. Yet these neighborhoods hardly exist any longer and neither do their temples. The privatization of housing after the 1980s greatly disrupted earlier residential patterns. The massive scale of continuous urban renewal in all of China's eastern cities has further scattered the old residents and broken up old neighborhoods.

Finally, the startling increase in migrants since the 1990s continues to transform those patterns.

A survey of "Buddhist" temples in Nanjing in 1951, for example, lists 298 different sites, only a few of which had a city-wide or larger influence.[12] While it has been possible to rebuild temples since the 1980s, almost none of those hundreds of neighborhood ones have come back to life. The same is true for mosques (serving Nanjing's historically important Hui community), where a pattern of neighborhood and occupation-based mosques has been replaced by just a handful of mosques intended to serve the city as a whole. The reason is not simply the political barriers to religion. It is also that the neighborhoods that supported these institutions no longer exist.

The weakening of a neighborhood base means that strong, multistranded ties, including the ties to religious institutions that we discussed in the preceding chapter, are increasingly unlikely in large urban contexts. The decline of kinship associations (they are no longer very important in any of the cities we studied) further encourages new kinds of ties. There are still networks of course, but the ties are more likely to be single stranded – colleagues at work, parents of children studying piano with the same teacher, and people who visit the same parks (although the people in the building next door may be utter strangers). For these reasons, social capital is thinner as well, making it more difficult to mobilize people but easier to break out of the status quo.

This mix has been favorable to innovations in engaged religion. The crucial step is to link across the thin ties that connect networks, combining them into something new. Scaling up an organization will always involve linking up with or forging new networks, and thus will challenge old forms of social capital. The large scale on which temples in major cities now build their base of support itself challenges old patterns of social capital. Urbanization is not the only factor that encourages scaling up, but it has been an important one in our cases.

At the same time, of course, larger-scale organizations must also tap into (and create) other fields of social capital. In the case of Malacca's Cheng Hoon Teng, for example, the core leadership remains closely tied to power-holders in the Straits Chinese community, even though the political and religious leadership functions have been formally split since the founding of the Chinese political party, the Malaysia Chinese Association. Tianhou Temple in Lukang similarly remains tied to powerful men in the larger community, as it always did. And we have already discussed at some length in Chapter 3 how reconstructed temples in Chinese cities must tie into local political power structures. The innovation occurs instead in the ways these temples interact with the broader community by mobilizing large numbers of people, controlling

[12] Yang, *Buddhist and Daoist Temples of Nanjing*, 550–558.

flows of information, and attracting large sums of money. These are, of course, the very features that make those temples attractive to the local state and other powerful actors.

Thus, for example, both Cheng Hoon Teng and Tianhou Temple attract throngs of visitors from far outside the political power base of their managers. In Malacca it allows the Chinese community to present itself as part of Malaysia's multiethnic state. In the case of Lukang, it is enough to alter the local economy significantly and to bring large amounts of money into the temple. The situation is even clearer for the large urban temples that have been rebuilt in China. The successful ones garner donations of all kinds, from a few coins dropped in the ubiquitous donation boxes to massive amounts of money given by devoted entrepreneurs. The constant stream of people means that weak ties (like a single visit in passing) always have the potential to bring new people into the network, who may in turn draw on their own micro-networks to further enhance the group.

As an example of the complex ways in which such a network can be constructed, we can look briefly at Qianyuan Guan (乾元观), one of several important temples on Maoshan (茅山) – a major Daoist center in southern Jiangsu with a very long history. When the local Religious Affairs Bureau decided to rebuild the temple, they finally settled on a relatively young Daoist nun, Yin Xinhui (尹信慧).[13] From a derelict site without even electricity or running water, the temple is now a complex of large, ornate buildings with several halls for worship and housing, a restaurant for visitors, a library, and more construction ongoing.

The government did not contribute any money at all toward the enormous expense involved, but it was crucial at the beginning in providing links between networks. For example, Yin said that the first really significant funding – 50,000 RMB (roughly 8,500 USD) – came as a loan from the largest mosque in Changzhou. This is hardly a standard form of funding for Daoists, but shows the way a politically required thin tie like monthly political study meetings for all local leaders of the five official religions can be turned into unexpected gain.

Major Buddhist temples, like their Daoist counterparts, stitch together large and scattered constituencies, sometimes with few ties to their immediate neighborhoods. Followers may not have any formally registered connection to Buddhism (making them difficult to count), but simply frequent certain temples, recite some sutras, attend lectures or watch television broadcasts of clergy, or perhaps take some Buddhist vows. Institutional ties do not engulf entire communities like temple worship does, but instead typically involve vertical ties of master and follower; people who come to a Buddhist event typically

[13] For more details on the reconstruction, see Johnson, "Two Sides of a Mountain."

do not represent a geographical community and often do not even know each other. They are a community only for the occasion – at most something more like a congregation than a neighborhood. Although the followers often include micro-networks with strong ties, in general only a single strand ties everyone at a Buddhist temple together – the tie to the temple itself.

A few cases in recent decades have been able to create vast Buddhist networks even outside the confines of temple institutions. We have already noted the striking success of Tzu Chi. As another example, the Pure Land monk Jingkong (Chin Kong), whom we mentioned in the previous chapter, has achieved broad global influence with no clear institutional base in a temple and without connections to the officially sanctioned Buddhist Association. His ideas have spread throughout China mostly through circulation of media, which one can find in almost any temple on tables where free religious literature is available. We have seen his books and DVDs in vegetarian restaurants, at major Daoist temples, and in Buddhist temples, even those where at least some of the clergy take a dim view of the movement. This was for a long time the liveliest and most innovative Buddhist movement in China, offering a populist version of Buddhism with little reliance on clergy and a strong commitment to social engagement based on individual devotion.[14] All of these new Buddhist movements organize people on an enormous scale where face-to-face ties become impossible. All also have a strong commitment to philanthropic work.

Christian churches may foster tighter, more multistranded connections in many cases, but they too are good at bridging networks. We can see this in fund raising, for example. The rural Anhui church studied by Zhou Dian'en raised money for its initial construction and later reconstruction on a larger scale by turning to older congregations in the surrounding regions.[15] These were not ties of denomination, nor were they politically mediated by the local religious affairs authorities. Instead they relied on the narrow bridge of personal contacts, usually of just one individual, to the other congregations.

In our own research area in Jiangsu, a very successful Xuzhou Protestant nursing home illustrates the same point. Founded by a retired pastor and lay members of Xuzhou churches, this nursing home was not part of a church. Ms. Wang, a senior volunteer explained:

> We started with 6,000 RMB of donations from Christian brothers and sisters. The churches refused to support us because they said that worship was more important than taking care of old people. So we sought funding from the Amity Foundation, who gave us 50,000 RMB, and the Social Service Department of the joint committee of the Chinese Christian Council and Three-Self Patriotic Association of Christianity. Later we connected with the United Christian Nethersole Community Health Service (UCN)

[14] See Sun, "Religious Dynamics in a Fragmented Authoritarian State."

[15] Zhou, "Experiential Belief, Habitual Ritual and Social Capital."

in Hong Kong through the Amity Foundation. They paid us a visit and donated medical appliances since most of our elderly need in-house medical assistance.

Here again we see the ability to scale up support by patching together thin ties to other networks. We can also see how innovation – Protestants donating money for a nursing home instead of directly for worship and church construction – required moving outside the usual sets of social connections from within existing churches.

Charismatic Connections

The literature on social capital sometimes downplays vertical connections, like patron–client ties, because they cannot create reciprocal trust in the same ways that horizontal and voluntary ties do.[16] Nevertheless, charisma-based ties to the center of very large religious organizations may have a thick aspect that evokes trust, even though they are vertical. Sometimes members of large-scale religious groups have very little contact at all with each other, but they often have direct contact with the leader, or at least the feeling of direct contact through videos, texts, circulating objects, and pilgrimages to a central headquarters.[17] Charisma can provide the powerful motivational force that we might otherwise expect only from the multistranded ties of local communities. This kind of vertical tie can be just as effective in mobilizing people as any horizontal tie. Charismatic ties differ from thick ties of local social capital by being removed from all the bounds of age, class, and gender that typify social relationships in small communities. That is, like the abilities to repurpose latent ties or to use weak ties to unite across networks that we have been discussing, charisma enables innovation.

Let us begin with an example from a rural field site in Handan (Hebei). Near the outskirts of Lin Family Village, a large temple complex rises layer by layer up a rocky hillside. The beginnings of the temple go back to the 1950s, when a young woman from Henan married into the Lin clan. The woman had extraordinary healing powers. Even though claims of such healing were discouraged during that period as "feudal superstition," and even though folk healers were often made targets of political campaigns during land reform and collectivization, a steady stream of people began coming to seek relief from psychological and physical distress through this woman's laying on of hands. They came from all around the area, not just from the Lin community. The tragic and chaotic experiences of the Great Leap Forward and the Cultural Revolution saw no slowing of the need for healing.

[16] For example, Putnam, *Making Democracy Work*.

[17] See, for instance, Weller and Huang, "Charisma in Motion."

The woman, so the story goes, did not accept payment for herself. Nevertheless, people who are healed by a god are supposed to give something in return to the healer and to the cosmic forces that made the healing possible. During the late 1950s and 1960s, people had few resources to pay their spiritual debts; they faced harsh political punishments for even trying. The repayment was thus more in the form of nonmaterial promises than actual material gifts. As the religious repression of the Cultural Revolution era lifted, however, the accumulated promises began to become actualized. Beneficiaries of the woman's spiritual healing began to contribute money and labor to build pavilions and temples to various deities scattered over the mountain.

The effort has escalated over the past twenty years and now the whole hillside is covered with temple pavilions, which are much more artfully constructed than any other buildings in the region. They enshrine large, ornately carved images of many different deities. Perhaps as befits its piecemeal construction, the temple is completely eclectic. It contains Buddhist bodhisattvas, Daoist immortals, deified local heroes, gods of heaven and earth, Guandi (the god of warfare and commerce, 关帝), the Nainai (grandmother, 奶奶) goddess who ensures the birth of both boys and girls, and the Eternal Mother (无生老母), whose promise to transform this world was once the basis for rebellions like the White Lotus. On auspicious dates in the lunar calendar, tens of thousands of people converge on the area for huge temple festivals. The temple is now building an adjacent guesthouse to accommodate some of the pilgrims.

The woman whose healing has inspired this outpouring of devotion is still alive as of this writing. She was eighty-two years old in 2009, when one of us visited. She still receives seekers, some of whom come from far away. At least one was an overseas Chinese woman who came all the way from Australia, after visiting famous shrines all over China looking in vain for relief from her psychological illness. Finally, she was steered to this out-of-the-way local temple in Lin Village. She spent an hour and a half with the healer and came out cured. In gratitude she has donated large sums of money to the temple.

While drawing on many elements of Chinese tradition – rituals of religious Daoism, shamanistic healing practices, a pantheon of popular deities, and festivals during auspicious dates on the lunar calendar – the temple does not simply reproduce "traditional" religious practices. For one thing, local deity temples were usually built and maintained by a village or small town and held the gods that protected the local community. This temple is instead supported by a wide, loose network of individuals, not related by kinship or residence, who come from near and far after hearing about its healing powers. Theirs is an individualistic devotion, a repaying of personal debts to the healer and the gods who support her. The gods themselves do not even form a community. The temple in the mountain is a collection of individual pavilions, added one by one over several decades (and continuing to be built), with different gods in each pavilion and no discernible order among them.

It is too much to expect the local government to actively support mystical faith healing and a burgeoning but somewhat incoherent mélange of shrines to traditional deities. Nonetheless, the old healer's temple could not exist without a modicum of official toleration. It turns out that the temple has been planting evergreen trees on the barren hillside surrounding it. These trees are said to play an important role in combating erosion. The local government has now designated the area an "ecological reserve" and encourages the temple to do more planting and fire protection. This is how even a place like this can gain political merit while still expanding its network of followers. The healer's temple is like a supermarket of deities, with something for every kind of devotion to meet the individual needs of every kind of seeker. It has created a following that reaches even beyond the borders of China in an idiosyncratic temple setting that shows the ability of a single charismatic individual to break the bonds of the ordinary.

Hanshan Temple in Suzhou provides a similar case of charismatic connections overriding horizontal community ties to support new philanthropic activities. The former abbot Master Xiangkong's personal charisma and good vertical relationships with government leaders allowed him to build the first grassroots religious institution in the region to get a "government project" – the Charitable Supermarket that we discussed earlier. The current abbot, Master Qiushuang, like many second-generation charismatic leaders, shared some of the charisma of Master Xingkong. He, too, wrote calligraphy, for instance, as a method of both self-cultivation and cultivation of vertical ties with followers. In 2014, Hanshan Temple organized an auction of calligraphy and paintings in Hehe Foundation's charitable fund-raising event. They began with a briefing in which Master Qiushuang and municipal government officials gave speeches on the connection between religious philanthropy and the slogan of the new Xi Jinping regime – "China Dream." Afterwards invited participants (mostly regular donors and entrepreneurs) were led to an upstairs exhibition hall. Not only was the abbot's own work offered for bidding; many local calligraphers and painters also exhibited their works under the urging of the abbot (see Figure 6.1). Several of them even came to the auction and wrote new works then and there. The participants could witness the artistic creation process and then take home the artwork. All the funds raised would go to the Hehe Foundation, the philanthropic branch of temple, which would distribute the funds to their various projects. One volunteer estimated that the Hehe Foundation raised a total of 400,000 RMB (roughly 66,000 USD at that time) during the one-day auction.

Many local entrepreneurs came to support the abbot's work. As one of us asked some entrepreneurs what they got at the auction, they happily

Figure 6.1 Charitable fundraising of the Suzhou Hehe Foundation. The banner reads: "Hehe Dream; China Dream; One Dream."

replied: "We are very lucky to have won the bidding for a piece of calligraphy by the abbot himself. It is very hard to get anything by him nowadays. And he is doing this solely for charity. We are very happy that we could support him and support the public good through him" (see Figure 6.2). Though Hanshan Temple was in many ways a "local" temple in the sense that it has been in the same neighborhood for hundreds of years, it is hardly a local temple anymore, not only because the local neighborhoods have gone through substantial changes but also because the temple does not depend on immediate local communities to raise money, nor does the temple offer charity to that community. Instead, major donations to the Hehe Foundation are often from entrepreneurs who are attracted to the new industrial parks in Suzhou. In this case, vertical ties to the charismatic religious leader were able to combine small networks of loose horizontal ties among small groups of entrepreneurs and other donors to foster innovations in philanthropy.

The True Jesus Church in Nanjing provides another kind of example. The True Jesus Church stems from an indigenous charismatic Christianity that spread widely in China during the 1920s and 1930s.[18] Its headquarters moved from Nanjing to Taiwan after the Revolution, and the church was founded again there only in 1993. Like the Handan healer's temple, the True Jesus Church is "engaged" only within the strict confines of its religious activities: the Handan

[18] See Lian, *Redeemed by Fire*, chapter 2; Bays, *A New History of Christianity in China*; Inouye, "Miraculous Mundane."

Figure 6.2 The abbot and one bidder standing in the auction hall. The large calligraphy to the left of the abbot is the Chinese character for "dream."

temple heals in a way not recognized by most health-oriented NGOs, and the True Jesus Church is "engaged" only with eternity. Yet both involved important structural innovations through charisma.

The key actor for Nanjing's True Jesus Church was Luo Xiaoxia (罗晓霞). Luo had been a Presbyterian for about a decade before she discovered the True Jesus Church. She organized a Presbyterian house church in the 1980s with about forty people who often attended. The Presbyterian group could be considered evangelical, with a strict theology based on Biblical inerrancy. At the same time, Luo was working and taking some classes at Nanjing's seminary. She traveled with about a dozen others in 1992 to see a True Jesus preacher in Fujian, where she had dramatic battles with demons (鬼), followed by her first experience of speaking in tongues. She soon was baptized in the True Jesus way, with total immersion in a river.

When she returned to her Presbyterian house church group in Nanjing, she faced a dilemma. On the first day she planned to preach her usual kind of thing about salvation. The small congregation was gathered in one room, and she was waiting in the next. As she told the story to one of us:

It was time for me to go out there, but there was no door in the room! No windows! People in the other room said "It's time, hurry up." I said, "I'm coming," but … no door, no windows! I knew there must be something wrong with me. It's not like other people couldn't leave the room; only me. So I got on my knees and prayed. I told God, "I know

I have done something wrong, but I don't know what it is and I really have to go preach now. Let me do that, and then I'll come back and fix whatever I did wrong. I'm willing to change, but I just have to go preach first." Then God told me I had to preach on *Acts*, chapter 2. And there was the door!

The problem was, she had no idea what *Acts* 2 actually said; she explained that she did not really know the Bible that well back then. She stood in front of the group, opened her Bible, and saw in the first few lines that it is the core charismatic text, which describes the Pentecost and speaking in tongues. She realized then that God had been forcing her to preach about the True Jesus Church, and so she described her experiences in Fujian and her new faith. The audience was completely rapt, she said, not like their usual wandering off to the bathroom or to get a drink of water while she preached. After half an hour, she said "I am a follower of the True Church. My house church is now a True Jesus church. If you want to come, then come." And in fact, she said, most of them joined her. In the more than two decades since then, the group has reported about 1,800 baptisms and they are centered in a downtown church that seats about 400 and fills up completely for their Saturday services.[19]

Luo's innovations, like the healer in Handan, are primarily institutional. She broke with the lines of trust that had previously supported her in the Presbyterian Church and the Protestant seminary. She created more than just a new church – it was a new kind of church (at least for her and her followers) that valued embodied experience as much as theology. This kind of innovation was possible only through her own charismatic leadership and her ability to transform most of her original congregation and then to bring in large numbers of other people.

The most obvious case of charisma in the world of Chinese engaged religions is of course Tzu Chi's founder and leader, Cheng Yen. The story of her charisma has been told elsewhere, so we will only note that we too have frequently seen it in action. Members of the group often tell stories of how they burst into uncontrollable tears when they see and hear her for the first time (even if only on video or audio cassettes). We have seen followers coming up to her, falling to their knees, and handing her a large donation in a red envelope, with their hands shaking from the experience of being in her presence. People endure long waiting lists to volunteer for a few days at a Tzu Chi hospital for the opportunity it can provide to see her for a few moments. Rather than continuing with this, however, let us give a more extended example of the Tzu Chi branch in Malacca to show how the various modes of innovation we have been discussing – repurposing latent ties, combining disparate networks through weak ties, and charisma – can interrelate in practice.

[19] *True Jesus Church*, 8.

Combining Innovative Techniques: Tzu Chi in Malacca

Tzu Chi in Malacca was able to transcend the limits of social capital by activating latent connections of cosmopolitan aspiration and gender, making links across very different kinds of social networks, and through direct charismatic connections to Cheng Yen (even though she was never physically present). People with no ties or only weak ties became united in ways never before possible. One crucial result of these processes in Malacca is that Tzu Chi has broken through the bonds of Chinese ethnicity in a way that temples with stronger ties to traditional social capital (like the Cheng Hoon Teng) have not.

The Tzu Chi free clinic distinguishes the group most clearly from local Chinese religious medical initiatives. Tzu Chi is the only such organization that actively provides medical services to non-Chinese groups and even institutionalizes this outreach orientation. The medical care mission has been the major lever allowing Tzu Chi to reach beyond the Chinese diaspora. The waiting area of the Free Clinic in Malacca regularly fills up with a mixture of Indian, Malay, and *orang asli* (indigenous peoples), with Chinese and a handful of Indian volunteers tending to them.[20]

In addition, they run a regular mobile free clinic, which frequents settlements of the orang asli in Tebong, Masjid Tanah, and Lubuk China in the state of Malacca. On the day that one of us took part, the clinic team consisted of fewer than ten people, including one nurse practitioner and the rest volunteers. The team left early in the morning from the Malacca branch office in one minivan of medical equipment and one compact car. As soon as they arrived at the estate, staff members were divided up to carry out different tasks, with the medical staff and volunteer leaders directing other volunteers to households according to a list generated on previous visits, checking on each patient in his or her house. The locals appeared to be relatively familiar with the Tzu Chi team, with adults conversing in Bahasa Malaysia while children curiously followed the team around as they navigated the woods and houses. The entire visit was short and efficient, and strictly medical. There was no attempt to distribute Tzu Chi information.

Tzu Chi in Malaysia first collaborated with the UN Refugee Agency (UN High Commissioner for Refugees [UNHCR]) in 2004 when it provided medical outreach to the Myanmar Muslim Religious School in Malaysia. In 2005 and again in 2007, UNHCR again appointed Tzu Chi Kuala Lumpur as a partner, operating to provide medical and dental assistance on a monthly basis to refugees and detainees in detention camps.[21] In addition, the Tzu

[20] Huang visited the Free Clinic during fieldwork in 2004, 2006, and 2008. She also participated once in their mobile medical clinic.

[21] *Tzu Chi & UNHCR: Collaboration & Activities.*

Chi International Medical Association (TIMA, modeled on Doctors Without Borders) has been holding free clinics, often quite large-scale, in various locations. For example, for three days in 2007, TIMA of Singapore, Malaysia, and Indonesia jointly held the Ninth Free Clinic on Batam Island. The program involved more than 100 medical personnel and 300 volunteers, and a total of 4,245 patients received treatment.[22]

Unlike all of its Chinese religious counterparts in Malacca and Malaysia more generally, Tzu Chi has successfully shifted from serving only the diasporic Chinese (and Taiwanese) ethnic community in its outreach programs (including charity and environmental protection as well as medical care) to providing ecumenical services across the ethnic spectrum of Malaysia. Their medical outreach has become complementary to public medical care, and the group' s charity and environmental initiatives have received awards from high-ranking officials including the chief minister and the prime minister.

We can trace the group's success in transcending local social capital by looking at the history of the Malacca branch. This branch was established in 1992, and it became the main office for all of Malaysia. The Malacca branch was founded and continues to be led by Mr. and Mrs. Liu. The Lius have long been pious Buddhists, taking refuge with a monk in Taiwan prior to their migration. Mr. Liu distinguishes Tzu Chi from his previous Buddhist practice, saying that: "Our 'Pure Land' practice used to involve only chanting scriptures every day. The Dharma gate of Tzu Chi, which we now identify with, is more 'practical.'" Such stories are quite typical for people who become strongly committed to Tzu Chi.

We can follow the evolution of Tzu Chi Malacca through several stages of expanding and tapping into social networks of nonmembers and members. The story traces back first to economic migration, as the Lius moved from Taiwan to Malaysia in 1988 to set up a garment factory in Malacca's free trade zone. They were part of the general movement of labor-intensive factories out of Taiwan toward regions with cheaper labor costs at that time. On one of her visits back to Taiwan, Mrs. Liu read a Tzu Chi newsletter and then took a trip to its headquarters. She was very touched and wanted to begin fund-raising in Malaysia, but she had trouble getting a branch organized.

The initial migration was further combined with Buddhist transnational practice, as Mrs. Liu continued to carry Buddhist media between Taiwan and Malaysia. Moreover, the Lius' Buddhist practice became transnationally dyadic, as they became followers of a Buddhist monk in Malaysia at the same time they were frequenting the Tzu Chi headquarters in Taiwan. The Malaysia-based monk eventually connected Mrs. Liu to a handful of Chinese Malaysian

[22] Tzu Chi Medical Care, "9th Free Clinic Visitation at Batam Island, Indonesia."

Tzu Chi pioneers in Perak, who gave Mrs. Liu hands-on instruction in carrying out charity work. These followers gave her the key she felt she needed to make the branch successful – she had to build it around practical activities rather than fund-raising. At this point she and some of her workers began to volunteer regularly by cleaning houses of poor local seniors, most of whom were Chinese and Indians.

At this point, through a structural passageway between two different social networks, the Taiwan–Malaysia transnational Buddhist network became connected to the local Buddhist network in Malaysia. However, according to Mr. Liu, the pioneers in Perak eventually disappeared and did not serve as a significant long-term link between Taiwanese transnational Buddhists and Tzu Chi Malaysia networks. Rather, the connection to local trust networks took place in the Lius' garment factory, from the clerks to the factory workers, and from there to the workers' neighborhoods.

Most proselytizing occurred among the clerks, who had already been responding to Mrs. Liu' s Buddhist charitable causes even before she developed her Tzu Chi connection. At the same time, information flowed through the pool of factory workers, who helped both in discovering prospective charity recipients and in publicizing the nascent Tzu Chi Malacca by expanding the number of participants for Tzu Chi events. Through these networks, for example, they learned about a nursing home that needed volunteers. In addition, the female factory workers informed them of individuals and families in need of help. "Because of their own living environment, they're more likely to know people who have been suffering, and they reported to us," as the former accountant of Mr. Liu' s factory explained. He continued:

> We followed the address as reported to us … And when we visited one house, their neighbors were curious … Why had this isolated household suddenly gotten so many visitors? We told them we're here to help. They would report other families who also needed help. So we had more and more cases … Then we held a reception at Mrs. Liu's office, and told everyone to bring their friends and family here to learn about Tzu Chi.[23]

Many devotees came to Tzu Chi during this early stage, which they often refer to as the "Shangqiao period," after the name of the Lius' garment factory. Tzu Chi held their activities in the canteen of the factory complex prior to the completion of their Still Thoughts Hall in Malacca's free trade zone in 1997.

As early as 1995, Mrs. Liu began to tap into various other smaller networks to build her branch. One of the first was the Chinese language education system, which is one of the most important Chinese Malaysian networks. At this point, the connection between Tzu Chi and the Chinese education system was Mr. Zhang, a supervisor at the Bureau of Education in the State of Malacca,

[23] Interview in Malacca, January 2004.

who met Mrs. Liu through the principal of a Chinese school in 1995. A pious and learned Buddhist, Mr. Zhang responded to Mrs. Liu' s proposal for Still Thoughts pedagogy and began to promote the group among the teachers of the Chinese education system while becoming an active devotee of Tzu Chi Malacca. Mr. Zhang was another key structural passageway between the Tzu Chi branch and other networks. The result was the formation of the Tzu Chi Teachers' Club, which extended the Lius' work-related and Taiwan-related networks to agents of Chinese schooling, which is one of the "three pillars" of Malaysian Chinese civil society.[24]

Tzu Chi tapped into the growth of Buddhist study clubs in colleges around 1997. The majority of the staff in the Malacca office as well as in the Kuala Lumpur and even Singapore offices began as former Tzu Chi college youths who related easily to each other through the typical college networks of class years and cohorts. They first encountered Tzu Chi through Buddhist clubs on campus, where they formed their own separate Tzu Chi groups and lived together off campus, a bit like a fraternity or sorority group, and mobilized students for Tzu Chi summer camps. Some became full-time, paid staff immediately upon graduation, and others worked elsewhere before they eventually "returned" to Tzu Chi. For example, Huiwan was from the second cohort of Tzu Chi youths during her college days. Eleven out of the twelve members in her cohort became full-time paid staff in Tzu Chi offices in Malacca, Kuala Lumpur, or Singapore. The one exception found other work because of pressure from his family, who regarded Tzu Chi jobs as underpaid underemployment.

Local Buddhist networks overlap with these social networks. The remaining devotees who did not belong to any of these social networks came to Tzu Chi through public events, such as "tea party" receptions. Some of them learned about the group through small announcements about the receptions in local Chinese newspapers. The majority learned the information through a friend from another Buddhist social network, whom they then accompanied to these events.

Even those who learned about Tzu Chi through newspapers made their initial visits as a result of being encouraged by fellow Buddhist friends. In other words, as early as the "Shangqiao period," Tzu Chi Malacca had begun to tap into and rework various kinds of smaller social networks. The Buddhist connections alone involved at least four sources. The first was the Buddhist study groups in neighborhoods, or "parks," as they are described locally (花园 in

[24] In 2003, there were sixty-five Chinese schools fully aided by government in Malacca. The total number of students was 21,082, and there were 1,090 teachers. There was only one independent secondary Chinese school in Malacca, Pay Fong Secondary School, which relies mainly on donations from the Chinese community. There were five more conventional schools in Malacca and one Chinese evening school. See Choy, "The Development of Education Culture and Arts of the Malacca Chinese."

Chinese, or *taman* in Malay). Sources also included Buddhist study groups at colleges/universities and sutra chanting classes and dharma events at local popular temples (especially Cheng Hoon Teng and Seck Khia Een). The final source included a variety of Buddhist associations. These associations ranged from the most organized, active, nationwide monastic network – the Malaysia Buddhist Association (马来西亚佛教总会, commonly referred to by its abbreviation, 马佛总) and the equally organized yet far more intellectual and publicly outspoken Young Buddhist Association of Malaysia (马来西亚佛教青年协会, commonly referred to by its abbreviation, 马佛青, or in English as YBAM) – to many other groups of much smaller scale, such as the Pure Land Study Association (净宗学会).

A closer look at members' personal histories shows that across all these types, most either began as Buddhists or felt strong personal ties to Mr. or Mrs. Liu. In sum, the proselytization of Tzu Chi's Malacca division was done mainly through Mr. and Mrs. Liu as network brokers, whose ties to more than one network allowed them to proselytize Taiwanese expats, factory employees, local Buddhist leaders, and the Chinese school system. In addition to the Lius' personal networks, the existing local Buddhist networks were sources for prospective followers through public events held by Tzu Chi. Finally, as always with this group, many of those who come to volunteer also feel a powerful personal connection to the charisma of Cheng Yen.

The Malacca branch of Tzu Chi has thus successfully broken through two kinds of ethnic enclaves. The first is the world of recent Taiwanese migrants. Although there are a handful of Tzu Chi branches around the world that have similarly appealed to local, non-Taiwanese populations (several cases in southern Africa, a few cases in the United States), the vast majority of branches consist predominantly of Taiwanese migrants. Under the leadership of the Lius, the Malacca branch has achieved a far greater local appeal by building connections across networks (Buddhist, educational, and factory-based) that would otherwise be quite separate. Second, especially in its service provision, Tzu Chi in Malacca has transcended the Chinese ethnic boundaries that limit almost all other engaged religious groups there. It has innovated beyond the possibilities that local social capital had been able to achieve by taking advantage of latent networks, weak ties, and charismatic vertical relations to create new possibilities.

The Anxieties and Limitations of Innovation

The examples we have been giving all appear to cast innovation in a positive light. There is nothing inherently good about innovation, however. Like social capital, innovation is only a tool; it can be used equally to harm and to help. In this section we discuss some of the difficulties that accompany innovation.

First, innovation nearly always challenges some aspect of the status quo, and will thus be met with resistance and friction. Second, innovations may not survive, but instead become compromised back into something like the status quo. Finally, innovation itself is not a permanent process. If it is successful, it creates a new status quo and a new reservoir of social capital, subject to all the same kinds of problems we discussed in the previous chapter.

We can see some of the challenges that innovations face by looking at how some Buddhist temples in China have managed to break out of the more standard mode, sometimes with charismatic leadership and often by building on weak ties. Suzhou's Xiyuan Temple (西园寺), for example, has embraced a number of innovative activities intended to reach out to a broader public, beginning around 2006. For example, they work with the local police department to provide dispute mediation, which brings them in touch with both officials (the police) and local households who might not normally have much contact with the temple. They have introduced the Guanyin Hotline (观音热线), which provides psychological counseling. The hotline has expanded into a drop-in center as well. Inspired by this endeavor, some Buddhist seminary teachers have specialized in researching and writing on the link between Buddhism and psychology. Xiyuan Temple has hosted five international forums on "Buddhism and Psychotherapy" involving speakers who include university professors, authors, and practitioners. They have been so successful in this "psychological charity" (as some monks call it) that it has become a trademark for the temple. They also run a very wide range of camps and educational programs that allow them to network into student groups in ways very similar to what we just saw for Tzu Chi in Malacca.

In fact, however, the leadership in the early 2000s intended to position the temple in a completely different way – as a leader in clerical education with their seminary as the major showcase. They showed no interest in developing charity or other forms of outreach. This was a very conventional and traditional goal for an old and established temple like this. They were pushed to the new strategy by a combination of lower-level leaders who were interested in new kinds of activities and pressures that came from outside the temple. For example, it was the police who broached the idea of a mediation program. And it was the Buddhist seminary teachers who initiated the counseling program, because they were constantly approached by visitors with life crises that they hoped to solve through Buddhist teachings. The abbot at the time was unenthusiastic about all of these new programs, feeling that they distracted from the proper cultivational goals of Buddhism. The eventual success of these new projects, however, changed the attitudes of the leadership.

The tension that this strategy engendered among the leadership is not at all unusual. Echoes of the exact same argument occur in Nanjing's Buddhist temples, for example. All the largest ones are involved in some forms of engaged religion, mostly because the government has made it such a clear priority, as we discussed in Chapter 3. Yet all of them also feel that it is somehow a distraction from the truly important goals of Buddhism, and none of them has embraced the idea the way Xiyuan Temple has. Their attitudes toward Tzu Chi seem similarly impatient, with frequent complaints that the group seriously underplays Buddhist clergy and learning, and that charity involves its own forms of self-interest. Some also pointed out that many Tzu Chi volunteers had first tried volunteering at their temples, but lacked what the clergy considered the seriousness and dedication to continue. The Tzu Chi people themselves often confirm their prior Buddhist experience, but explain the change instead as the sudden realization that Cheng Yen offered the path they had always been looking for.

Christians are just as torn about becoming broadly engaged. Many congregations criticize the Amity Foundation, for example, as having nothing to do with Christianity, and are unwilling to donate funds. The Christian nursing home in Xuzhou that we mentioned earlier is on a far smaller scale than Amity, but local churches also saw little reason to contribute money. From the point of view of those churches, it just bled away resources that could have been better used to support Christianity directly. Cao Nanlai describes another case in which a wealthy Wenzhou Christian created a foundation to do charitable work, but was widely criticized by the local churches.[25]

One problem with innovating beyond existing ties of social capital is thus that there will be opposition from people who prefer the status quo. Even simple scaling up will normally involve a challenge to some vested interests and is likely to attract some kind of opposition. Successful innovation always, to some extent, breaks out of the strong, bonding, horizontal community ties of social capital and in the process creates its own critics.

Another danger for innovation is that it can drift back into the old patterns of social capital that it meant to overcome. For example, in addition to Amity, a number of Christian groups have attempted to move to a more universal idea of charity rather than just a concern for the salvation of souls. The entrepreneur-led Suzhou Christian project to lift Yunnan farmers out of poverty through the development of gastrodiae rhizome, which we mentioned earlier, was open in principle to anyone in their target town of Shimenkan. Yet it is no coincidence that Shimenkan occupies an important position for Christians in China, because they frequently circulate stories of how selfless missionaries a century ago "civilized" the Miao people who live in the area, and how the Miao are now such devoted Christians. Alongside this social enterprise, the Suzhou Protestants also give living allowances to 500 local Yunnan Christian preachers

[25] Cao, "A Local Business Elite and Popular Christian Charity."

so that they would remain in their villages instead of becoming migrant workers in the cities. That is, the older Christian networks undercut some of the truly universalist goals that the leaders officially espoused. Other Christian moves toward universal charity have also sometimes also seen only limited success. Hangzhou's official Protestant association, for example, runs an old age home that is in principle open to anyone. When pressed, however, a church leader told us that 95 percent of the residents are in fact Christian, along with all of the staff. That is, in both the Hangzhou and Suzhou cases, an attempt to innovate by spreading benefits beyond the circle of fellow Christians ultimately had little effect, having been drawn back into the gravitational field of the status quo.

Breaking out of structures of social capital makes it possible to transcend the limitations that we discussed in the previous chapter. Yet, in the end it just creates new forms of social capital or actually returns to the old forms. Innovation itself is not necessarily constructive. The techniques we have described here – activating latent ties, using weak ties to connect networks, and charisma – are morally neutral. They can be used in ways most people consider socially useful, as is normally the case for religious engagement, but they can be used for any other purpose as well.

Although it has not been our primary theme here, we should recall that successful innovations in engaged religion (and elsewhere) typically reproduce both the advantages and limitations of social capital. That is, those visions of new forms for engaged religion or of new institutional structures achieve a status quo of their own if they are successful over the long term. They develop their own lines of authority, their own bureaucracies, and their own rationalities.[26]

Innovating Gender and the Good

Religions are sites for social capital formation, and this can work for both reproduction and innovation. Innovation in turn reproduces both advantages and limitations of social capital. The examples we have been discussing involve many forms of innovation, but there are two we particularly want to highlight: an enhanced leadership role for women and a rethinking of what constitutes "the good." Each of the interrelated processes we have been discussing involves activating ties in new ways or forging ties that may not have existed before. We have seen this, for example, in the way a charismatic leader can animate ties that previously existed only in potential (for instance, with

[26] One can see this particularly in the scandals that occasionally surround religious or charitable groups that have been very successful at developing new niches. Examples include the controversy surrounding Shaolin Monastery and its abbot, Shi Yongxin; the 2010 resignation of Li Yi as vice chair of the Chinese Daoist Association after a scandal; and the ongoing crisis of trust that has affected the Chinese Red Cross since problems in fund management first became apparent in 2011.

Tzu Chi and middle-class women), or in which weak links between networks can be united to create new forms of organization (such as a monastery for Daoist nuns or a Christian-inspired nursing home).

The first broad area of innovation is in gender relations. It was not our intention when designing this project to concentrate on gender in particular, yet as so many of these examples show, gender has been crucial in allowing these groups to escape the bonds of older forms of social capital. Although we have not analyzed them here beyond the brief discussion in Chapter 2, it is worth recalling that many of the redemptive societies of the first decades of the twentieth century were founded by women or offered them important roles.[27] Tzu Chi's founder Master Cheng Yen, and the origin story of the movement, emphasizes her separateness from Buddhist institutions and practices of the time – the difficulty in finding clergy to let her become a nun, the isolated cultivation in a hut in Taiwan's poor east coast, the refusal to perform rituals for money, and the initial following of all women.

Somewhat less dramatically, we have also seen Daoist master Yin Xinhui's construction of a rare monastery for Daoist nuns and her ability to differentiate it from the surrounding Daoist temples. There were also the cases of the healer and her patchwork temple in Lin Family Village; Luo Xiaoxia and her ability to split from the Presbyterian church for a radically new form of worship; the role of Catholic nuns in Jinde Charities; the Suzhou Protestant female entrepreneurs developing social enterprises in Yunnan; and the female spirit mediums acting to protect the local environment in China and Taiwan. Of course, not every case involves women. Nevertheless, our cases taken together do suggest a pattern in which women are one of the key forces that can break out of older patterns of social capital. Women in general were the least invested and least included in earlier forms of social capital. Especially when combined with the charisma we see in many of these same cases, it should not be too surprising that women often take the lead in such innovations.

Second, one theme we have stressed throughout this book is the way that the "good" itself can be understood differently over time and across places. It would be a mistake to think that concepts of what is good vary simply by theology. For many of the groups we have discussed here, a crucial aspect of the good is a broad-based humanistic universalism that involves medical care, emergency relief, education, old age care, and so on. This crosses religious and theological lines; we see it from Christians (Amity, Jinde Charities, the Xuzhou nursing home), Buddhists (Tzu Chi, Xiyuan Si, and many others), Daoists (Qianyuan Guan, though to a more limited extent), and even the popular temples of Lukang. Yet we also see branches of each of those religions that

[27] See Duara, *Sovereignty and Authenticity*, chapter 4.

reject those efforts as a watering down of crucial theological principles and ritual practices. There are Christians for whom salvation is the *only* important issue (for example, the True Jesus Church), Buddhists who see goodness in rituals like reciting the Buddha's name or in practices such as releasing animals, and many local temples for whom the good is defined only locally and personally. In many cases, those groups actively oppose the more universalistic and humanistic practices as a waste of money and effort on things that are not fundamentally important.

In spite of this continuing diversity in images of the good, however, probably the most striking change since the 1980s has been the trend across religious lines toward the more universalizing kind of charity for the public good, rather than for the particular theological, ritual, or social interests of a religious group. As we mentioned in the previous chapter, universalism is not at all new in China. Nevertheless, the general convergence toward this idea was a definite departure from the previous history of most of the religious groups we have been discussing. In this chapter, we have tried to explain just one of the reasons behind the change: the way that breaking the bonds of older social capital has allowed people to reimagine what religious organizations can and should do. This is accomplished through ways that much theorizing about the positive role of social capital in fostering social welfare has tended to take too lightly: the ability to catalyze dormant potential networks of gender or class; the possibility of repurposing networks; the creation of connections that utilize weak ties to unite separate strong networks; and the use of vertical, charismatic ties to build new networks.

7 Alternative Goodness

When we ran focus groups with religious leaders from Nanjing, Suzhou, and Shanghai, one of our questions concerned the religious nature of "goodness."[1] We pointed to the common Chinese axiom that all religions urge people to pursue goodness (劝人为善), but wondered whether it was possible that all religions really meant the same thing by the term. When these religious professionals encouraged compassionate goodness (a literal translation of 慈善, charity) or preached that people should do good deeds (做善事, 行善), were there any differences in what they had in mind? Why did their concrete activities look so similar across such wide religious divides?

To our disappointment, each focus group was initially baffled by the question. *Of course* they all mean the same thing; *of course* all their activities are similar: good is good. Yet things began to change when we pressed on more specific details. Does releasing living animals count as charity? Emphatically yes for the Buddhists, but certainly not for the Christians or Muslims. The same goes for conducting a ritual to provide salvation for ghosts after a natural disaster. In the same way, leading someone to embrace monotheism and stop burning incense to his or her ancestors was a good for the Christians, but not for the Buddhists or Daoists. That is, religions in China have not lost their unique world views and moral orders. Nevertheless, in public discourse about charity and even about goodness itself, religious leaders are quick to abandon any claim to a particular religious point of view in favor of the generic embrace of a desacralized goodness. As one Buddhist monk, who is very active in setting up charities through his monastery, said at one of these focus groups, "If you want to do charity on a large scale, you have to take out the religious content."

Although he spoke specifically about mainland China, where the pressures against public religion are strong, he and all the others were describing a situation we found to be true in Taiwan and Malaysia as well: there is

[1] These sessions took place in Nanjing and Shanghai in May and June, 2014. They included Buddhist, Christian, Muslim, and Daoist leaders with an interest in charity. Some were involved in the state-sanctioned religious associations and others were not; some were based in religious institutions and others in nongovernmental organizations (NGOs) or the private sector.

a remarkable degree of similarity in the forms and rationalities of religious engagement across political regimes, from one religious tradition to another, and at both large and small scales of organization. At least within the confines of these activities, "goodness" has become universal and singular, pursued in much the same ways and for the same purposes by everyone.

"Goodness" and its carriers, as the focus group responses indicate, have become generalized common sense, no longer tied to specific religious views of the moral world. That is why the list of engaged religious activities looks so similar to any list of the programs offered by secular NGOs or state agencies. Yet even though this new "good" has no clear religious basis, it does show certain basic characteristics. That is, even though it may appear as naturalized and obvious to people promoting it, it is actually tied to its own specific moral order, reworked in each national and religious context, and fully part of the political and social institutions of the market economy in the late twentieth century and beyond. It is an imagined image of an unbounded and unlimited good – not limited by religious belief or community boundary, and not by economic scarcity or class structure. Much of this book so far has been devoted to explaining how this came to pass.

Nevertheless, even in the midst of this strong convergence toward shared rationales for engaged religion, the seeds of other visions of philanthropy and of goodness itself continue to exist, forming an important counterbalance. The trend toward a singular goodness has only been partial and has not silenced alternative forms of goodness. The imagination of an unbound, unlimited, and generic good in religious philanthropy, which has risen to such prominence across the Chinese world, still has no monopoly on religious engagement. In this chapter we briefly look over those parts of the religious field that have managed to avoid the broad trend toward a singular concept of the good, the ones that have maintained a heteromorphism of the good across Chinese societies. We turn to other ways of imagining "goodness" and other ways of thinking about what it means to be "engaged" through religion. This diversity of goodness, we will suggest, provides an important resource for pluralism and empathy.

Other Goods

We have documented the rise of a philanthropic package based around what we have called industrialized religious charity: an image of the universal good, carried through the love exhibited by autonomous decision makers, institutionalized through national laws concerning social organizations and NGOs, and open to surveillance and audit. Every aspect of this package has been molded by the specific experiences of the twentieth century at our field sites. To some extent, even our concept of "engaged religions," or the more commonly used "faith-based organizations," reflects an organization of knowledge fundamentally different from earlier Chinese ways of thinking about these issues. A concept such as engaged religion, for example, implies that the default status of religion is to be confined to a "religious" sphere, from which such groups can choose to emerge to "engage" with the separate sphere of society. They can also use the ideas and beliefs of that discrete religious sphere to inspire their work in the secular organizational form of an NGO (as implied by the faith-based organizations idea) – the twentieth-century institutional carrier of the idea of the unbounded social good. There is nothing natural or obvious, however, about this treatment of religion as a separate entity. As we have seen, what we now call religion was rarely separated from society in this way in Chinese practice before the twentieth century.

"Engaged religion" as an idea has been very useful to shed light on the convergences that developed late in the twentieth century, but we can also broaden the concept to open up other forms of engagement whose fit with the model of faith-based organizations is much more awkward. We do not need to assume, for instance, that "religion" needs to be constituted as something separate from a "society" with which it can then engage. It may be worth remembering that the modern word for "society" in Chinese (社会) originally referred to the social group with joint responsibility to worship the local shrine to the earth.[2] Nor do we need to assume that the secular NGO is the most logical model for such engagement. And finally, we need to recognize that the unbounded, universalized good is not the only possible good.

As a way of rounding out this study, we thus turn to forms of engagement based on alternative visions of what counts as the good. Even though the industrialized model of religious philanthropy has become so widespread across religions and across regions, these alternatives remain vibrant and important. They are not simply remnants of earlier religious modes, but continue to help people make sense of their lives today, and maybe most importantly, they offer the potential seeds of other visions for a religious and social future. We will discuss four main alternatives to the idea of an unlimited good carried by NGO-like institutions: (1) community ritual, which rejects the flattening universalism of the industrialized model; (2) cultural heritage, which repackages religious engagement toward community identity and development; (3) spiritual life, which retains core ideas of religious difference; and (4) problem-solving, by which we mean uniquely religious solutions to problems, such as sickness or unemployment, that the industrialized model tends to address with secular mechanisms.

[2] See Katz, *Demon Hordes and Burning Boats*, 188.

Community Ritual as Public Good

Let us begin with community ritual in Chinese societies, much of which rejects the idea of the unbounded good in favor of a local good. Village and neighborhood deities protect their turf. Miracle stories thus always involve local people, sometimes at the expense of those from elsewhere. The good here is fundamentally communitarian, not universal. Thus people in Sanhsia still tell stories about the time when Taiwanese men were drafted to fight for the Japanese army in Southeast Asia during the Second World War. Sanhsia's patron deity frequently communicated directly to local men, warning them of impending air raids so they could run to safety. Other soldiers, even those from other parts of Taiwan, were left to face the bombs. This pattern of local deities intervening only in local life recurs in all Chinese societies.[3]

Such religion also rejects core ideas that had spread across Chinese societies from early in the twentieth century, especially the movement toward political secularization that was so important in defining the religious project after the end of the Qing dynasty. This kind of local religion instead continued to intertwine temples, politics, social organizations, and family life. Such temple-based religion is oriented above all toward ritual action – this is what creates the community that the god protects, what calls down the protection of the god for the locality and its families, and what empowers the deity itself in the sense that an exciting ritual is a clear sign of a vital god. It is also the key material mobilization of the political power and social resources of the community.

The secularism that began in Chinese societies in the early twentieth century marked the beginnings of the separation of religion as a discrete category and the introduction of a definition of religion strongly influenced by Protestantism, as we have discussed.[4] It also shared with Protestantism a strong suspicion of ritual, which appears especially clearly in the emphasis on belief over outward performance, as we can see, for example, in Martin Luther's embrace of *sola fide* (by belief alone) as a fundamental tenet in the movement's radical dismantling of Catholic ritual.[5]

Part of the heritage of the globalization of these ideas in the construction of national constitutions in Asia and elsewhere is a continuing suspicion of ritual. It is no coincidence that the Chinese Constitution guarantees freedom of religious belief, but not freedom of practice (that is, ritual). This suspicion also helps explain why the most strongly ritualized traditions, those most embodied and least theological – above all local temple religion in the Chinese context – have been defined outside of "religion" since the early twentieth century. Their

[3] For more examples, see Chau, *Miraculous Response*, 2005, chapter 5.

[4] See especially Goossaert and Palmer, *The Religious Question in Modern China*, 2011.

[5] Seligman et al., *Ritual and Its Consequences*.

survival, reconstruction, and flowering in many parts of the Chinese world today remind us of the limits on the global spread of a Protestant-inflected secularism and on the more recent spread of an image of the unbounded good. It also shows us how such religions can be socially engaged, even if in ways quite foreign to the usual NGO vision – not engaged in philanthropy per se, but in the construction of society itself.

Villages and neighborhoods across China have long organized public processions and festivals, and we can see how they embed an alternative concept of goodness. This tradition continues or has been revived across many parts of China, Taiwan, and Malaysia. The ability to organize events that typically involve complex coordination and often attract tens of thousands of worshipers is a strong indication of local society's capacity to organize itself without the direct involvement of the state.

Much of this fits a standard Durkheimian view of ritual as a way of marking boundaries and increasing solidarity within the group. The boundary marking is particularly clear when gods leave their temples in processions to tour their territories, carefully marking the edges of their turf. These events recall, and to some extent mimic, late imperial magistrates touring the boundaries of the areas they controlled. Just as a touring magistrate would bring an escort of civilian aides and military guards, gods bring their own retinues of heralds, secondary gods, and spirit soldiers. While the god is typically embodied in a wooden statue and carried in a sedan chair, the retinue consists of local young men (and occasionally women) dressed in appropriate costume and make-up. Infused with the power of the god, some performers may bloody themselves with ritual weapons (especially in Taiwan, Malaysia, and the far south of China) and others perform intricate martial routines, complete with spears, swords, and shields.

Boundary creation is clear here, since these processions almost always mark off a god's turf and its underlying social organization; they show communities in space. Yet processions and festivals also bring us directly to the boundary crossing work of ritual.[6] Visits between temples provide one way in which this occurs. Among the most elaborate of these are visits back to a temple of origin. This has been increasingly important in Taiwan as the possibility of return to the mainland has opened up. The huge parade to welcome Mazu back to Lukang after she had visited the mother temple on the mainland, which we discussed in Chapter 5, provides a typical example. In one sense this was about Tianhou Temple etching and reinforcing its historical claims and mobilizing the social capital it controls within its territory. Yet in another sense the event provided a stage for the collaboration between temples. Performing groups

[6] See Seligman and Weller, *Rethinking Pluralism.*

from other temples, along with their own gods in sedan chairs, led the procession. That is, gods were greeting each other across temple boundaries, rather than Mazu simply reiterating her own boundaries.

On a smaller scale, something similar happened in front of Tianhou Temple almost every day, as gods from all over Taiwan would come to visit. The details varied widely from one group to the next, but the basic structure of the ritual was always the same. The visiting deity, sitting in his sedan chair, would stop before the entrance to the temple while his retinue exorcised the temple plaza and showed its respect (and the visiting deity's power). They accomplished this through the performance of traditional martial displays such as a dragon dance or the popular form in Taiwan called the Eight Infernal Generals.[7] Possessed mediums would also perform until their blood flowed. Finally, the visiting god would approach the temple in three rapid thrusts and retreats before finally entering, the equivalent of a kowtow. The visiting god's followers trailed close behind, and they would burn incense to honor the host goddess. Community boundaries are certainly marked here, but in a way that allows them to be crossed through godly versions of human etiquette. In China, with its history of intervillage feuding (械斗), such boundary crossing could be a significant social contribution.

The anthropological literature tends to emphasize the boundary-creating aspects of ritual over the idea that ritual is fundamental to the ability to cross community boundaries – to maintain civil relations among groups whose competing interests may create tension between them. In Chinese understandings of ritual (礼), however, the ability to cross boundaries while still maintaining them is central. Much of the ritual so emphasized in the Confucian tradition was interpersonal. Recognizing that people's interests and desires differed, putting them into positions of potential conflict, the Confucian answer was mutual acceptance of ritual – rituals of etiquette to deal with interpersonal relations, rituals of diplomacy to foster international contacts, and cosmic rituals to deal with the broader, nonhuman forces of the universe. All such ritual was an act of showing respect (the basic meaning of *bai* 拜, the most common term for worship). Actually *feeling* respect could come later.

Ritual, with its simultaneous creation and crossing of boundaries, was the key mechanism for addressing all kinds of social difference. Even some of the most august neo-Confucian thinkers thus spent time writing manuals of everyday etiquette (礼貌, literally "ritual appearances") because they thought it was the key to social peace and civility. For much of the imperial period, the Board of Rites (礼部) was responsible for diplomatic relations, which illustrates the same principle. And, of course, ritual also guided people in their relationship

[7] Sutton, *Steps of Perfection*; Boretz, *Gods, Ghosts, and Gangsters*.

to the otherness of the spirit world. This idea thus leads to a completely different way of thinking about goodness, in which divisions among people are natural and our goal is to find ways of living together socially in spite of those differences. In contrast, the industrialized goodness of modern philanthropy sees everyone as fundamentally the same everywhere, and there should be no divisions among people.

Although the Tianhou Temple example comes from Taiwan, it represents the continuation of a cultural pattern that predates the political separation of the island from the mainland in 1895. We can find equivalents today in China, for example, when different villages in Handan (Hebei) cooperate to put on a local festival by contributing different resources or different kinds of performing groups. For example, Guyi Village of Wu'an City has since 1987 renewed its masked performance (傩戏) for local gods to help drive away the Yellow Demon, a bringer of danger and harm. More than 600 performers take part, accompanied by another 400 assistants, organized into troupes to enact the masked performance and various other processions and routines. Like most local festivals, this one also attracts hundreds of traders and petty merchants from Hebei and Shanxi Provinces to conduct business. Every family in Guyi Village invites relatives from other villages, even from far away, to witness the performances.[8] Similar to the Taiwan case, the ritual does not simply consolidate community boundaries, but also encourages movement across them.

Another example comes from the mountains of Yunnan, where an ethnically, religiously, and linguistically very mixed population has a long history of living together harmoniously. Here too we see shared ritual playing a key role as people make space for the religious needs of others.[9] At funerals, for example, not only are ethnic boundaries crossed – everyone in the same village regardless of ethnic identification has to participate in the ritual – but borders between otherwise more clearly maintained religious boundaries are transcended. The Buddhist mourners will arrange to have nonalcoholic drinks for the Protestants who are not allowed to drink in this part of the region. Moreover, the Protestants cannot eat animal blood, unlike the local custom. As a result, separate cooking pots are set up for the Protestant relatives and their fellow-villagers. However, Protestants, Buddhists and nonreligious people work side by side in carving the coffin, executing the burial and other funeral-related activities. The funeral, therefore, serves as a boundary-crossing ritual in this pluralistic society, even while maintaining the existing categories of difference.

Sometimes people even create a secularized space at these funerals for officially atheistic cadres to make speeches, after which they change the mode to their familiar rituals. Again, in a Catholic funeral where the deceased was

[8] Du, "Welcoming the Gods and Performing Nuo Ritual."

[9] This is based on results from another research project conducted by Keping Wu.

a schoolteacher, the county-level educational bureau cadres decided to honor the late teacher by giving him a socialist funeral, in which the head of the bureau recalled the teacher's life according to the official files, the other officials displayed big paper flower bouquets (花圈), and all participants spent three minutes in silence with their heads bowed while listening to the standard Chinese funeral music. Once the cadres finished their performance, they got in their cars and left. The Catholic priest then resumed his position and said a prayer before the coffin was slung over the villagers' shoulders and slowly carried into the church, where the formal Catholic funeral continued. When the Catholic part was finished, the villagers proceeded to the nearby hill according to the local custom and start digging and constructing the grave. Every villager carried bricks (for building the grave) and drinks (alcohol for Buddhists and Catholics; soda for Protestants) all the way up the hill to the preselected burial site. After the person was buried under the supervision of the Catholic priest, people rested next to the graveyard by having drinks and chatting before they finally went down to the village to enjoy a big feast. The funeral thus became a space in which all kinds of boundaries were reshuffled; in usual circumstances it would be extremely rare for a Catholic priest to be standing at the same podium as the head of the education bureau, or for a Protestant pastor to be digging the grave next to the Catholic priest. Though the boundaries resume their positions when life goes back to normal, what remains is an opportunity of interaction that would be perceived as impossible when we see these boundaries as concretized objects. Ritual here provides a crucial public good – a space for intergroup cooperation. It is highly "engaged," but not in a way usually recognized in the world of religious philanthropy.

Sometimes groups pursuing engaged religion ritualize their activities in ways that are not directly religious, but still serve to forge them into an effective social unit. For instance, part of the attraction of a group like Tzu Chi for people in Malacca is that it allows them an opportunity to share a portion of their lives with each other, from drinking tea to volunteering in a health clinic. This is the ritual of etiquette in its most secular sense, but it can be just as important as other forms of ritualization. In Taiwan as well, we have also seen them undertake activities such as arranging an outing to a forest for core members. This is purely for enjoyment, not for any charitable mission, and they were even reminded not to wear their uniforms.[10]

There is, of course, always the danger that these forms of spiritual etiquette can break down – just like secular etiquette. Gods, like humans, can snub each other by refusing to visit each other's temples or to act respectfully. Martial performance groups from different villages usually dealt with each other with

[10] Huang, *Charisma and Compassion*, 2009.

ritual care, but could occasionally come to blows if they accidentally came face to face. Rituals do not make underlying tensions disappear, but they do create a mechanism for living with them. Harmony, after all, is not sameness, but the coordination of difference, and so there is always some risk involved.

Human history so far has granted us no guarantees of living in harmony. Nevertheless, it may be worth reconsidering the potential role of ritual in allowing us to live with difference without denying it. Both the Confucian and other ritual traditions recognize real boundaries, and they also help us learn to how to cross them.[11] In doing so they also contribute to the public good in a way that is not often recognized and that has been almost entirely omitted from the universalizing and unlimited good that we have seen so powerfully influencing contemporary philanthropy.

Nanjing offers a small example of the consequences of taking ritual lightly. Even though the city lies outside the traditional area where Mazu is an important goddess, it has two functioning Mazu temples. One was originally the guild hall for merchants from Mazu's stronghold in Fujian and the other was founded by Zheng He in gratitude for Mazu's protection during one of his great ocean voyages during the Ming dynasty. Both were brought back to life rather late in the process of China's religious renaissance, largely because the United Front Work Department of the Communist Party (which is in charge of cross-Strait policy as well as religion) felt that it was a useful gesture to Taiwanese investors.[12] This was especially important because Nanjing is the capital of a province that benefits enormously from Taiwanese investment, as well as being the nominal capital of the Republic of China.

In Taiwan and parts of Fujian, Mazu's birthday is usually the high point of the ritual year. The smaller of Nanjing's Mazu temples does not even attempt a ritual, but the larger one, called Tianfei Gong (天妃宫, using another of Mazu's imperial titles), has had a procession for many years. In 2014, when one of us took part, the birthday ritual attracted several hundred people and featured banners bearing the names of companies that had given large donations. Important donors wore conspicuous yellow sashes and filled the temple courtyard, while local people stood around the edges to watch.

The ceremony began with speeches on a temporary stage constructed across from the main hall of the temple. This space might have housed an opera performance in a Taiwanese temple, but this time there were mostly only government officials from the Tourism Department of the city government and

[11] Seligman and Weller, *Rethinking Pluralism*.

[12] It is unusual that the Party would encourage temples to folk deities, which are not normally recognized as religion. To legitimize these temples, one was given to the Daoist Association to manage, and the other to the Buddhist Association.

Figure 7.1 Impatient dragon dancers.

top leaders from the district government. The Tourism Department "owns" the temple because it stands in a public park. The audience stood facing them, some chatting on their phones. Two dragon dance troupes fidgeted at the sides – speeches by officials were no moment for the hot and noisy excitement of dancing dragons, or for popular temple ritual in general (see Figure 7.1). When the speeches finally ended, we all turned to face the temple but the only ritual was an attempt at a very formal Confucian offering of incense, where a leader slowly called out "Bow the first time," and the second, and the third. This was followed by "Offer the first stick of incense," and then the second, and the third, and so on. The pace remained glacial as the audience grew increasingly restless. Finally, the big donors were allowed to make their offerings and the attempts to keep the crowd neatly ordered finally edged a little bit toward the more usual feelings of chaos.

The problem was that, unlike such temples in Fujian or Taiwan, there were no Buddhist or Daoist priests to lead the ritual, which created the jury-rigged and amateur impression the performance seemed to evoke for most participants. This temple is actually run by Buddhists, but the monk in charge said that while he had no objection to the ceremony, there was nothing Buddhist about it and he had no interest in taking part. A government clearly uncomfortable with religious ritual, and especially with the carnivalesque aspect of most popular temple ritual, was still fumbling to find an alternative.

In prior years, this ceremony had then moved outside the temple in a procession through the local neighborhood. People would come out to watch, and sometimes to make offerings or burn incense.[13] The problem in 2014 was that the city government had decided that the procession could not take place out on the streets, but must instead happen within the large park that houses the temple. As a result, almost no one came out to watch, which meant that the dragon dancers and other costumed performers soon stopped performing. Once the image arrived, after an arduous climb, at a pavilion at the other end of the park, the ceremony simply petered out.

Perhaps the most conspicuous feature of this event was an absence: there were no Taiwanese. It is in this sense that the ritual, what there was of it, failed. The government allowed this event and had encouraged the reconstruction of the temple only because it thought it was important to cross-Strait relations. The temple thus proudly displays photographs of Lian Chan's visits there when he came to China representing the Guomindang; his name is carved into the wall along with other donors. Nevertheless, Taiwanese business people say that they do not go because the ritual is all wrong. The basic problem is that the city government cannot bring itself to sponsor something that the Taiwanese would recognize as a proper ritual, and so the potential of ritual to bridge differences is never met. We are not suggesting that this weak ritualization is actually creating any problems, but it is causing the temple itself to fail to build bridges to the Taiwanese – the very purpose for which it was reconstructed.

Cultural Heritage and Community Identity

A second form of alternative goodness is most obvious now in the widespread attempts to treat religion as cultural heritage (although this has so far been less relevant for Christianity than for all the others). This possibility became increasingly important after 2003 when UNESCO introduced the category of intangible cultural heritage. All three of our research areas have embraced some form of this idea, with China in particular registering large numbers of such sites and creating a hierarchy of lesser designations of national, provincial, and local cultural heritage sites. This has been particularly important because the designation created a new channel through which religious practice could be legitimized – even temple worship, which does not count as religion in China, can now be justified as an important aspect of cultural heritage. In a place where "culture" (文化) had been used to mean something like high educational achievement and urban middle-class values, this is an interesting change. Culture in the UNESCO sense has become a much broader concept, entwined with questions of local and national identity.

13 We are grateful to the Nanjing Normal University anthropologist Bai Li, who has been observing the festival for many years, for providing information on previous versions.

Enshrining temples or belief systems as cultural heritage is a way of concretizing memory, of saving it from the ravages of time. Jan Assmann drew a useful distinction between what he called everyday memory and collective or cultural memory.[14] Everyday memories are the ones we personally experienced, and that we may share with friends or our children. They may thus outlive us, but they are unlikely to outlive the next generation; Assmann gives them a lifespan of 80–100 years at most. We can, however, alter those memories in an attempt at creating permanence – cultural memory. This happens when we write histories or build museums and memorials; it happens when we claim that temples and festivals are really cultural heritage rather than religion. Such exercises are crucial for the creation of identity over time, even if they also threaten to alter some of the original context of temples and festivals. This creation of local identity, and the social life that accompanies such identities, is another form of the "good" that Chinese religions are now sometimes providing, even if it is far from the universalized goods of philanthropic poverty donations or medical aid.

For instance, Martin Saxer has recently shown how Buddhism in Tibet found a new space for political acceptance via the idea of intangible cultural heritage, instead of being condemned as superstition (much as happens in Han China) or as evidence of separatist tendencies.[15] Traditional Tibetan monastic debates, for example, became something to be proud of, and something to schedule for the convenience of tourists. After 2003, this process allowed Buddhism to be partially reincorporated as part of Tibetan ethnic identity, for the first time under the People's Republic. As Saxer also notes, however, more ritualized practices of Tibetan Buddhism, such as pilgrimage or circumambulation, have not been recognized in the same way. The embrace of some aspects of the religion as cultural heritage means that these excluded forms, while not illegal, are more likely to be seen as politically inspired and therefore dangerous. Here we have a combination of the fostering of a kind of identity through the designation of cultural heritage and the alienation of ritual in a way that handicaps religion's possibility of crossing over boundaries of identity, just as we saw in the earlier discussion of the Mazu temple in Nanjing.

The temple-museum built in Handan for Lin Xiangru (藺相如) offers another example of the attempt to construct local cultural heritage. It is located not far from the spirit medium's temple complex that we discussed in Chapter 6. Unlike her temple, however, with its very shallow history and ties to a form of spirit mediumship that China is certainly not eager to claim as "culture," the temple to Lin Xiangru commemorates a historically important figure from the Warring States period, known nationally but active in this area, which had

[14] Assmann, "Collective Memory and Cultural Identity."
[15] Saxer, "Re-Fusing Ethnicity and Religion."

been the center of the state of Zhao. An old temple to Lin had been destroyed in the Cultural Revolution. When local villagers began planning to rebuild the shrine in 1997, members of the county government gave significant support because they saw this project as a way of building both a local identity and a tourist attraction as the home of such a famous historical figure. That is why the temple is also billed as a museum. Similar stories have been reported all over China, and usually show the same awkward compromise between local interpretations of a site or practice (Lin Xiangru as god) and state attempts to overwrite those interpretations with their own (Lin Xiangru as a local hero with national historical importance).[16]

The mainland Chinese government has invested much more into the formal recognition of cultural heritage than our other field sites, but similar processes are at work there too. For example, an extensive renovation project at Malacca's Cheng Hoon Teng earned a UNESCO Asia-Pacific Heritage Conservation Award in 2002. This was an important step in their political merit-making, in part because of the temple's importance as a tourist attraction and a symbol of the Chinese community. The temple itself highlights the identity function of this exercise in materialized memory. As the chairman of the temple's board said at the time, "We want to pass this legacy to our children, to our grandchildren, and our great grandchildren. They have as much right to this heritage as we have. We must not allow our efforts of perpetuating our culture and traditions to fade away with the passing of time. We must preserve our heritage for the sake of our descendants."[17]

Taiwan plays the same game, with the Ministry of Culture designating various festivals as intangible cultural heritage. In this case it is not a direct response to international opportunity, because Taiwan's liminal diplomatic position makes it impossible to earn UNESCO recognition. Nevertheless, the indirect influences of such programs are obvious enough, as is the feeling that they are competing with the mainland for claims on Chinese cultural heritage. Added to this, Taiwan also shows very clearly the immediate effects of a newfound search for identity that became so important on the island after democratization, and the demarcation of cultural heritage is a good way to mark off identity as memory. The famous Mazu temples are a clear example. Mainland China has earned a place for "Mazu beliefs and customs" on UNESCO's representative list of the "Intangible Cultural Heritage of Humanity," and Taiwan has responded by placing Mazu on its own lists. Mazu has thus been promoted in some ways as a symbol of a uniquely Taiwanese cultural identity, concretized in bigger festivals than ever before, through academic conferences and

[16] For similar examples, see Liang, "Turning Gwer Sa La Festival into Intangible Cultural Heritage"; Gao, "An Ethnography of a Building Both as Museum and Temple."

[17] See their web page, "Welcome to Cheng Hoon Teng Temple."

writings on the goddess as intangible cultural heritage, and by taking the goddess to New York to promote Taiwan's perennial attempt to join the United Nations. They have even constructed bigger statues than ever before – including what claims to be the largest in the world, on the island of Matsu, staring at the mainland across the short distance of water that separates them.

Elana Chipman points out in a study of Beigang, which is another Taiwanese town known primarily for the Mazu temple that dominates its economy, government support for local cultural history workshops has strengthened two aspects of the search for identity. The first is a unifying island-wide identity separate from the mainland, and the second is a purely local identity that, for example, makes Beigang's Mazu worship different from Lukang's. As she writes:

> To culture workers, their agenda is a local authenticity that they can imagine as belonging to the town itself. Excluded from most forms of power or social capital, they craft narratives of the local past which critique contemporary distributions of power. Yet, since their work is ultimately the product of a state-driven nation-building project, it is never merely local.[18]

Collective memory in these cases, whether or not it takes the official United Nations form of "cultural heritage," materializes identities for people.

"Cultural heritage" does not set out to alleviate poverty, cure disease, or provide blankets and water for victims of natural disasters. Its "good" is not the sort of thing that our informants (including those in the government) usually thought of when we asked them about the religious performance of charity ("benevolent good," 慈善). Nevertheless, it is a form of good through concretized identity that many communities value and that has long engaged religion.

Preserving culture as "heritage," however, runs the danger of discouraging change and flexibility. China already has the problem that new temples cannot use this strategy because they must be able to document a pre-1949 history. Even successful use of the strategy by carving identity and memory into stone and wood, or printing it in books, of course, can be equally problematic given the potential to build walls between competing community or national identities. Nevertheless, this experiment is still young, and we have yet to see the problems that this form of goodness may also bring.

Spiritual Goods and Religious Differences

Yet another kind of goodness stems from the spiritual contributions that many already associate with religion, but that almost never play into discussions of charity, philanthropy, or the public good. In fact, these were exactly the features of religion that people downplayed when we asked them about their charitable

[18] Chipman, "Our Beigang," 21.

activities. Spiritual "goods" are what differentiate religions from each other, but our informants usually emphasized those elements of charity that instead made them sound indistinguishable from each other. All religions are not the same, however. We can see this most clearly in a minority of religious specialists who refuse the cosmopolitan practices of the unbounded and industrialized good exactly because they distract from what these people see as more fundamental kinds of good. Such people exist in each of the religious traditions, keeping their distance from the pressures of political merit-making in all its forms, and promoting instead more religion-centered images of the good.

A few important Buddhist temples in China thus manage completely to avoid forms of engagement like charity that would pull them away from the cultivation that they see as the core of the Buddha's teachings. For example, Master Mingxue, the abbot of the Lingyan Shan temple in Suzhou, thinks that they should help people deal with the most basic problems of death, which will eradicate the problem of suffering from its root, instead of worrying too much about feeding another hungry man. He belongs to the older generation of monks who were born and educated during the Republican era. He played a crucial role in the recovery of Buddhism in the early 1980s, but nevertheless refused the government's original plan to turn Lingyan Shan into a tourist spot. He also turned down funding to build a road that would provide direct automobile access up the mountain to the temple. And he capped the entrance fee at 1¥ for years despite government pressure to raise the price. He has refused even modern rest room facilities for tourists.

In recent years, Master Mingxue has also ignored the government's call for Buddhism to be more institutionally involved in philanthropy. He described how "a Religious Affairs Bureau official drove to the foot of Lingyan Shan in his car. He wanted me to participate in social philanthropy. I gave him 20,000 of my own savings and donated an equal amount from the Temple's account. I totally agree that helping others is very important, but we should only do what we are capable of." Unlike most major Buddhist temples in the region, this one still refuses to do any more systematic forms of philanthropy. Because of Mingxue's status and reputation in the Buddhist world, nobody challenged him.

Most other temples are not able (or not eager) to take such an extreme position, but instead find ways to balance the tension between different conceptions of the good. Some do just enough charity to earn some political merit, but their lack of enthusiasm is clear in conversation. A monk at one of Nanjing's most important temples, for instance, had little interest in describing their charitable activities and explained that he thought their primary contribution was in Buddhist education instead. "You have to remember," he said, "that everyone who does charity is also hoping to gain something for themselves." Later in the conversation he brought up the *Diamond Sutra*, a core Buddhist text, as something that everyone should read. It echoes his comments on charity, where the Buddha explains that "In the practice of charity, bodhisattvas should abide in nothing whatsoever. That is, to practice charity without attachment to form, sound, smell, taste, touch, or dharmas." Yet this is almost impossible for anyone to do. As the text later points out, giving away vast amounts of wealth earns enormous merit, but not nearly as much as reading just a few lines from the sutra. Why? Because (as another Buddhist cleric explained to one of us) the sutra teaches us the possibility of achieving enlightenment by giving up all attachments, while charity usually just creates more attachments. We should still be charitable, but it is only a crude first step on the path to enlightenment.

Partly for these reasons, many Buddhist monks and nuns in southern Jiangsu expressed a combination of admiration and disdain for Tzu Chi, which has recently gained a significant following in the area. As one said, "It's really just a secular NGO with a little Buddhist flavor added in." Instead, those temples that have not whole-heartedly embraced charity emphasize education in Buddhist principles (usually through a seminary), Buddhist forms of cultivation (reciting the Buddha's name or practicing Chan meditation, for instance), and rituals based around sutra recitation (including those to release animals). Most temples in practice do some mix of all of these things. Only a few temples these days spurn industrialized philanthropy altogether, but almost all of them also embrace other forms of the good with far more powerful roots in Buddhist thought and ritual.

The Daoist Qianyuan Guan also chooses to do only a minimum of charity as it balances the tension between pursuing generic and secular images of unbounded good through political merit-making and the desire to create a uniquely Daoist center for self-cultivation. Led by the innovative nun Yin Xinhui (see Chapter 6), the temple carries out some minor charity, giving ad hoc donations to needy individuals drawn to its attention, and sending a small number of volunteers into the local county villages to help people. These activities are minimal, however, ranking far behind ritual performance and meditational self-cultivation for the temple's nuns. Following much the same logic, this temple also largely shuns the commercial opportunities that dominate the other important Maoshan temples. Because they charge only a nominal entrance fee of 10¥, for instance, tour bus companies do not come – their cut of those fees is too low. Access to the other temples on Maoshan, in contrast, cost 120¥ in 2014, and tour buses flock to them.

As we have emphasized throughout, our evidence contradicts the idea that Christianity simply brought "modern" ideas of charity to China. In addition to what we have described in earlier chapters, we can add here that Christians are as deeply immersed in debates about the proper role of charity as Buddhists and Daoists. Many are in fact very uncomfortable with industrialized charity and see it as a dangerous distraction from the real good of saving souls. Recall, for example, the Christian nursing home in Xuzhou (discussed in Chapter 6), which found itself in financial difficulties when none of the local churches felt it was appropriate to provide support for charity. Preachers in Nanjing's True Jesus Church, the Pentecostal-like movement that we mentioned earlier, similarly felt no need at all to do such charity. Registered with the Religious Affairs Bureau but not affiliated with the official Three Self Movement, they have little possibility of earning much political merit. For them the only thing that mattered was saving souls. As one of them said, "We really don't care about the state. Governments are temporary. What we care about is eternity." The same, of course, goes for other "temporary" problems such as poverty, sickness, and disaster.[19]

The one major religious tradition in Chinese societies that most unambiguously embraces charity is Islam, where charitable giving (*zakat*, 天课) is one of the fundamental requirements for every Muslim. That tradition, however, has not succumbed to the pull of the universal good but retains its roots in the Islamic community. While there are forms of Islamic charity that can be universal, *zakat* itself must be returned to needy Muslims in the community.[20] This is based on the idea that the wealthy have a particular responsibility for those people who allowed them to become wealthy.

All forms of religion across Chinese societies have felt a strong push toward industrialized philanthropy based on ideas of universal love, autonomous individual hearts, and modern accounting. As these examples show, though, all also continue to foster their own visions of goodness. Some religious organizations have completely embraced the universalizing model, but all also have at least a minority of clergy and temples or churches that locate goodness instead in various concepts of community instead of autonomous individuals, and in forms of the good that have little to do with state visions of the public good, from giving up worldly attachments to saving souls.

Solving Life's Problems

Beyond the conventions of the rituals we discussed earlier, much of the "goodness" that Chinese religion offers has always been votive – making offerings to deities in the hopes of solving concrete problems. People offer incense to get pregnant, pass exams, start a successful business, and so forth. Even major temple rituals include an aspect of guaranteeing spiritual protection for the

[19] Nanlai Cao's study of a Christian philanthropic entrepreneur in Wenzhou also shows that most of the members of the church disagreed with his charitable initiative. Cao, "A Local Business Elite and Popular Christian Charity."

[20] For an example of Islamic NGO-type philanthropy in China, see Man and Hao, "Islamic Philanthropies."

entire community. When asked why they go to temples, many Chinese people will reply that they go in order to maintain a life of peace (保平安), meaning a life without financial crisis, serious illness, or domestic strife. "Peace" in this sense is the final form of goodness that we will discuss here.

Healing has been one of the most important and influential of these forms of goodness. For instance, one of us watched in 2014 as an ill patient approached a spirit medium in the outskirts of a southern Jiangsu city. She offered incense to the medium's image of the Buddha Sakyamuni, but he quickly told her to wait outside in the courtyard. While she waited he chatted to several of us about how there seemed to be so many evil things (邪东西) harassing local people in recent months. When asked for an example, he pointed to the woman. After about ten minutes he suddenly slipped into what appeared to be a mild trance in which he was possessed by the Buddha himself. He commanded the woman to return and to prostrate herself repeatedly in front of the altar, more or less as would happen in a Buddhist temple. Soon she began to hiccough and belch; after a few more minutes she began to weep.

The medium had been sitting at his desk, watching her and occasionally invoking a deity with a hand sign. As the possessing demon began to manifest itself through the woman's tears and belches, however, he stood up, walked over to her, and placed his hands at various points on her face and head. As he touched the top of her head, she began to shake violently. And when he touched her temples the demon – a monkey spirit, as we later learned – began to scold and curse the medium. Its final words were "I'm only a little weaker than you. I will be back to fight you again!" Though more treatments would still be needed, the medium reports that she was eventually cured.

This medium was very influential in the area, and many of his cured patients had become lesser mediums who could cure still more people. The large scale of this network was unusual in our experience, but we give the example here mostly because of its typicality in other aspects. Healing of more or less this kind is common across Chinese societies. Visiting temples to burn incense as part of a request to a god for similar favors is even more widespread than spirit mediumship, and has been documented in the anthropological literature since scholars first began to pay attention to local religion. Even officially institutionalized religions, such as Buddhism or Daoism in the mainland context, do this to some extent. Many Daoist temples can write amulets (符) to help heal diseases or help people in other ways. We have had interviews interrupted as a Buddhist monk dashed off to heal a child. At another Buddhist temple an enthusiastic lay follower explained how her daughter's insanity had been healed when the abbot told the follower to read a particular sutra. The monk himself had a more Buddhist and less magical explanation: he emphasized that he had told her to take the daughter to a hospital as well, but if the problem were a blockage in her karma, then reading the sutra would help. The main point for all of these examples is that engaged religion also includes these forms of material help for people, but provided in ways that are religiously unique and not recognized by the mechanisms of secular charity or its modern religious equivalents.

The same processes are just as important to Chinese Christianity, especially in the more charismatic forms that have been growing rapidly on the mainland (as in much of the world) and have strong footholds as well in Taiwan and Malaysia. The True Jesus church, for example, which was active in all of our field sites, consistently emphasizes God's healing power. The Malacca branch, for example, was founded in 1961 in thanks for an act of healing.[21] Pastors from the Nanjing church, when asked how they differed from other Protestants, emphasized divine healing and speaking in tongues, along with ritual details (such as full body baptism) and a literal interpretation of the Bible. They were quick to share testimonials from followers who had been healed by prayers from the congregation. When one of their preachers spoke at a service targeting young people as potential converts, he especially emphasized the votive aspects of the religion. The Bible, he claimed, was the key to getting rich, to feeling a sense of equanimity in life, and to staying healthy. Many rural congregations – some in the official church and others not – also recruit primarily through healing.[22]

Forms of the Good

Of course, these "goods" are exactly what more standard versions of charity offer as well – economic benefits, health improvements, stronger family and community lives. Nevertheless, neither the literature on religious philanthropy nor our informants tend to think of Doctors Without Borders and spirit mediums as belonging to the same category. One belongs to the world of NGOs and states, and the other to temples and churches. This distinction itself has deep roots in the modernist projects of the twentieth century. In our field sites, these projects began from the secularism of the early twentieth-century Asian constitutions, which separated and isolated religion from the rest of social life. They have continued and strengthened further with the "neoliberal" governance trends of the 1980s and beyond, which have promoted and industrialized an image of a boundless good over the unique goods of particular religions.

This chapter is only a brief summary of alternative forms of the good that continue to be important in Chinese societies. By touching on the variety of these forms we have hoped to show two things. First, the universalizing,

[21] "My Church – Malacca."

[22] See, e.g., Zhou, "Experiential Belief, Habitual Ritual, and Social Capital"; Lian, *Redeemed by Fire*.

unbounded goodness championed by philanthropy, as it has been conceived in the early twenty-first century, is only one of many possible visions of goodness. This vision of the good has been thoroughly naturalized by the international community and many of our informants to the point where it seems like obvious common sense to many of them. Nevertheless, as these examples have shown, it is just one way of conceptualizing the good, and one that has been shaped by its own historical and social contexts just as much as any of the others.

Second, even where specific views of goodness coincide (better health, higher standards of living for the poor, and so on), the means to achieve them can be totally different. The industrialization of religious and other philanthropy through secular state regulation and auditing procedures is utterly different from the nonindustrial production of the good through prayer, ritual, or spirit mediumship. Alternatives thus continue to thrive. The very fact that they are not industrialized, universalized, and secularized means that they cannot easily become general "common sense" the way state and NGO concepts of philanthropy have. They are too rooted instead in local visions of goodness and in the specifics of different religious traditions. Nevertheless, they continue to exert important impacts on people's lives.

8 Conclusion: The Unlimited Good in Context

This book responds, in part, to recent calls for the development of an anthropology of the good.[1] We begin here, however, with an earlier generation of anthropological thinking about the good, especially as it contrasts with the kinds of goodness we have seen in our three cases. Half a century ago, George Foster identified an "image of the limited good," which he thought characterized "peasants" everywhere.[2] The article was strongly influential at the time, helping to shape both academic anthropology and development policy during the heyday of modernization theory. While Foster's assumptions have long been questioned and the article no longer holds its earlier authority, his analysis is still a useful foil for understanding the very different images of goodness that we have been discussing. His taken-for-granted notion of a "modern good" that contrasted with the image of the limited good reveals the nature of the notions that have become naturalized in much of the world, including much of what we saw in our research.

In a typically anthropological way, Foster was trying to explain the sense behind behavior that North American and European observers (especially development professionals) found irrational. In doing so, he implied a contrast between a peasant view of goodness and the one that people from "modern" societies were taking for granted as natural and normal. He never spelled out the "modern" half of this contrast, but his implied concept of modern goodness nevertheless helps reveal the contours of what we mean by an image of the boundless good – the sort of good that has animated many of the people we have been writing about here.

The premodern limited good had several key aspects for Foster. First, it permeated all aspects of life. If one person grew rich, it must be at the expense of someone else; friendship with one person could only strengthen at the cost of other friendships. Health and honor were similarly limited so that one person's gain was always another's loss. Even a mother's love was limited, giving rise to endemic sibling rivalry.[3] This is a world where goodness could neither be

[1] Robbins, "Beyond the Suffering Subject: Toward an Anthropology of the Good."
[2] Foster, "Peasant Society and the Image of Limited Good."
[3] Ibid., 298.

created nor destroyed, but where it flowed toward some and away from others. Second, it was strongly bound in by a muscular culture (a fundamental and shared "cognitive orientation" in his terms). That is, individual agency was relatively powerless to affect the basic concept, even though individuals could make choices about how to maximize their own good. Foster's ideas linked to an anthropological form of modernization theory, as made clear in one of the few passages where he points explicitly toward a nonpeasant image of the good, writing that "the primary task in development is … to try to change the peasants' view of his social and economic universe, away from an Image of Limited Good toward that of expanding opportunity in an open system."[4]

We bring this up not because Foster's image of the limited good resonates very closely with the alternative forms of goodness we have been describing in Chinese societies: it does not. Rather, his implied opposite – an expanding good in an open system – tells us a lot about the broader secularized idea of goodness that has now become important in Chinese societies, and indeed in much of the world. This comment of Foster's about expansion and openness sheds light on the image of unlimited good that he appeared to take for granted as normal and natural.[5] In this good, the primary unit of agency is not a culturally determined "cognitive orientation" like that of peasants, but the autonomous individual making decisions in an open system. For purposes of engaged religions, we might say that the unit is the individual heart. This was constantly emphasized by nearly everyone in our study as the most important element for intervention. The hearts of people need to change so that they themselves will want to help others instead of pursuing only self-interest. Christians talked about this through the image of God's love, and Buddhists through that of an enlightened heart (菩提心, bodhicitta), like that of a bodhisattva. The main goal of modern charity is also to change the hearts of others, to reform and transform them, much as Foster's "development" aimed to transform the hearts of peasants.

Just as the autonomous heart is the main unit of intervention, love is the main currency. This is not the limited love of Foster's peasant mother, but the infinite and inexhaustible love – Jesus' love, a bodhisattva's love, the Chinese idea of a Great Love (大爱, 兼爱, 博爱) – that has become so crucial in the discourse of charity in China, Malaysia, and Taiwan.[6] As we have discussed,

[4] Ibid., 310.

[5] Others have also discussed the concept of unlimited good as a contrast with Foster's work, most notably Nash, *Practicing Ethnography in a Globalizing World*, 35–54. They use it, however, to examine only the economic aspect of capitalism, and to criticize its unlimited drive to consume and amass wealth. Here we stress, like Foster, that the concept actually reaches far beyond the economic sphere, affecting philanthropy as much as production and consumption.

[6] Note that the character for love (爱) is not very common in early Chinese texts, with the exception of Mozi's anti-Confucian promotion of the idea of universal love (兼爱). Nor is it important in the major Buddhist sutras. Nevertheless, the term continued to constitute a minor theme

love has become a dominant trope over the past few decades, fully permeating engaged religions, but also central to state and secular discussions of charity.

Finally, let us note that the image of unlimited goodness-as-love also accepts no national or class boundaries, at least in principle. This is emphatically not the image of local charity that grows out of the thick ties of social capital we discussed in Chapter 5, nor is it the Confucian one that carefully calibrates the quality of the unequal relationships between people (see Chapter 4). Tzu Chi's international work is the clearest example in our research, but many groups are crossing, or at least claiming to cross religious, class, and geographic lines. The idea links closely to the rise of the conception of an inclusive "public," which should share in the general love, rather than the overlapping and interested spheres of an earlier Chinese view of humanity.

Chinese Contexts of the Unlimited Good

One of our goals has been to explain the timing of this revaluation of ideas about goodness in Chinese societies. A retired official of the United Front Work Department (which is responsible for religious policy, among other things) in Shanghai offered us her own observations about how different Shanghai's religious charity was now from the situation in the 1950s and earlier. Back then, she said, there were two crucial differences from today. First, religious charity tended to be specialized as each group pursued its own path. Catholics, for instance, specialized in orphanages. Native place associations (originally always organized with altars) specialized in charitable graveyards (as they still do in Malacca). Each had its own niche based on both theology and history. Now, however, most charity looks alike across all the religions. Second, she said, religions and other social organizations in the past generally helped only their own groups. Now they all help anyone in need.

This may be somewhat overstated, given the evidence for the continuation of alternate ideas about goodness that we outlined in the previous chapter. Nevertheless, her summary identifies a general trend that we have seen in all of our field sites to various degrees, and which we date roughly to the 1980s. This postdates Foster's implied vision of the naturalized "modern" unlimited good by several decades. Nevertheless, we would not reduce the current situation in Chinese societies to a simple reiteration of a vision of goodness that modernization theorists like Foster took for granted. The ideas are related, but our

in Chinese thought throughout the historical period, as for instance with Zhang Zai (張載, 1020–1077): "Show deep love toward the orphaned and the weak … Even those who are tired, infirm, crippled, or sick; those who have no brothers or children, wives or husbands, are all my brothers who are in distress and have no one to turn to," in Chan, *A Source Book in Chinese Philosophy*, 497.

basic argument is that all ideas of goodness are shaped by unique historical, social, and political circumstances. For that reason, we would expect to see important variations molded by both time and place. In this section we review some of the most important characteristics of the unlimited good as it took form in our three Chinese societies toward the end of the twentieth century, and as it continues today.

As we discussed in the chapters on social capital and innovation, one of the reasons for the timing of the change has to do with the clearing away or at least diminishing of many of the social forms that supported older and more particularistic forms of charity. Rapid urbanization and high population mobility, especially in Taiwan and China, meant that rural temples no longer served the same kinds of communities. In poor areas, villages often lack the working-age adults who are crucial for temple functions. In the cities where they arrive, massive urban renewal has generally broken up and scattered old neighborhoods and their temples (although exceptions such as Lukang remind us of what it used to be like more generally).

Other factors have also weakened older power structures. This is most obvious in China, where campaigns to disempower alternate forms of authority began systematically in the 1950s with attacks on lineages, native place associations, and religion in general. Neither Taiwan nor Malaysia had such a drastic experience, but both have still felt changes of their own. Taiwan's land reform, although very different from China's, also undercut the communal economic base of many forms of association. The Guomindang government during the authoritarian period allowed little space for alternate forms of social authority. Although Malaysian Chinese preserved more of these earlier forms, even they felt the influence of migration and economic change. Recent Taiwanese migrants to Malaysia, for instance, were crucial in importing Tzu Chi's new vision of what engaged religion could be. For all these reasons, lines of social authority have been in flux, with the 1980s having been a crucial period especially for migration and urbanization in all three places. The formations of power dominated by place-based, middle-aged and older, wealthy men have declined in many areas, and are being replaced by new forms as a result of both economic change and state policy.

The weakening of older structures of power and authority thus created an opportunity for innovation, although of course it did not determine what those innovations would be. Among the most important forms of innovation that we identified in Chapter 6 were greater leadership roles for women and a universalizing image of what charity should be – one crucial aspect of the image of the unlimited good. These changes were made possible by a general decline in the strength of earlier forms of social capital across the region, which had previously helped channel religious engagement toward local and particularistic purposes generally under the control of older, wealthier men. In contrast to much of the literature on the contributions of social capital to social well-being, our cases show that sometimes breaking down such ties is a crucial step in developing new forms social engagement. We also saw how these processes helped encourage a change in the nature of the gift itself, fostering a greatly increased role for gifts through intermediaries and as indicators of a generically loving heart, rather than the earlier primary emphasis on gifts as creators of direct social and emotional bonds between givers and recipients.

The weakening of the older forms of religious charity provides a partial answer to the question of why we see these changes in the 1980s, but it does not address the reasons behind the particular change to an image of the unlimited good and a practice of industrialized philanthropy. We have identified several primary mechanisms to help explain those developments. In our cases one of those primary concerns is how states shape the niches to which engaged religions must adapt (see especially Chapter 3). The three relevant governments in our cases have been influenced by global trends, for instance in the rapid embrace of nongovernmental organizations (NGOs), but always adapted to their local needs and interests. In each case, the state is strong enough to have a powerful shaping influence on the resulting world of engaged religion.

The primary carriers of this engaged religion are the religious institutions themselves and the NGOs they sometimes foster. Even though some of these act on an international scale, all of them are very much shaped by political agendas, laws, and regulations that each state has developed. For instance, restrictions on conversion and worship greatly alter the religious field in each of our sites. China allows no religious activity that attempts to convert minors and none that takes place outside of designated religious sites. This makes it almost impossible to emphasize religious content while providing charity. Malaysia permits no attempts to convert Muslims, and this has helped keep engaged religion there bunkered into ethnic enclaves. Only Taiwan has no comparable restrictions and thus yet another pattern of engagement.

Each place also has very different structures for defining nonprofits, social organizations, foundations and other forms of NGO. Tzu Chi in China thus takes a very different institutional form from the same group in Malaysia or Taiwan. Similarly, we showed at the beginning of Chapter 3 how these differences pushed Tzu Chi into quite different land acquisition strategies under each of these regimes. States thus continue to matter and to shape variations in how religious philanthropy can take place.

State rules about the operation of NGOs, in spite of their differences, have also promoted some cross-national similarities in the management of engaged religion as well as in its content. The process of applying for money from the state or from international NGOs forces religious (and other) groups into particular rhetorical and organizational modes. They need to direct their efforts in directions that the funders favor, which tends to push all groups to act in similar ways. Thus in China we see widespread interest in constructing old age homes across the entire religious spectrum. This is because the government recognizes the impending consequences of decades of the one-child policy; it is thus willing to make resources available to such efforts and engaged religious groups have thus converged on this kind of project.

The rules governing nonprofits and religious organizations have further promoted a convergence toward similar ideas of goodness and structures for enacting it. Traditional mechanisms of transparent religious finance – like posting the names and amounts of donations outside a temple – are no longer sufficient. All three states we studied increasingly require modern accounting methods, enforced through the threat of audit. Some of these work through tax laws concerning nonprofit status and the treatment of donations; others involve restrictions on how NGOs handle funds or minimum amounts of endowment they must hold; still others involve direct regulation of religion. No matter what the specifics are, however, the result is a kind of "audit culture" that pushes all engaged religion toward one particular mold.[7]

As we discussed in Chapter 3, the various regimes we are studying here have each reached rather different accommodations with engaged religions. China's enormous power over the sector has put engaged religions into a defensive posture, where they need to earn political merit with the state in order to carry out their activities. In postdemocratic Taiwan, however, the relationship is much more mutualist. Engaged religions still need to earn merit with the state, but politicians also rely on the mobilizational potential of religion. Finally, in Malaysia, with a mode of governance built around clearly marked ethnoreligious lines, engaged religions usually take the form of enclaves, each working primarily within its own ethnic bunker. These findings undermine the idea that private forms of welfare (such as NGOs or engaged religions) thrive primarily in situations of state failure or state retrenchment. None of these are failed states and none exactly resemble the retrenched welfare states of West Europe.

They also undermine the idea that greater authoritarian control means less effective social engagement. Both China and Taiwan before democratization had something like a defensive form of political merit-making, but such forms can be both important and effective. These cases remind us not to make any simple reductions to authoritarian versus democratic rule. Both bring their own range of variations. The mechanisms of defensive merit-making in China today and Taiwan before 1987 were quite different from each other, because of Taiwan's tradition (at that time) of avoiding state responsibility for welfare as much as possible, and China's socialist tradition of embracing it as much as

[7] See Strathern, *Audit Cultures*.

possible. Malaysia and post-1987 Taiwan are both democratic, and both indeed show aspects of mutualist political merit-making, but their patterns of engaged religion are again quite different because of Malaysia's heritage of ethnic separation. All three of our polities have thus encouraged a convergence toward industrialized philanthropy, but it will never be total because of continuing difference between state structures and goals.

Another mechanism fostering the convergence in the ideals and forms of religious philanthropy that began in the 1980s is direct interaction among engaged religious groups – those driven by the competition between groups for resources and supporters leading to emulation of successful strategies, rather than those driven by the more vertical processes of politics. The two forms interact, of course, because political resources are some of the most significant ones over which groups compete.

It is tempting to think that the rise of modern engaged religion is an emulation of the welfare-oriented strategies carried to China by missionaries in the late nineteenth and early twentieth centuries. There is no doubt that they promoted a strong religious identity to the provision of medical care, education, disaster relief and many other areas in ways that closely resemble the modern pattern. Nevertheless, such an explanation is surely wrong, or at best very partial, as we have argued. First, it fails to address the time gap of very roughly a century between the introduction of this movement and the convergence toward a similar model that began in the 1980s. Second, it ignores the close connections between belief systems and social engagement that already had a very long history in China. While some of these were explicitly Buddhist, many others were based in local temple religion or in Confucian thought, and thus not recognized as religion by either the missionaries or the Republican and then Communist governments of China. Nevertheless, there is no compelling reason for us to accept such a very narrow and ultimately Protestant-inspired concept of religion. Instead, we place far more emphasis on the adaptation of existing social and cultural resources to a new image of the unlimited good.

The example we gave in Chapter 4 of the Presbyterians in Lukang showed the kind of transformation we have in mind. For George Mackay, the early Presbyterian missionary who first spread his faith in Taiwan, providing medical help for non-Christians was an example of God's infinite love – *caritas*, a version of the unlimited good – in addition to being a technique to gain converts. Nevertheless, the Presbyterians in Lukang increasingly served only their own congregation throughout most of the twentieth century, becoming more like a Chinese model of localist good. Only in the 1980s did they begin to look outwards again, inspired not so much by an ideology of caritas, we suggested, as by the great successes of Tzu Chi.

We are thus proposing that the idea of caritas and the entire Christian theological armature that supports it is not an especially important factor in driving the changes we have documented. Even in North America and West Europe this particular version of caritas became important primarily only in the nineteenth century – it is not somehow primordially Christian.[8] In the various Chinese societies we are discussing here, the image of the unlimited good and the timing of its growth stems much more from the changes in political and social space in the 1980s and 1990s that we have been discussing than from a direct emulation of Christianity.

This certainly seems to be true of Tzu Chi, which has been among the most influential modern movements of engaged religion in our study areas. Of course, there is a Catholic side to Tzu Chi's origin story, as we have discussed. Nevertheless, the group never simply emulated Christian models. From the beginning it was rooted in a Buddhist conception of the self and the universe. Part of its genius was the ability to make an image of the unlimited good – whose origins lie in the logic of the market economy and the demands of the nation-state as much as in any religious tradition – appeal to people through a familiar Buddhist language. This quickly swept Taiwan and then the entire Chinese world.

One of the areas in which Tzu Chi has departed from older Christian missionary models of social engagement is in its ability to create deployable agents who enact the group's unbounded love (see Chapter 4). Note that this idea too is integral to the image of the unlimited good. Recall that for Foster, as for modernization theory more generally, non-Western people like "peasants" were held back by the iron grip of a muscle-bound culture. The implied opposite was the idea of a fully autonomous individual, operating in a world where everyone might eventually achieve maximal goodness. Here we have people whose utility is universal love, to be maximized as a realization of God's caritas (for the Christians) or as the bodhisattva's drive to salvation for all living things. In a way parallel to the economy, the ability to make autonomous choices results in individuals (factory workers, Tzu Chi volunteers) who can be deployed toward the general good (profit for the factory, healing for the sick). This idea of the individual as a deployable agent in service of a greater good, a loving heart placed within a universe of civic harmony, is what we have called "civic selving."

The volunteering that goes hand in hand with civic selving is not new in Buddhist temples. They have long had groups of lay Buddhists who take part in rituals and help out around the temple by cooking or cleaning. This was primarily a form of personal religious cultivation for the people involved. With Tzu Chi, however, we see a completely new model as their masses of volunteers became deployable agents who could be directed toward all kinds of

[8] Two of us have discussed this briefly in Huang and Weller "Merit and Mothering."

projects. While Buddhist cultivation remains a goal for some of these people, it is no longer the primary issue, and in fact volunteers need not think of themselves as Buddhists at all, as we discussed in Chapter 4.

This change in the nature of volunteering toward deployable agency now exists far beyond Tzu Chi. The difference between the two models of Buddhist volunteering was palpable when one of us attended the ceremony to seat the new abbot of a large temple in Nanjing in 2014. Such events do not happen frequently, so the Buddhist leadership of the entire city was in attendance along with hundreds of monks and nuns. There were hundreds of volunteers as well, because many temples had mobilized their lay followers to help out. A quick glance was enough to differentiate the two kinds of volunteers. Two or three hundred wore black Buddhist robes (海清) that serious lay Buddhists buy for themselves. These people were mostly in their sixties and seventies, and spent their time milling about the temple courtyards and chatting to each other. All of these were the cultivational model of volunteer and they came from most of the larger temples in the city.

The other model was represented by about 150 volunteers, probably twenty or thirty years younger on average, standing in ordered ranks and wearing identical red vests bearing the name of their temple, the Qingliang Si (清凉寺). As all the other abbots entered the restricted area where the main ceremony would take place, their abbot stood in front of his volunteers, carefully instructing them about what they should do and where they should go. He was, in brief, deploying his agents, these civic selves, making this group stand out from all the others with its efficiency and organization (see Figure 8.1).

Christians do not look very different. The closest to the Tzu Chi model of deployable agency is probably China's Amity Foundation, as we have discussed. Like Tzu Chi, they have a core of employed professionals as well as a large reserve of volunteers whom they deploy on all kinds of projects. YMCAs in Hangzhou and Nanjing that we examined have the same structure, though on a smaller scale. Volunteers for Amity or the YMCA need not be Christian at all, and many are not. In some cases, they may not even realize that they are working for Christian groups. That is, they are being deployed for "good," but this good is generic and universal rather than being the product of a specific religious tradition. And this very form of volunteering is equally ubiquitous and not tied to any religious tradition. It is, of course, quite typical of a wide range of purely secular NGOs as well as these religious groups.

This convergence toward similar models of the unlimited good requires us to go beyond any simple evocation of "globalization" as an explanation. Our cases point to the importance of both power and competition. We saw power primarily operating through what we called political merit-making. Even this, however, has an element of imitation in the way that various regimes have converged in certain features (e.g., auditing and reporting requirements) even

Figure 8.1 New-style volunteers, Nanjing 2013.

as they maintain their own differences (e.g., in how they define the religious field). The early twentieth century saw something similar (as we outlined more briefly in Chapter 2) when states throughout the world began to adopt constitutions involving some form of separation of church and state and began the push toward secularism that we saw especially clearly in Taiwan and China. There was thus both imitation and competition as states learned from each other, and the deployment of power as they put their new rules into effect in ways that continue to shape the religious fields we see today.

Saying that there was imitation or globalization, however, really offers very little explanatory power.[9] Imitation always involves some form of adaptation, and does not occur at all unless the imitation makes sense to people. Tzu Chi may indeed have served as a catalyst for some contemporary engaged religion, but pure imitation is not an explanation. For the same reasons, Cheng Yen's argument with Catholic nuns did not result in a simple Tzu Chi imitation of an existing Christian model. Rather, the unlimited good and its deployable agents became convincing to people toward the end of the twentieth century because it meshed with such a wide range of their life experience. In this period of rapid economic growth in all three of our study areas, the economic experience of individual agency and an idea of unlimited progress made compelling sense. Socially there was the idea of unlimited improvement that could be shared by everyone, even those whom the economic system had shunted aside. We might

[9] We are inspired in part here by the work of Gabriel Tarde at the turn of the previous century: Tarde, *The Laws of Imitation*.

see both the early missionaries and the later Tzu Chi as catalytic moments in this process, but catalysts work only when the rest of the chemistry is right, which happened especially in the 1980s in the regions we examined.

Other Contexts

We have seen how an industrialized religious philanthropy based on the idea of autonomous volunteers rose to prominence across our three Chinese polities and across our religious traditions in the 1980s. The change had a powerful effect on the practice of engaged religion, and an even stronger influence on the rhetoric of what religious philanthropy should be, to the extent that many informants could articulate only a single idea of goodness, even when their own practice partially drew on other ideas. All of this, we have argued, tied to larger changes happening during the period: rapid economic growth, significant political loosening (though taking quite different forms in each of our cases), a growing ease and speed of communication through new media, increasing mobility within and across national borders, and new senses of selfhood.

We can see similar phenomena occurring in many societies at the time, and so perhaps it should not surprise us that several other recent studies have identified comparable changes in religious philanthropy during the 1980s beyond the Chinese world. We will discuss in particular two recent books that identify changes in religious philanthropy during roughly the same period: Mona Atia's study of what she calls "pious neoliberalism" in Egypt and Andrea Muehlebach's work on "moral neoliberals" in Italy.[10] These cases closely resemble ours, especially as the changes those authors document have constructed a new subjectivity built around volunteering, "loving" individuals and a "rationalization" of the process from ad hoc charity to what we have called industrialized philanthropy. Just as within our own examples, however, there are significant differences, which help to clarify the significance of the various Chinese contexts we have been discussing.

In both the Italian and Egyptian cases we can see state policies and international precedents that encouraged the development of industrial-scaled religious philanthropies. In Italy this was primarily the result of classic neoliberal policies where the state systematically moved away from a vision of welfare as a fundamental responsibility of the social contract with the state to a vision of having people take care of themselves without state interference (what we have been calling state retrenchment). Egypt was politically very different, of course, both in the relative financial inability of the state to provide welfare benefits, and in its construction as an authoritarian government. Nevertheless,

[10] Atia, *Building a House in Heaven*; Muehlebach, *The Moral Neoliberal.*

both developed forms of industrialized philanthropy. As Atia describes the "pious neoliberalism" that resulted in Egypt: "Associations used intensive social research systems to ensure that their money was going toward the right kind of poor. They shifted their charity work to a development model and emphasized market-based solutions to poverty, such as employment, upgrading skills, and microenterprises."[11]

In both cases, the process encouraged new kinds of subjectivities. In Egypt, for example, recipients of aid sometimes had "to attend moral and religious instruction (*irshad dini*) on topics such as cleanliness, organization, honesty, consistency between words and actions, neighborly relations, relationships with relatives, marital relations, and other disciplinary and behavioral issues."[12] This process was just as important for the donors and volunteers as for the recipients of such aid: "Individuals discipline the subjects they seek to help and in turn are also disciplined by the associations for which they volunteer."[13] This is strikingly similar to Tzu Chi's early slogan of providing "relief for the poor and instruction for the rich," which we mentioned in Chapter 4.

While in Egypt these changes encouraged a kind of privatized Islamic piety, the new subjectivity in Italy strongly echoed the emphasis on loving hearts that we have seen across our Chinese cases.

> When government agencies call for a 'citizenship to be lived with the heart'... , or when volunteers themselves state that the services they render are animated by 'love,' they all participate in generating a public fantasy of affectively animated individuals made productive through state law, policy, and citizens' sentiments themselves.[14]

Just as in our Chinese cases, Egypt and Italy show the rise of new forms of religious philanthropy that depend on changing concepts of selfhood that emphasize autonomous "loving" selves and deployable agents. Muehlebach even documents changes in the notion of the gift that are very consistent with what we have seen, where "the ethos of the gift, rather than disappearing under neoliberal conditions, is reappearing in its ideologically most heightened form – as magnanimous, selfless, unrequited acts of voluntary generosity performed by what appear as disembedded individuals."[15]

Both Atia and Muehlebach are concerned to show that neoliberalism is fully consistent with ideas of personal piety, loving hearts, and voluntary generosity. Much the same could be said about the Chinese cases. Unlike those authors, however, we have chosen not to highlight the concept of neoliberalism to the same degree in our analysis. One reason for this is that the concept seems

[11] Atia, *Building a House in Heaven*, 132.
[12] Ibid., 56.
[13] Ibid., 160.
[14] Muehlebach, *The Moral Neoliberal*, 10.
[15] Ibid., viii.

like too blunt an instrument – the political and economic situations in Egypt, Italy, China, Taiwan, and Malaysia do indeed share some important similarities, but the differences loom just as large and have just as powerful an effect on how engaged religions work. Of all these cases, for instance, only Italy had attempted a classic European welfare state, and thus only in Italy has the state been desacralized and the society sacralized to the same extent.[16]

The closest example in our study might be mainland China, where the Communist state before the reform period that began around 1979 made strong claims about its care for the welfare of all the people. It would be an enormous stretch of the term, however, to describe China today as neoliberal.[17] The state (like the Party) is consistently present in China, continuing to emphasize its critical role in all aspects of society. It has little interest in ideological claims of neoliberalism, even if some aspects of the regime do use techniques of neoliberal policy and governance.[18] Or again, in Egypt Atia describes how religious charities "deploy a neoliberal definition of social justice that sees job creation as a substitute for distributive justice."[19] Job creation and similar broad economic responsibility, however, was rarely stressed in any of the Malaysian, Taiwanese, and mainland Chinese cases we have examined. Every case responds to widely shared global pressures and to its own awareness of what other places are doing.

Final Thoughts

Thus, although we agree that there are powerful global trends at work here, we should not lose sight of crucial differences in how those trends are experienced and reworked from one place to another. For that reason, we have hesitated to reduce our cases to another example of moral or pious neoliberalism. These globalizing changes have been crucial in shaping religious engagement since the 1980s, as we have shown for all our sites. Nevertheless, combining everything under the simple label of some kind of religious neoliberalism risks losing sight of the variations that still characterize our cases, and which may prove to be crucial as these systems continue to evolve.

The forces that encouraged a partial convergence among our cases, with the 1980s providing an especially consequential turning point, led to a remarkable transnational and trans-religious cross-fertilization in organizational techniques, financial arrangements, and even the repertoire of activities undertaken.

16 Ibid., 92.

17 See Nonini, "Is China Becoming Neoliberal?," 2008.

18 We draw here to some extent on Larner's distinction between several types of neoliberalism. See Larner, "Neo-Liberalism: Policy, Ideology, Governmentality."

19 Atia, *Building a House in Heaven*, 26.

Explaining this change and exploring its limits has brought us into dialogue with several large theoretical trends.

First, globalization is obviously an important factor in the limited sense that our various states and religions are well aware of trends in other parts of the world, and they interact with those trends as they develop their own strategies. None of our cases, however, shows globalization as a straightforward, top-down process of imitation in which new practices are passed along as naturally as water flows downhill. For example, all three places we discuss felt the powerful effects of the worldwide trend toward secularism in the early twentieth century, but the actual institutionalization of religion/state relations in China, Malaysia, and Taiwan is very different, and this has changed the possibilities for engaged religions. All three places also felt powerful effects from the neoliberal policy fads that followed from the Reagan and Thatcher era. This led to many of the organizational and financial forms that we saw develop from the 1980s on, but all three places also have fundamental differences in how social organizations are defined, regulated, and audited.

In addition, we found little support for the idea that the globalization of nineteenth-century Christian ideas of charity was the primary shaper of current practice. Those ideas were certainly one factor in the general evolution of engaged religion, but there is little direct continuity between those missionary projects and current practice. What we have seen in our cases owes at least as much to Buddhist and what we might loosely call Confucian ideas of charity as to anything that came in from outside.

Second, national histories have influenced engaged religions in surprising ways. For example, we see the strongest continuities with traditional patterns of religious charity where colonialism lasted the longest (Malaysia), while China has the strongest rupture, even though it was the least colonized. The cross-national comparison also led us to reject zero-sum theories of the relation between state and social responsibility for social well-being. None of our cases involve failed states (or even very weak states) or clear retrenchment from earlier welfare goals (with the partial exception of the Chinese mainland). Yet all have made increasing space for charity through religious and other social organizations. The comparison also reminds us that the nation-state (including a political entity like Taiwan that functions as a state even without the diplomatic trappings) is still a crucial unit of power, not just shaping the religious and philanthropic fields, but providing the grounds for the political merit-making projects that are so central to engaged religion, in different ways, in each of our field sites.

Finally, perhaps our most important point for the general understanding of philanthropy is that no absolute "goodness" exists, except within the frames of just some of our religious traditions. All charity implies some concept of doing "good," and this is usually quite explicit in the religious forms. We have identified a strong tendency for engaged religion everywhere in our study to converge toward just one rhetorical version of the good – the one we have labeled as the image of the unlimited good. This is a universalist and ameliorist concept, realized through a limited repertoire of actions (disaster relief, public health and old age care, poverty programs, etc.), organized with the technology of secular NGOs, and supervised through the surveillance of an audit culture. Much of the literature on philanthropy assumes this form of goodness to be natural and obvious enough not to merit discussion. There is nothing natural about it, however. It developed under specific historical conditions, and became naturalized in the Chinese societies we have examined only in the 1980s and beyond.

This idea of goodness has spread powerfully through the mechanisms we have been discussing, including the weakening of earlier forms of social capital that supported alternate visions of the good, the processes of political merit-making, and the appeal of "loving hearts" as a means to creating civic selves. Yet there continue to be important differences across national and religious lines. We have seen, for example, that political merit-making works quite differently across our three polities, taking defensive, mutualist, or enclaved forms depending on local political and historical patterns. And although every religious tradition that we have examined has felt the powerful influence of these global trends, the image of the unlimited good still has not achieved a total monopoly on goodness. We think it is important that alternate conceptions of the good continue to exist, from spirit mediums to theologians, refusing and resisting the powerful pressures to become merged into a generic discourse of universal charity. A diversity of goodness gives us the resources to deal with future changes, and it encourages us to continue finding ways to help others in those areas to which the currently hegemonic "good" may be blind.

References

"A Brief History of the Cheng Hoon Teng, Melaka." Unpublished pamphlet. Malacca, n.d.

Allahyari, Rebecca Anne. *Visions of Charity: Volunteer Workers and Moral Community.* Berkeley: University of California Press, 2000.

Appadurai, Arjun. *Modernity at Large: Cultural Dimensions of Globalization.* Minneapolis: University of Minnesota Press, 1996.

Ashiwa, Yoshiko, and David Wank, eds. *Making Religion, Making the State: The Politics of Religion in Modern China.* Stanford, CA: Stanford University Press, 2009.

Assmann, Jan. "Collective Memory and Cultural Identity." Translated by John Czaplicka. *New German Critique*, April 1, 1995, 125–33.

Atia, Mona. *Building a House in Heaven: Pious Neoliberalism and Islamic Charity in Egypt.* Minneapolis: University of Minnesota Press, 2013.

Bays, Daniel H. *A New History of Christianity in China.* Malden, MA: Wiley-Blackwell, 2011.

Berger, Peter L. "Pluralism, Protestantization, and the Voluntary Principle." In *Democracy and the New Religious Pluralism*, edited by Thomas Banchoff, 19–29. New York: Oxford University Press, 2007.

Berger, Peter L., Brigitte Berger, and Hansfried Kellner. *The Homeless Mind: Modernization and Consciousness.* New York: Vintage, 1974.

Bian, Yanjie. "Review of 'The Flow of Gifts,' by Yunxiang Yan." *China Quarterly*, no. 150 (1997): 474–75.

Boretz, Avron. *Gods, Ghosts, and Gangsters: Ritual Violence, Martial Arts, and Masculinity on the Margins of Chinese Society.* Honolulu: University of Hawaii Press, 2010.

Bourdieu, Pierre. *Outline of a Theory of Practice.* Translated by Richard Nice. Cambridge: Cambridge University Press, 1977.

"The Forms of Capital." In *Handbook of Theory and Research for the Sociology of Education*, edited by J. Richardson, 241–58. New York: Greenwood, 1986.

Brokaw, Cynthia Joanne. *The Ledgers of Merit and Demerit: Social Change and Moral Order in Late Imperial China.* Princeton, NJ: Princeton University Press, 1991.

"Buddhist Tzu Chi Foundation Fact Sheet." www.us.tzuchi.org/us/en/index.php?option=com_content&view=article&id=308&Itemid=282&lang=en (Accessed May 16, 2017).

Cammett, Melani, and Sukriti Issar. "Bricks and Mortar Clientalism: Sectarianism and the Logics of Welfare Allocation in Lebanon." *World Politics* 62, no. 3 (2010): 381–421.

Campany, Robert Ford. *Signs from the Unseen Realm: Buddhist Miracle Tales from Early Medieval China*. Honolulu: University of Hawaii Press, 2012.

Cao, Nanlai (曹南来). ("A Local Business Elite and Popular Christian Charity.") "地方商业精英与民间基督教慈善." In (*Religion and Public Life in the Jiangnan Region*) 江南地区的宗教与公共生活, edited by Robert P. Weller (魏乐博) and Lizhu Fan (范丽珠), 237–58. 上海: 上海人民出版社, 2015.

Cao, Xinyu. "From Famine History to Crisis Metaphor: Social Memory and Cultural Identity in Chinese Rural Society." *Chinese Studies in History* 44, no. 1–2 (2010): 156–71.

Chan, Wing-Tsit. *A Source Book in Chinese Philosophy*. Princeton, NJ: Princeton University Press, 1969.

Chandler, Stuart. *Establishing a Pure Land on Earth*. Honolulu: University of Hawaii Press, 2004.

Chau, Adam Yuet. *Miraculous Response: Doing Popular Religion in Contemporary China*. Stanford, CA: Stanford University Press, 2005.

Chipman, Elana. *Our Beigang: Culture Work, Ritual and Community in a Taiwanese Town*. PhD dissertation, Cornell University, 2007.

Choy, T. Y. "The Development of Education Culture and Arts of the Malacca Chinese." Working paper. The Melaka Story. Malacca: Melaka Chinese Assembly Hall, January 15, 2003.

Chu, Ruey-ling. "Charity and Altruistic Behavior in Chinese Societies." *Bulletin of the Institute of Ethnology, Academia Sinica* 75 (1993): 105–32.

Csikszentmihalyi, Mark. "Finding Altruism in China: The Confucian Corpus and the Quest for Universal Benevolence." Unpublished paper, n.d. www.academia.edu/6214406/Finding_Altruism_in_China (Accessed May 16, 2017).

Dan, Wenjing (單文經). (*Lukang Gazetteer: Education.*) *鹿港镇志：教育篇*. 鹿港：鹿港镇公所, 2000.

DeBernardi, Jean. *Rites of Belonging: Memory, Modernity, and Identity in a Malaysian Chinese Community*. Stanford, CA: Stanford University Press, 2004.

DeGlopper, Donald R. *Lukang: Commerce and Community in a Chinese City*. Albany: State University of New York Press, 1995.

Du, Xuede (杜学得). ("Welcoming the Gods and Peforming Nuo Ritual in Guyi Village of Wu'an City.") 武安市固义村迎神祭祀暨社火傩戏." In (*Collected Research on Popular Culture in North Chinese Villages: Records Popular Customs of the Handan Region*) *华北农村民间文化研究丛书：邯郸地区民俗记录*, edited by Daniel L. Overmyer and Lizhu Fan(范丽珠). 天津：天津古籍出版, 2006.

Duara, Prasenjit. "The Discourse of Civilization and Pan-Asianism." *Journal of World History* 12, no. 1 (2001): 99–130.

Sovereignty and Authenticity: Manchukuo and the East Asian Modern. Lanham, MD: Rowman & Littlefield, 2004.

"Superscribing Symbols: The Myth of Guandi, Chinese God of War." *The Journal of Asian Studies* 47, no. 4 (1988): 778–95.

"Transnationalism and the Predicament of Sovereignty: China, 1900–1945." *The American Historical Review* 102, no. 4 (1997): 1030–51.

DuBois, Thomas David. "Before the NGO: Chinese Charities in Historical Perspective." *Asian Studies Review* 39, no. 4 (2015): 541–53.

"Public Health and Private Charity in Northeast China, 1905–1945." *Frontiers of History in China* 9, no. 4 (2014): 506–33.

Embong, Abdul Rahman. "The Culture and Practice of Pluralism in Postcolonial Malaysia." In *The Politics of Multiculturalism: Pluralism and Citizenship in Malaysia, Singapore, and Indonesia*, edited by Robert W. Hefner, 59–85. Honolulu: University of Hawaii Press, 2001.

Eno, Robert. "The Analects of Confucius: An Online Teaching Translation," 2015. www.indiana.edu/~p374/Analects_of_Confucius_(Eno-2012).pdf (Accessed December 12, 2016).

"The Great Learning and the Doctrine of the Mean: An Online Teaching Translation," 2016. www.indiana.edu/~p374/Daxue-Zhongyong.pdf (Accessed December 12, 2016).

Fassin, Didier. "Introduction: Toward a Critical Moral Anthropology." In *A Companion to Moral Anthropology*, 1–17. Chichester, West Sussex, UK; Malden, MA: Wiley-Blackwell, 2012.

Fassin, Didier, and Richard Rechtman. *The Empire of Trauma: An Inquiry into the Condition of Victimhood*. Princeton, NJ: Princeton University Press, 2009.

Faubion, James D. *An Anthropology of Ethics*. Cambridge: Cambridge University Press, 2011.

Faure, David. *Emperor and Ancestor: State and Lineage in South China*. Stanford, CA: Stanford University Press, 2007.

Fisher, Gareth. *From Comrades to Bodhisattvas: Moral Dimensions of Lay Buddhist Practice in Contemporary China*. Honolulu: University of Hawaii Press, 2014.

Formoso, Bernard. *De Jiao – A Religious Movement in Contemporary China and Overseas: Purple Qi from the East*. Singapore: NUS Press, 2010.

Foster, George M. "Peasant Society and the Image of Limited Good." *American Anthropologist* 67 (1965): 293–315.

Freedman, Maurice. *The Chinese in Southeast Asia: A Longer View*. London: The China Society, 1965.

Freedman, Maurice, and Marjorie Topley. "Religion and Social Realignment among the Chinese in Singapore." *The Journal of Asian Studies* 21, no. 1 (1961): 3–23.

Fuma, Susumu (夫馬進). *(History of Chinese Benevolent Halls and Associations.) 中国善堂善会史*. 北京：商务印书馆, 2005.

Fung, Heidi. "Becoming a Moral Child: The Socialization of Shame among Young Chinese Children." *Ethos* 27, no. 2 (1999): 180–209.

Gao, Bingzhong (高丙中). ("An Ethnography of a Building Both as Museum and Temple: On the Double-Naming Method as an Art of Politics.") 一座博物馆--庙宇建筑的民族志: 论成为政治艺术的双名制." 社会学研究, no. 121 (2006): 154–68.

Gao, Shining (高师宁). ("The Positive Role of Religion in Society.") "试论宗教在社会中的积极作用." *The Chinese Scholarship on Religion*, 2012. http://iwr.cass.cn/zjyzz/201204/t20120405_10303.htm.

Giddens, Anthony. *The Consequences of Modernity*. Stanford, CA: Stanford University Press, 1990.

Goossaert, Vincent. "Republican Church Engineering: The National Religious Associations in 1912 China." In *Chinese Religiosities: Afflictions of Modernity and State Formation*, edited by Mayfair Mei-hui Yang, 209–32. Berkeley: University of California Press, 2008.

Goossaert, Vincent, and David A. Palmer. *The Religious Question in Modern China*. Chicago: University of Chicago Press, 2011.

Granovetter, Mark S. "The Strength of Weak Ties." *American Journal of Sociology* 78, no. 6 (May 1, 1973): 1360–80.

Harrison, Henrietta. *The Missionary's Curse and Other Tales from a Chinese Catholic Village*. Stanford, CA: Stanford University Press, 2013.

Hefner, Robert W. "Introduction." In *The Politics of Multiculturalism: Pluralism and Citizenship in Malaysia, Singapore, and Indonesia*, edited by Robert W. Hefner, 1–58. Honolulu: University of Hawaii Press, 2001.

"Multiple Modernities: Christianity, Islam and Hinduism in a Globalizing Age." *Annual Review of Anthropology* 27 (1998): 83–104.

Hirschman, Charles. "Demographic Trends in Peninsular Malaysia, 1947–1975." *Population and Development Review* 6, no. 1 (1980): 103–25.

Huang, Chien-Yu Julia, and Robert P. Weller. "Merit and Mothering: Women and Social Welfare in Taiwanese Buddhism." *The Journal of Asian Studies* 57 (1998): 379–96.

Huang, C. Julia. *Charisma and Compassion: Cheng Yen and the Buddhist Tzu Chi Movement*. Cambridge, MA: Harvard University Press, 2009.

"*Provider and Facilitator: Religion and Social Capital among the Chinese in Malacca, Malaysia*." University of Toronto, 2009.

Huang, Minzhi (黄敏枝). (*Collected Essays on the Song Buddhist Economy*.) *宋代佛教经济史论集*. 台北：台湾学生出版社, 1989.

Huang, Shiun-wey. "Accepting the Best, Revealing the Difference – Borrowing and Identity in an Ami Village." In *Religion in Modern Taiwan: Tradition and Innovation in a Changing Society*, edited by Philip Clart and Charles Brewer Jones, 257–79. Honolulu: University of Hawaii Press, 2003.

(黄宣衛). ("The Historical Construction and Imagination of Foreigners: Analysis of Ami Cultural Identity through the Example of Three Leaders.") "历史建构与异族意像 – 以三个村落领袖为例： 初探阿美族的文化认同." In (*Han Society and Culture Seen from the Frontier*), *从周边看汉人的社会与文化*, edited by Yinggui Huang (黄应贵) and Chunrong Ye (叶春荣), 167–203. 台北：中央研究院民族学研究所, 1997.

Huang, Xiuzheng (黄秀政). (*Lukang Gazetteer: History*.) *鹿港镇志：沿革篇*. 鹿港：鹿港镇公所, 2000.

Hunt, Robert, Kam Hing Lee, and John Roxborogh. *Christianity in Malaysia: A Denominational History*. Petaling Jaya: Pelanduk Publications, 1992.

Inda, Jonathan Xavier, and Renato Rosaldo, eds. *The Anthropology of Globalization: A Reader*, 2nd ed. Malden, MA: Wiley-Blackwell, 2007.

Inouye, Melissa. "Miraculous Mundane: The True Jesus Church and Chinese Christianity in the Twentieth Century." ProQuest Dissertations Publishing, 2011. http://search.proquest.com/docview/856603282/ (Accessed July 27, 2016).

Introduction to the Quanzhou Guild. *泉郊简介*. 鹿港：金昌顺泉郊基金会, 1995.

James, Erica Caple. *Democratic Insecurities: Violence, Trauma, and Intervention in Haiti*. Berkeley: University of California Press, 2010.

"Haiti, Insecurity, and the Politics of Asylum: Haiti, Insecurity, and the Politics of Asylum." *Medical Anthropology Quarterly* 25, no. 3 (2011): 357–76.

Jing, Jun. "Environmental Protests in Rural China." In *Chinese Society: Change, Conflict and Resistance*, edited by Mark Selden and Elizabeth J. Perry, 197–214. New York: Routledge, 2000.

Johnson, Ian. "Two Sides of a Mountain: The Modern Transformation of Maoshan." *Journal of Daoist Studies* 5 (2012): 89–116.

Katz, Paul R. *Demon Hordes and Burning Boats: The Cult of Marshal Wen in Late Imperial Chekiang*. Albany: State University of New York Press, 1995.

"The Religious Life of a Renowned Shanghai Businessman and Philanthropist, Wang Yiting." Unpublished paper. Institute of Modern History, Academia Sinica, Taiwan, 2006.

Kieschnick, John. *The Impact of Buddhism on Chinese Material Culture*. Princeton, NJ: Princeton University Press, 2003.

Kipnis, Andrew B. *Producing Guanxi: Sentiment, Self, and Subculture in a North China Village*. Durham, NC: Duke University Press, 1997.

Knoblock, John, and Jeffrey Riegel. *Mozi: A Study and Translation of the Ethical and Political Writings*. Berkeley, CA: Institute of East Asian Studies, 2013.

Laidlaw, James. "For an Anthropology of Ethics and Freedom." *The Journal of the Royal Anthropological Institute* 8, no. 2 (2002): 311–32.

The Subject of Virtue: An Anthropology of Ethics and Freedom. Cambridge: Cambridge University Press, 2014.

Laliberté, André. "The Growth of a Taiwanese Buddhist Association in China: Soft Power and Institutional Learning." *China Information* 27, no. 1 (2013): 81–105.

"Religions and Philanthropy in Chinese Societies Since 1978." In *Modern Chinese Religion, 1850–2015*, edited by Vincent Goossaert, Jan Kiely, and John Lagerway, 2:613–48. Leiden: Brill, 2016.

Larner, Wendy. "Neo-Liberalism: Policy, Ideology, Governmentality." *Studies in Political Economy* 63 (2000): 5–25.

"Laws of Malaysia: Act 15 – Sedition Act 1948, Incorporating All Amendments up to 1 January 2006." The Commissioner of Law Revision, Malaysia, under the Authority of the Revision of Laws Act 1968, in collaboration with Malayan Law Journal SDN Bhd and Percetakan Nasional Malaysia Bhd, 2006.

Lee, Anru. "Subway as a Space of Cultural Intimacy: The Mass Rapid Transit System in Taipei, Taiwan." *China Journal* 58, no. 2 (2007): 31–55.

Lee, Raymond L. M., and Susan E. Ackerman. *Sacred Tensions: Modernity and Religious Transformation in Malaysia*. Columbia: University of South Carolina Press, 1997.

Leung, Angela Ki Che (梁其姿). (*Charity and Jiaohua: Philanthropic Groups in Ming and Qing China.*) *施善与教化：明清的慈善组织*. 石家庄：河北教育出版社, 2001.

Li, Yih-yuan (李亦园). (*An Immigrant Town: Life in an Overseas Community in Southern Malaya.*) *一个移殖的市镇：马来西亚华人市镇生活的调查研究*. 台北：正中书局, 1985.

Li, Zhigang (李志刚). (*The History of Early Christian Missionaries to China.*) *基督教早期在华传教士*. 台北：台湾商务印书馆, 1984.

Lian, Xi. *Redeemed by Fire: The Rise of Popular Christianity in Modern China*. New Haven, CT: Yale University Press, 2010.

Liang, Yongjia. "Turning Gwer Sa La Festival into Intangible Cultural Heritage: State Superscription of Popular Religion in Southwest China." *China: An International Journal* 11, no. 2 (2013): 58–75.

Lim, Khay Thiong (林开忠). (*Constructing Chinese Culture: An Ethnic-Based State and the Chinese Language Education Movement.*) *建构中的华人文化：族群属性国家与华教运动*. Hong Kong: 华社研究中心, 1999.

Liu, Shufen (刘淑芬). (*Medieval Buddhism and Society.*) 中古的佛教与社会. 上海：上海古籍出版社, 1991.

Liu, Ying. "Love and Faith: An Empirical Study on the Current Situation of Christian Charity in Jiangsu." In *Christianity and Social Development in China*, edited by Theresa C. Cariño, 251–69. Hong Kong: Amity Foundation, 2014.

Lozada, Eriberto. *God Aboveground: Catholic Church, Postsocialist State, and Transnational Processes in a Chinese Village*. Stanford, CA: Stanford University Press, 2001.

Luo, Jingshan (骆静山). ("The Past and Present of Chinese Religion in the Malay Peninsula.") "大马半岛华人宗教的今昔." In (*History of the Chinese in Malaysia*) *马来西亚华人史*, edited by Shuigao Lin (林水檺) and Jingshan Luo (骆静山), 409–45. Kuala Lumpur: 马来西亚留台校友会联合中会, 1984.

Lynn, Richard John, trans. *The Classic of Changes: A New Translation of the I Ching as Interpreted by Wang Bi*. New York: Columbia University Press, 1994.

Malinowski, Bronislaw. *Argonauts of the Western Pacific*. London: Routledge, 1932.

Man, Ke, and Sumin Hao. "Islamic Philanthropies in Northwest China: The Perspectives of Individuals and NGOs." In *Religion and Development in China: Innovations and Implications*, edited by Keping Wu and Michael Feener, 52–65. Singapore: National University of Singapore, 2015.

Mauss, Marcel. *The Gift: The Form and Reason for Exchange in Archaic Societies*. Translated by W. D. Halls. London: W. W. Norton, 2000.

McCarthy, Susan K. "Serving Society, Repurposing the State: Religious Charity and Resistance in China." *The China Journal*, no. 70 (July 2013): 48–72.

Menegon, Eugenio. *Ancestors, Virgins, & Friars: Christianity as a Local Religion in Late Imperial China*. Cambridge, MA: Harvard University Asia Center for the Harvard-Yenching Institute, 2009.

Mollier, Christine. "Karma and the Bonds of Kinship in Medeval Daoism: Reconciling the Irreconcilable." In *India in the Chinese Imagination: Myth, Religion, and Thought*, edited by John Kieschnick and Meir Shahar, 171–81. Philadelphia: University of Pennsylvania Press, 2013.

Moskowitz, Marc L. *Cries of Joy, Songs of Sorrow: Chinese Pop Music and Its Cultural Connotations*. Honolulu: University of Hawaii Press, 2010.

Muehlebach, Andrea. *The Moral Neoliberal: Welfare and Citizenship in Italy*. Chicago: University of Chicago Press, 2012.

"My Church – Malacca." http://members.tjc.org/sites/en/my/sr/mlc/mychurch.aspx (Accessed August 5, 2014).

Nagata, Judith. "Christianity among Transnational Chinese: Religious versus (Sub)ethnic Affiliation." *International Migration* 43, no. 3 (2005): 99–128.

"The Globalisation of Buddhism and the Emergence of Religious Civil Society: The Case of the Taiwanese Fo Kuang Shan Movement in Asia and the West." *Communal/Plural* 7, no. 2 (1999): 231–48.

Nash, June C. *Practicing Ethnography in a Globalizing World: An Anthropological Odyssey*. Rowman Altamira, 2007.

Nedostup, Rebecca. *Superstitious Regimes: Religion and the Politics of Chinese Modernity*. Cambridge, MA: Harvard University Asia Center, 2010.

"(Nirvana Sutra)." "大般涅盘经." *CBETA*, November 4, 2002. http://buddhism.lib.ntu.edu.tw/BDLM/sutra/chi_pdf/sutra7/T12n0374.pdf (Accessed December 12, 2016).

Nonini, Donald M. "Is China Becoming Neoliberal?" *Critique of Anthropology* 28, (2008): 145–76.

Ong, Aihwa. *Flexible Citizenship: The Cultural Logics of Transnationality*. Durham, NC: Duke University Press, 1999.

Oxfeld, Ellen. *Drink Water, but Remember the Source: Moral Discourse in a Chinese Village*. Berkeley: University of California Press, 2010.

Pacey, Scott Thomas. *From Taixu to Shengyan: Legitimizing Modern Buddhism in China and Taiwan*. PhD dissertation, Australian National University, 2011.

Paulo, Craig J. N. de, and Leonid Rudnytzky. "Introduction." In *Confession of Love: The Ambiguities of Greek Eros and Latin Caritas*, edited by Craig J. N. de Paulo, 1–15. New York: Peter Lang, 2010.

Pittman, Don A. *Toward a Modern Chinese Buddhism: Taixu's Reforms*. Honolulu: University of Hawaii Press, 2001.

Portes, Alejandro. "Social Capital: Its Origins and Applications in Modern Sociology." *Annual Review of Sociology* 24 (1998): 1–24.

Putnam, Robert D. *Bowling Alone*. New York: Simon & Schuster, 2000.

Making Democracy Work: Civic Traditions in Modern Italy. Princeton, NJ: Princeton University Press, 1993.

Quan, Hansheng (全汉昇). ("Causes of Charity in Medieval Buddhist Monasteries.") "中古佛教寺院的慈善事业." In (*Fifty Years of Research on Buddhist Monasteries from Han to Tang*) *五十年来汉唐佛教寺院经济研究*, edited by Ziquan He (何兹全). 北京：北京师范大学出版社, 1986.

Queen, Christopher S., and Sallie B. King. *Engaged Buddhism: Buddhist Liberation Movements in Asia*. Albany: State University of New York Press, 1996.

Reardon-Anderson, James. *Pollution, Politics, and Foreign Investment in Taiwan: The Lukang Rebellion*. Armonk, NY: M E Sharpe, 1997.

Redfield, Peter. "Humanitarianism." In *A Companion to Moral Anthropology*, edited by Didier Fassin, 451–67. Malden, MA: Wiley-Blackwell, 2012.

Robbins, Joel. *Becoming Sinners: Christianity and Moral Torment in a Papua New Guinea Society*. Berkeley: University of California Press, 2004.

"Beyond the Suffering Subject: Toward an Anthropology of the Good." *Journal of the Royal Anthropological Institute* 19 (2013): 447–62.

Rowe, William T. *Hankow: Conflict and Community in a Chinese City, 1796–1895*. Stanford, CA: Stanford University Press, 1992.

"The Public Sphere in Modern China." *Modern China* 16, no. 3 (1990): 309–29.

Samuels, Jeffrey. "*Buddhist Temple Networks across the Indian Ocean: Capital, Resources, and Minority Identity Formation*." Singapore, 2010.

Sangren, P. Steven. "Traditional Chinese Corporations: Beyond Kinship." *The Journal of Asian Studies* 43 (1984): 391–415.

Saxer, Martin. "Re-Fusing Ethnicity and Religion: An Experiment on Tibetan Grounds." *Journal of Current Chinese Affairs* 43, no. 2 (July 9, 2014): 181–204.

Seligman, Adam B., and Robert P. Weller. *Rethinking Pluralism: Ritual, Experience, and Ambiguity*. New York: Oxford University Press, 2012.

Seligman, Adam B., Robert P. Weller, Michael J. Puett, and Bennett Simon. *Ritual and Its Consequences: An Essay on the Limits of Sincerity*. New York: Oxford University Press, 2008.

Shen, Hsiu-hua. "'The First Taiwanese Wives' and 'The Chinese Mistresses': The International Division of Labour in Familial and Intimate Relations across the Taiwan Strait." *Global Networks* 5, no. 4 (2005): 419–37.

Simon, Scott. "Negotiating Power: Elections and the Constitution of Indigenous Taiwan." *American Ethnologist* 37, no. 4 (2010): 726–40.

Smith, Joanna Handlin. *The Art of Doing Good: Charity in Late Ming China*. Berkeley: University of California Press, 2009.

Soo, Khin Wah (苏庆华). (*Studies of the Chinese in Malaysia and Singapore: A Collection of Soo Khin Wah's Works*.) *马新华人研究：苏庆华论文选集*. Kuala Lumpur: 马来西亚创价学会, 2004.

Strathern, Marilyn, ed. *Audit Cultures: Anthropological Studies in Accountability, Ethics and the Academy*. London: Routledge, 2000.

Su, Long. "Master Xingkong – Standing Member of Municipal Political Consultative Conference and the Abbot of Hanshan Temple." *Member Profiles (Weiyuan Fengcai)* 1 (2004). www.hanshansi.org/download/zx/200401/200401f018.htm (Accessed October 21, 2014).

Sum, Chun-Yi. *'Therefore I Am Made Indifferent": Morality and Agency among University Students in China*. PhD dissertation, Boston University, 2015.

Sun, Yanfei. "The Chinese Buddhist Ecology in Post-Mao China: Contours, Types and Dynamics." *Social Compass* 58, no. 4 (2011): 498–510.

Religious Dynamics in a Fragmented Authoritarian State: Explaining the Differentiated Growth of the Chinese Buddhist Establishment and the Newly Rising Jingkong Buddhist Force. Manuscript. n.p., 2011.

Sutton, Donald S. *Steps of Perfection: Exorcistic Performers and Chinese Religion in Twentieth-Century Taiwan*. Cambridge, MA: Harvard University Asia Center, 2003.

Tambiah, Stanley J. "The Ideology of Merit and the Social Correlations of Buddhism in a Thai Village." In *Dialectics in Practical Religion*, edited by Edmund R. Leach, 41–121. Cambridge: Cambridge University Press, 1968.

Tan, Changguo (谭昌国). (The Paiwan People.) *排湾族*. 台北：三民书局.

Tan, Chee Beng. *The Baba of Melaka: Culture and Identity of a Chinese Peranakan Community in Malaysia*. Petaling Jaya: Pelanduk Publications, 1988.

(陈志明) ("The Chinese in the Strait Settlements – The Society and Culture of the Baba Chinese.") "海峡殖民地的华人 – 峇峇华人的社会与文化." In (*The History of the Chinese in Malaysia*) *马来西亚华人史*, edited by Shuigao Lin (林水檺) and Jingshan Luo (骆静山), 167–200. Kuala Lumpur: 马来西亚留台校友会联合中会, 1984.

Development and Distribution of Dejiao Associations in Malaysia and Singapore: A Study on a Chinese Religious Organization. Singapore: Institute of Southeast Asian Studies, 1986.

"Shantang: Charitable Temples in China, Singapore, and Malaysia." *Asian Ethnology* 71, no. 1 (January 1, 2012): 75–107.

Tan, Kevin YL, and Li-Ann Thio. *Constitutional Law in Malaysia and Singapore*. Singapore: LexisNexis, 2010.

Tarde, Gabriel de. *The Laws of Imitation*. Translated by Elsie Worthington Clews Parsons. New York: H. Holt and Co., 1903.

Teiser, Stephen F. *The Scripture on the Ten Kings and the Making of Purgatory in Medieval Chinese Buddhism*. Honolulu: University of Hawaii Press, 2003.

Tocqueville, Alexis de. *Democracy in America*. Translated by Gerald Bevan. London: Penguin Classics, 2003.

Tomlinson, John. *Globalization and Culture*. Chicago: University of Chicago Press, 1999.

True Jesus Church: Special Issue on the Twentieth Anniversary of the Nanjing Congregation. 真耶稣教，南京教会纪念特刊20周年. Nanjing: n.p., 2013.

Tsu, Yu-Yue. *The Spirit of Chinese Philanthropy: A Study in Mutual Aid*. PhD dissertation, Columbia University, 1912.

Tzu Chi Medical Care. "9th Free Clinic Visitation at Batam Island, Indonesia." *Medicine with Humanity* 8 (2007): 45.

Tzu Chi & UNHCR: Collaboration & Activities. Kuala Lumpur: Taiwan Buddhist Tzu Chi Foundation Malaysia (Kuala Lumpur Branch), n.d.

Wagner, Rudolf G. "Fate's Gift Economy: The Chinese Case of Coping with the Asymmetry between Man and Fate." In *Money as God? The Monetization of the Market and Its Impact on Religion, Politics, Law, and Ethics*, edited by Jürgen von Hagen and Michael Welker. Cambridge: Cambridge University Press, 2014.

Wakeman, Frederic. "The Civil Society and Public Sphere Debate: Western Reflections on Chinese Political Culture." *Modern China* 19, no. 2 (1993): 108–38.

Watson, James L., ed. *Golden Arches East: McDonald's in East Asia*. Stanford, CA: Stanford University Press, 1997.

Weber, Max. "The Protestant Sects and the Spirit of Capitalism." In *From Max Weber: Essays in Sociology*, edited by H. H. Gerth and C. Wright Mills, 302–22. New York: Oxford University Press, 1946.

Welch, Holmes. *The Practice of Chinese Buddhism, 1900–1950*. Cambridge, MA: Harvard University Press, 1967.

"Welcome to Cheng Hoon Teng Temple." www.chenghoonteng.org.my/restoration .html (Accessed July 1, 2017).

Weller, Robert P. *Alternate Civilities: Democracy and Culture in China and Taiwan*. Boulder, CO: Westview Press, 1999.

Discovering Nature: Globalization and Environmental Culture in China and Taiwan. Cambridge: Cambridge University Press, 2006.

Unities and Diversities in Chinese Religion. Seattle: University of Washington Press, 1987.

Weller, Robert P., and Chien-Yu Julia Huang. "Charisma in Motion: The Compassion Relief Movement in Taiwan, the United States, Japan, and Malaysia." In *Cities in Motion*, edited by Sherman Cochran and David Strand, 272–94. Berkeley: Institute of East Asian Studies, 2008.

Wielander, Gerda. *Christian Values in Communist China*. New York: Routledge, 2013.

Wu, Keping. "Negotiating the 'Grey Zone': Buddhist and Protestant Philanthropies in Contemporary Southeast China." In *Religion and the Politics of Development*, edited by P. Fountain, R. Bush, and R. M. Feener, 129–54. Basingstoke: Palgrave-Macmillan, 2015.

Wuthnow, Robert. *Saving America?: Faith-Based Services and the Future of Civil Society*. Princeton, NJ: Princeton University Press, 2004.

Xu, Xueji (许雪姬). (*Lukang Gazetteer: Religion*) *鹿港镇志：宗教篇*. 鹿港：鹿港镇公所, 2000.

Yan, Yunxiang. *The Flow of Gifts: Reciprocity and Social Networks in a Chinese Village*. Stanford, CA: Stanford University Press, 1996.

Private Life under Socialism: Love, Intimacy, and Family Change in a Chinese Village, 1949–1999, 1st ed. Stanford, CA: Stanford University Press, 2003.

Yang, Fenggang. "The Red, Black, and Gray Markets of Religion in China." *Sociological Quarterly* 47, no. 1 (2006): 93–122.

Yang, Lien-sheng. "The Concept of Pao as a Basis for Social Relations in China." In *Chinese Thought and Institutions*, edited by John King Fairbank, 291–309. Chicago: University of Chicago Press, 1957.

Yang, Lin. *The Funeral Pattern of Tzu Chi Shanghai*. MA thesis, Tzu Chi University, 2009.

Yang, Mayfair Mei-hui. *Gifts, Favors, and Banquets: The Art of Social Relationships in China*. Ithaca, NY: Cornell University Press, 1994.

"Mass Media and Transnational Subjectivity in Shanghai: Notes on (Re) Cosmopolitanism in a Chinese Metropolis." In *Media Worlds*, edited by Faye D. Ginsburg, Lila Abu-Lughod, and Brian Larkin, 189–210. Berkeley: University of California Press, 2002.

Yang, Xinhua (杨新华). (*Buddhist and Daoist Temples of Nanjing*.)*金陵佛寺大观*. 南京: 方志出版社, 2003.

Yen, Jing-hwang. "Historical Background." In *The Chinese in Malaysia*, edited by Kam Hing Lee and Chee-Beng Tan, 1–36. Kuala Lumpur: Oxford University Press, 2000.

Yuan, Guang-yi. "A Research of the Theory of 'Chengfu' of Tai Ping Classic." *Journal of Religion and Culture of the National Cheng Kung University* 2 (2002): 167–209.

Zeng, Yuchi (曾钰琪). ("Inescapable Network of Human Emotion (Renqing) and Connection (Guanxi): An Analysis of the Social Capital and Renqing Guanxi Network in Community Participation and Communication among Hakka Women's Volunteer Services.") 逃不開的人情關係網絡？--從客家婦女的志願性服務工作探討社區參與和溝通中的社會資本與人情關係網絡." MA thesis in Sociology, National Tsing Hua University, 2004.

Zhong, Xin (仲鑫). (*Contemporary Buddhist Philanthropic Organizations and Their Activities–The Case of the Ciji Foundation in Nanjing*.) *当代佛教慈济公益组织及其活动的研究－以慈济基金会南京会所为例*. Manuscript, n.p., 2014.

Zhou, Dian'en (周典恩). ("Experiential Belief, Habitual Ritual and Social Capital: The Life History of a Rural Christian.") 信仰实践与社会资本：一个乡村基督徒的个人生活史研究." Paper delivered at the Conference on Religion and Philanthropy in Jiangnan, Shanghai, 2012.

Zhuang, Yingzhang (庄英章). (*Lukang Gazetteer: Kinship*.) *鹿港镇志：氏族篇*. 鹿港: 鹿港镇公所, 2000.

Zigon, Jarrett. "Moral Breakdown and the Ethical Demand: A Theoretical Framework for an Anthropology of Moralities." *Anthropological Theory* 7, no. 2 (2007): 131–50.

Zuo, Furong (左芙蓉). (*Social Gospel, Social Service and Social Reform: A Historical Study of the Beijing YMCA 1909–1949*.) *社会福音，社会服务与社会改造：北京基督教青年会历史研究，1909*–1949. 北京：宗教文化出版社, 2005.

Index